AFTER JIHAD

AFTER JIHAD

AMERICA AND THE STRUGGLE
FOR ISLAMIC DEMOCRACY

—◆—

NOAH FELDMAN

FARRAR, STRAUS AND GIROUX

NEW YORK

FARRAR, STRAUS AND GIROUX

19 Union Square West, New York 10003

Library of Congress Cataloging-in-Publication Data

Feldman, Noah, 1970–

    After Jihad: America and the struggle for Islamic democracy / Noah Feldman.

        p. cm.

    Includes bibliographical references and index.

    ISBN 0-374-17769-4 (hc : alk. paper)

    1. Democracy—Religious aspects—Islam. 2. Islam and world politics. 3. Religion and politics—Islamic countries. 4. United States—Relations—Islamic countries. 5. Islamic countries—Relations—United States. 6. Islamic countries—Politics and government. I. Title.

BP190.5.D45F45 2003

321.8'0917'671—dc21

2002192524

Designed by Amy Trombat

www.fsgbooks.com

1 3 5 7 9 10 8 6 4 2

FOR JEANNIE

The Prophet, upon whom be prayer and peace, was returning from one of their battles, when he said, prayer and peace be upon him, "You have made the finest of returns; you have returned from the lesser jihad to the greater jihad."

They said, "And what is the greater jihad?"

He answered, "Man's struggle against his desires."

———◆———

"We have returned from the lesser jihad to the greater jihad."

They said, "And what is the greater jihad?"

He said, "The jihad of the heart."

CONTENTS

THE REVOLUTION THAT WASN'T...3

ISLAM AND DEMOCRACY IN CONTACT.......................................6

§

PART ONE

The Idea of Islamic Democracy

ISLAMIC DEMOCRACY, NOT ISLAMIST DEMOCRACY.....................19

ISLAM, THE WEST, AND THE QUESTION OF OPPOSITION.............26

ISLAM AND DEMOCRACY AS MOBILE IDEAS............................31

THE RESILIENCE OF ISLAM...38

GOD'S RULE AND THE PEOPLE'S RULE..................................51

ISLAMIC EQUALITY...62

ISLAMIC LIBERTY..69

THE UNIVERSALITY OF MOBILE IDEAS..................................75

§

PART TWO

Varieties of Islamic Democracy

DEMOCRATIZATION AND MUSLIM REALITY: AN OVERVIEW...........81

IRAN: ISLAMIC DEMOCRACY IN THE BALANCE.........................87

TURKEY: THE OUTLIER..101

ISLAM AND DEMOCRACY IN SOUTH AND SOUTHEAST ASIA:
MOBILITY AND POSSIBILITY...113

PAKISTAN: THE ISLAMIC STATE AND THE
STRUGGLE FOR STABILITY..119

THE DIVERSITY OF THE ARABS...131

MONARCHIES WITH OIL: THE RENTIER STATE IN ACTION...........137

KINGS WITHOUT OIL...148

THE DICTATORS AND THE ISLAMISTS:
THE PUZZLE OF EGYPT..162

REGIME CHANGE AND ITS CONSEQUENCES:
DICTATORS WITH OIL...174

THE BIG PICTURE: ISLAM, DEMOCRACY, AND THE
CONTACT OF MOBILE IDEAS...182

§

PART THREE

The Necessity of Islamic Democracy

WHY DEMOCRACY? THE PRAGMATIC ARGUMENT.......................189

NEUTRALIZING ANTI-AMERICANISM BY REFUTING IT.................199

DOING THE RIGHT THING..204

HOW TO DO IT..210

DEMOCRACY'S MUSLIM ALLIES..222

IMAGINING AN ISLAMIC DEMOCRACY...................................228

AFTER JIHAD..232

NOTES 235
ACKNOWLEDGMENTS..253
INDEX..255

AFTER JIHAD

The Revolution That Wasn't

Can democracy be made to flourish in the lands where Islam prevails? Today this might be the single most pressing question for American foreign policy, and this book sets out to answer it. But more than a decade ago, before jihad became a household word, before the most senior voices in the U.S. government began to speculate about a democratic Iraq, democracy had a trial run in an Arab state outside the international spotlight. What happened there set the course for the U.S. policies that are now being reforged in the crucible of the war on terror. It is there that the story of the encounter between America and Islamic democracy begins.

In 1989, that year of revolutions, unglamorous Algeria was an unlikely candidate for democratic change. Perched on the rim of North Africa, far from the upheavals of Eastern Europe, Algeria had been home to a romantic liberation movement that had evicted the French after a hard-fought guerrilla war. Yet the liberation movement had morphed, by way of a 1965 coup, into an autocratic, quasi-military, socialist regime. The sole political party, the Front de Libération National, had not permitted real elections since shortly after independence.

Starting in late 1988, young Algerians began a series of protests that led to a new constitution promising fundamental rights and political parties other than the FLN. The spirit of 1989 was abroad. In June 1990, in the first local elections under the new constitution, a newly formed Islamic party, the Front Islamique du Salut (FIS), came more or less from nowhere to win 62 percent of the votes cast. The FLN, which could boast that it had liberated Algeria from the French, came in at 28 percent.

One could almost hear the whispered soul-searching starting in Western foreign ministries. If elections were going to replace dictators in the Arab and Muslim worlds, as they seemed to be doing in the Eastern bloc and beyond, would Islamic parties do this well everywhere? Would democratically elected Islamic governments be good or bad for Western interests? Although democracy seemed like the desirable result of victory in the Cold War, the Algerian election suggested otherwise: Could democracy be an unalloyed good if Muslim states chose fundamentalist leaders?

Of course these were still just local elections. Perhaps the Islamists of the FIS had succeeded because no one else had had time to organize effective political parties in the short period between the ratification of the new constitution and the local elections. Unlike political parties, Islam itself had never been illegal, so Islamist politicians could use mosques as centers for organization, recruitment, and advertising—a built-in infrastructure that other parties lacked. Or perhaps Algerians who were not deeply sympathetic to fundamentalist Islam had voted against the old-guard FLN as a protest against dictatorship. In the national elections, with more at stake, people might vote more moderately.

The leadership of the FIS was almost as surprised as everyone else at the party's success in the local elections. The FIS was suddenly a major political force, and needed to explain to the newly minted electorate what its policies would actually be. No one had ever run a democratic Islamic government before, and the FIS leaders were not of one mind about the relationship between Islam and democracy. In the event, the ruling FLN effectively decided election strategy for them. In the run-up to the December 1991 national elections, it put the two most prominent FIS leaders in jail. This deterrent failed, and the FIS went on to win more seats than any other party: 188 out of a total of 429. The FLN got just 15 seats. The constitution called for a second round of elections; if the votes remained steady, the FIS was headed for a national victory.

Now the success of the Islamists became the stuff of high-level policy-making. In Washington, the experts were divided on how to react. Some sincerely worried that if the Islamists took office, they might abolish elections. Others focused on the strategic interests of the United States. As the example of Iran showed, states run by Islamist parties could be terribly anti-American, and might export terror. Still others, either optimistic or pragmatic, pointed out that the United States could form a friendship with an Islamic state. After all, America's close ally Saudi Arabia was a traditional monarchy in which Islamic law prevailed.

Then a remarkable thing happened. At the insistence of the Algerian generals, the FLN canceled the second round of elections. It retroactively called off the first round, and in effect the municipal elections, too. It banned the FIS and jailed the rest of its leaders. Its party banned, its leaders jailed, and many of its activists arrested, the FIS split in two and turned to armed resistance.

The French, worried about the influence that Islamic fundamentalism might have on the millions of Algerians who lived in France, acquiesced in what was essentially a preemptive coup d'état against the almost-elected FIS. The United States decided to go along with French policy. In a speech that has cast long shadows over subsequent American policy, then–Assistant Secretary of State Edward Djerejian explained that while the United States favored democracy, it opposed elections that would provide for "one person, one vote, one time." By implication, elections won by Islamists were elections that would lead not to more democracy but to less.

Algeria was plunged into a bloody civil war that has since killed at least 100,000 people. The experiment with Islamic democracy was over before it could get started. American policy was now firmly on the side of the autocrats against the Islamic democrats.

ISLAM AND DEMOCRACY IN CONTACT

The compressed drama of Algeria's flirtation with democracy foreshadowed a new, democratic direction for Islam, a harsh response from most Muslim monarchs and dictators, and acquiescence in repression on the part of the U.S. and Europe. In the decade since the collapse of the Algerian experiment, a handful of Islamist extremists have grabbed headlines by perpetrating violent terror, most spectacularly the September 11 attacks. The United States has been inexorably drawn into political and military engagement with the Muslim world. But during the same decade, outside the headlines, many more committed Muslims have sought to participate in the electoral politics of the countries where they live. Moving beyond the fantasy of violent revolution and Islamic utopia that some Islamist extremists entertain, they have turned toward persuasion and pragmatism.

So, contrary to what is sometimes believed in the U.S., Islam is not inherently committed to the overthrow of Western ideals. To the contrary, many, though by no means all, Muslims find the combination of Islamic ideals and democratic values appealing. Today Muslims around the world embrace the elegance, logic, and depth of Islam perhaps more warmly than at any time in a century. In Islam's language of justice, morality, hope, and commitment, they find not only religion, but a vital force in the realms of politics, society, and the spirit. At the same time, as their reliance on Islam grows, Muslims are also embracing the ideals of self-government and free-dom associated with democracy. To an increasing number of Muslims, these democratic values resonate with Islam and can develop in tandem with it. Wherever advocates have been free to speak out or run for office in the name of Islamic democracy, they have found an eager audience.

That freedom has certainly not been enjoyed everywhere. The quality of elections varies dramatically across the Muslim world. There are emerging democracies like Turkey and Indonesia, faltering quasi-democracies like Pakistan, and de facto presidential dictatorships like Egypt; there are constitutional monarchies like Jordan and Morocco; and in the monarchy of Saudi Arabia, where the king's word is law, there are no elections at all. Iran combines an elected president and legislature with an unelected Supreme Leader. Several of the Central Asian republics are run like the Soviet provincial satellites they once were.

Muslim countries, most of which are American allies in one sense or another, differ greatly in political system, degree of freedom, wealth, language, and culture. In nearly every Muslim country, however, there are voices today calling for greater democracy. Remarkably, the loudest voices are often those of Islamists, activists who believe that "Islam is the solution" to all problems in politics and private life alike.

The Islamists' call for democratic change in the Muslim world marks a fundamental shift in their strategy. For more than a decade after the Iranian Revolution of 1979, many Islamists sought to emulate the Iranian model by Islamizing their own countries through the revolutionary transformation of violent jihad. This violence was never embraced by every Islamist, but it was very much in the air, and few Islamists were prepared to condemn it. It brought about the assassination of President Sadat; it was also connected, more positively, to the Islamist resistance to the Soviet occupation of Afghanistan. The violence between the secular Algerian autocratic government and the Islamists after the cancellation of the Algerian elections certainly became jihad from the perspective of the Islamists themselves. A proliferation of so-called jihadi organizations throughout the Muslim world occurred during the 1980s, and the one that emerged as most prominent, Osama bin Laden's al-Qaeda, culminated its jihad with the horrifically successful attack on the World Trade Center and the Pentagon.

But September 11, and the sporadic attacks which have followed, are the last, desperate gasp of a tendency to violence that has lost most of its popular support. Al-Qaeda was itself a radical offshoot of the mainstream Islamist movement, politically irrelevant outside of its meddling in Taliban Afghanistan and Central Asia. Frustrated by Islamists' failure to effect actual change in the governments of the Muslim world, it concentrated on blowing up American targets because it had run out of other options. Al-Qaeda members may have believed that Muslims would rally to their cause and fight both the U.S. and their own governments, but that never happened. The notion that an Islamic state should be created through holy war is an idea whose time has passed among most in the Muslim world. The remaining jihadis may have a toehold in the predominantly Muslim republics of the former Soviet Union, and there are those inspired by bin Laden who will surely attempt further terrorist attacks against people whom they perceive as the enemies of Islam. For that matter, Pakistani-supported jihadis continue to operate in Kashmir, a phenomenon that has brought Pakistan and India to the brink of war. A worrisome number of Palestinians, some supported by Lebanese Hezbollah and Iran, are for the first time prepared to describe their battle against Israel in terms that would bring a smile to a jihadi's lips. But the fight for Palestine excepted, these extremists, frightening as they are, represent a fringe—the fringe not only to the great majority of Muslims, but even to committed Islamists.

One reason for the declining popularity of revolutionary jihad is that this approach was a signal failure. Of all the countries in the Muslim world, Islamists managed to take over just Sudan and Afghanistan. Today neither of those Islamist regimes remains in power. Violent jihad has popular support only where it has not yet failed: among Shi'is in southern Lebanon, where Hezbollah bombings helped drive Israel out; among those Palestinians who believe similar tactics might work for them; and among Pakistanis and Kashmiris who are fighting against India. It is no coincidence that all these conflicts, as well as that of the Chechens against Russia, are perceived by Muslims as wars of liberation. Jihad to take over Muslim countries or kill Western civilians is out of popular favor, but violent jihad has lost none of its luster where it is understood as self-defense.

That so many Islamists are now prepared to embrace democratic means to achieve their goals *within* their own countries, however, demonstrates an important development in the realm of ideas. For many of the world's Muslims, with a wide range of ideological standpoints, Islam and democracy are compatible. That was not true for much of the last century. It is a new circumstance that results from the global rise of democracy, the still-growing prestige and appeal of Islam, and the capacity of contemporary Islam to incorporate a broad range of nontraditional political ideas. In most of the Muslim world, people want democracy. And because Islam is also an essential part of political and religious life, most Muslims recognize that democracy will inevitably have to include the participation of Islamists. The Islamists may not dominate elections, as they were poised to do in Algeria, but they will certainly emerge as politically significant actors in almost any free, democratic Muslim state.

Autocratic Muslim governments are terribly threatened by even the possibility of democracy in their countries, and they have mostly stood firm against it. The Syrian dictatorship, which faced serious trouble after the flow of money and weapons from the Soviets slowed to a trickle, has shown no signs of democratization since. Maybe Syrians remember what happened in the town of Hama in 1982, when an Islamically inspired mini-rebellion against longtime dictator Hafez al-Asad led to the indiscriminate killing of between 5,000 and 30,000 civilians. When President Asad died in June 2000, his son Bashar immediately became dictator by descent—no election, no public discussion, just a seamless transition. Iraq was another totalitarian regime that might have felt the democratic aftershocks of 1989, but Saddam Hussein sidestepped the issue by invading Kuwait in August of 1990. In other, slightly less autocratic Muslim states, like Jordan and Egypt, the governments have allowed some Islamists to run for parliament, while keeping Islamism under tight control and surveillance.

Meanwhile, in the United States, the idea that promoting democracy abroad serves American values and interests was almost never considered applicable to the Muslim world until recent events began to suggest that many Muslims are unhappy with their own governments. During the 1990s, some influential American thinkers argued that Islam had inherited communism's mantle as the implacable opponent that democracy would have to confront in the future. A generation of thinkers reared on the incompatibility of communism and capitalist democracy tended to see Islam as a fighting faith that could not coexist without strife. The attacks of September 11 have fed the popular perception that all Islamists, perhaps even all Muslims, are the sort of fanatics whom one would not dare trust to govern themselves by democratic means. This perception will not easily be displaced so long as the most radical Islamists, who themselves deny that Islam and democracy can be reconciled, continue to underscore their words with violence.

Practical concerns also stand in the way of a policy that would actually encourage democratization in the Muslim world. The war on terror has pushed the United States to rely on its existing Muslim allies for intelligence and cooperation, and those allies are mostly autocrats. Democratization also carries risks, prominent among them the risk of instability, which in the Middle East and the Persian Gulf inevitably implicates the possibility of a rapid, economically dangerous rise in oil prices. So while the United States has made some gestures in the direction of supporting democracy in the Muslim world, such as President George W. Bush's call for an overhaul of the Palestinian Authority, and while Bush administration officials and some Democrats have spoken of the need to create democracy in a postwar Iraq, American policy has thus far done little to discourage Muslim autocrats from keeping their democratic opponents at bay. The legitimate fear that, as in Algeria, democracy might lead to Islamist politics has become a convenient partner to the cautious preference for stable autocracy and the steady flow of cheap oil. Since September 11, it has also become easier for the autocrats themselves to label every Islamically inspired opposition group a terrorist threat; and it seems unwise in the current American political climate to stick up for any Islamist group that might turn out to be less democratic than it appears on the surface.

Nonetheless, the absolutist thinking that insists on arraying movements like "democracy" and "Islam" against each other in inevitable conflict has led us badly astray. Shared by skeptical Westerners and some hard-line Islamists, it has led to mistaken reasoning, and hence to mistaken policies. Specifically, it has led the United States and Europe to ignore the possibility that Muslims want freedom as much as anybody else. It has led Western governments that pride themselves on their own democratic character to embrace dictators for reasons of short-term self-interest, forgetting that in the long run, the support of autocracy undermines their own democratic values and makes enemies of the people who are being oppressed with Western complicity. European countries have criticized America's heavy-handedness in the Muslim world, but they themselves have done almost nothing to advance the cause of democracy there, proving just as satisfied to deal with autocrats as the U.S. has been.

The once-entrenched American policy of preferring autocrats to elections in the Muslim world is neither necessary nor advisable. Ideas like democracy and Islam need not be opposed. Instead tentative, provisional compromises between these ideas might produce a synthesis capable of generating its own unique ideas and institutions—and that synthesis has already begun to be born. Islamic democracy, in its multiple potential forms, is not historically inevitable; but it is, just now, historically possible.

In the last two decades, the Muslim world has undergone extraordinary ferment and change. Visit a medium-sized town in almost any Arab country: where the outside world once arrived through an occasional newspaper read aloud to neighbors, there are now satellite dishes carrying not one, but half a dozen Arabic-language channels into even relatively modest homes. In Muslim cities from Kuala Lumpur to Casablanca, the well-off carry the same mobile telephones popular in Helsinki and San Francisco, complete with instant text-messaging in local languages. Islam itself has shown great internal flexibility alongside the rapid change in material culture. Even fundamentalists—nearly all of whom embrace and use the latest technology—are open to new ideas, and one can find numerous Internet discussions devoted to the proper Islamic perspective on globalization, politics, technological change, and, in fact, nearly any topic one could imagine.

Democracy and Islam are both what might be called mobile ideas—the kind that spread across the world, appealing to many people living in far-flung, strikingly different countries and societies. Because mobile ideas claim to work always and everywhere, they can clash. But mobile ideas also tend to be very flexible, and therefore capable of coming together in intriguing ways to produce unanticipated, new configurations. Islamic democracy is not a contradiction, because secularism of the Western variety is not a necessary condition of democracy. Separation of religion and state is not likely anywhere in the Muslim world in the immediately foreseeable future. But in a variety of places, Islam and democracy are starting to find means of mutual accommodation.

These first stirrings of Islamic democracy give hope for the future possibility of synthesis. Yet their fragility also suggests that without active encouragement and support, Islamic democracy may die on the vine. It is, therefore, not enough for the West merely to acknowledge the possibility of Islamic democracy—though that would be a start. The West, and particularly the United States, needs to change the incentives created by present foreign policy so as to facilitate, not discourage, democratic development in the Muslim world.

The democracy that might then emerge could take a number of forms. There are many ways for Muslims to embrace Islam without believing that Islam alone provides the answer to every question of life and politics. Our assumptions about what Islamic government means need to be revised. But each possible state would be a type of Islamic democracy: a state recognizably Islamic, populated by Muslims, and committed to the political principles of democracy.

Such democratic Islamic governance has never been tried. When it is, it will work very differently in practice than it sounds in theory. Certainly that has been true of every other political theory in human history—including, very prominently, the theory of democracy.

The need to ask how democracy and Islam interact with each other is especially pressing when we seem to be reaching a new juncture in the politics of the Muslim world. The autocrats are aging, and not all will be able to translate power to their sons as Asad did. Public reaction in the aftermath of the attacks of September 11 and to ongoing violence in the West Bank and Gaza revealed new instabilities in Muslim states. At the same time, democracy is struggling to emerge in small countries like Bahrain, whose emir has undertaken an experiment with free speech, political parties, and elections; in Iran, where democrats are locked in a difficult battle with mullahs who are loath to relinquish their power; in Morocco and Jordan, where young kings have been cautiously trying to balance economic liberalization with democratic politics; and elsewhere.

As increasing numbers of Muslims come to believe that Islamic democracy is not a paradox but a desirable synthesis, variants on the Algerian scenario are going to become more likely. In autumn 2002 elections in Morocco, Pakistan, and Turkey, Islamic parties exceeded all expectations to win unprecedented numbers of seats. Repressing elected Islamists has the potential to create disaster by driving them into violent opposition. It is difficult to maintain that the brutal civil war produced by the suppression of democracy in Algeria was a worthwhile sacrifice in some larger battle for freedom that may need to be repeated elsewhere. If the hard questions that result from the emergence of Islamic democracy are not addressed, the marriage of skepticism and self-interest that drives much U.S. and European policy on questions of democratization will persist, unacknowledged and unchallenged. Failure to engage the possibilities of Islamic democracy will have serious consequences for long-term American interests and values, to say nothing of its grave significance for the peoples of the Muslim world.

The stakes of America's decision either to maintain or to abandon the policy of embracing Muslim dictators are therefore extraordinarily high, and this is all the more true as the U.S. thinks about what governments should be created in the aftermath of regime change. It may appear that continuing to support Muslim autocrats is necessary to maintain stability, fight extremism, and avoid a rising tide of Islamist politics that might harm the security of the United States and Israel, America's staunchest regional ally. In the short term, it is true, existing alliances cannot be broken in the face of the necessities of regional war. So long as the Israeli-Palestinian conflict continues to claim lives daily, elected governments in the Muslim world would probably be even more anti-Israel than the unelected governments now in place. But these short-term realities must not be allowed to determine long-term policy without careful consideration of the costs of supporting dictators indefinitely. The U.S. will not always have troops in harm's way in the region, and Israeli-Palestinian violence must eventually be brought under control. Too exclusive a focus on perceived immediate concerns at the expense of the long view is part of what allowed the Taliban to take over Afghanistan and provide a home for al-Qaeda. That is the kind of mistake that the United States, and indeed Israel, can no longer afford.

Over the long run, the costs of sticking with the autocrats are great. Continuing this policy will array the United States and the West against the interests of ordinary Muslims, who will be unlikely to forget what they see as a betrayal of the values of freedom and self-government that the U.S. and the West represent to them. It will send the message to Muslims that democracy is less an animating aspiration at the core of American values than a tool to be deployed cynically and selectively. Existing Muslim dreams of democracy will sour. The autocratic governments of the Muslim world, already illegitimate in the eyes of many of their citizens and subjects, will continue to seem like creatures of the U.S. Frustrated dreams of self-determination will continue to attach themselves, however fleetingly, to any Muslim leader who purports to stand up to the U.S., even when he is a notorious butcher like Saddam or a marginal extremist like Osama bin Laden.

So long as the U.S. sides with the autocrats, true peace between Israel and her neighbors will remain elusive, rejected by the many Muslims who consider their leaders unfit to speak on their behalf and prepared to sell out the Palestinians to curry favor in Washington. Real normalization cannot occur unless ordinary Arabs take responsibility for the choice to make peace and accept the permanence and legitimacy of Israel's existence—and that will never happen so long as Arab leaders remain autocrats who do not speak or act for their people. When existing Muslim regimes falter or fall, Muslims will see the United States and the West as enemies who supported their oppressors, and the new governments that come to power will be neither democratic nor friendly to the West. Muslims themselves, who deserve democracy as much as any other people, will continue to suffer under repressive regimes.

Drastic change cannot happen overnight without drastic consequences. It would be naive and mistaken to demand the instant transformation of either Western policy or Muslim politics. But it would be equally mistaken and far more harmful to accept the status quo as inevitable. Long-term Western policy toward the Muslim world is in need of serious reconsideration; and the politics of the Muslim world cry out for self-transformation into new patterns, faithful both to democratic values and to the traditions of Islam as understood by Muslims themselves. Although the arguments for stasis deserve serious consideration, what now looks like caution may ultimately be the riskiest course when the winds have changed.

The hunger for Islamic democracy is growing. One sees this in the increasing number of Muslims who call for democracy. One sees it in the learned disquisitions, religious and secular, about the fundamental compatibility of Islamic and democratic institutions. And one sees it in a general trend away from the use of violence to bring about Islamic governance in Muslim countries. These developments warrant the question: What comes after jihad? What is the next step for Islamist movements that have not generated political transformation by the sword and are now interested in pursuing change by the ballot? What is the next step for Muslims who are not interested in bringing about change through violence but want change nonetheless?

It is not too soon to ask what comes after jihad, particularly when a new Muslim state is under construction in Afghanistan, and when it seems possible to imagine such a state being built in a post-Saddam Iraq. The memory of September 11 is still fresh, and that is as it should be. But the rubble of September 11 has been cleared, and that calls for constructing a plan for the future. American strategy for the Muslim world in the wake of September 11 rightly began by focusing on immediate questions of what could be done to punish and to prevent. Now a longer-term strategy must be developed, one that will serve American interests and American values, and one that will build on Muslims' capacities for shaping their own future in a peaceful and democratic way.

In what follows, I set out to address these questions by exploring the idea of Islamic democracy and the pressing need for it. Part One shows how Islam and democracy can come together to produce a synthesis that is true to both. Part Two evaluates the ways that the ideas of Islam and democracy are now interacting in the Muslim world. It looks closely at a number of Arab and non-Arab Muslim states to show how the encounter between Islam and democracy is shaping prospects for change. Part Three turns from analysis to argument, making the case that the West in general and the United States in particular must change their policies toward the Muslim world, encouraging democracy instead of impeding it. Such a change would serve long-term American interests and promote peace in the Middle East; it is also the right thing to do if the United States and Europe want to live up to their own deeply held values.

If the United States sticks to its present policies, and Islamic democracy does not emerge, it will be a tragedy for Muslims, and indeed for the rest of the world: change is needed before it is too late. This book provides an account of how Islamic democracy is possible in historical and theoretical terms; an argument for why the U.S. should help it to emerge; and a road map of constructive, practical steps to be taken to make Islamic democracy a reality.

————◦•◦•————

§

PART ONE

The Idea of Islamic Democracy

ISLAMIC DEMOCRACY,
NOT ISLAMIST DEMOCRACY

Where is the Muslim Solidarnosc? Critics generally pose this question to impugn the democratic possibilities of the Muslim world. The ideal of pro-democracy activism arising spontaneously from the shipyards of Gdansk stands for the hope that in every society, no matter how totalitarian or repressive, there are freedom-loving people who see clearly that democracy is the solution to what ails their country. Yet such popular democracy movements are hard to come by in the contemporary Muslim world.

One explanation is that repression works. All over the Muslim world, autocratic leaders of the kind who flourished during the Cold War—supported by the Soviets, by the United States, and occasionally (if they were very shrewd) by both—took careful note of the events of 1989–91 in Algeria. America's willingness to give tacit approval to the suppression of democracy, when presented as a defense against fundamentalism, emboldened autocrats in the Muslim world; wily about their own survival, the autocrats jailed and executed democracy activists. This well-proven tactic had the desired effect of encouraging other potential activists to keep a low profile or to emigrate. At the same time, until recently, most secular Muslim intellectuals were Marxists or socialists, drawn to familiar modes of anti-colonial and anti-imperial criticism rather than toward democratic ideologies.

But a great number of potential democracy activists in the Muslim world have turned toward Islamist criticism of government. Although autocratic governments repress all their critics, whether secular or Islamist, the Islamists have traditionally enjoyed a structural advantage. The governments of the Muslim world cannot fully suppress Islam and the mosque, which are too deeply a part of everyday culture and society. Islam, in its various forms, plays a central role in the lives of many people. Notwithstanding the failure of Islamist activists to overthrow governments by violent revolution, a large and growing number of Muslims, poor and rich, educated and illiterate, not only respect Islam as a source of personal faith but consider it relevant to government.

Secular nationalism was tried in the Arab world, in Iran, and even in Indonesia—and the consensus is that it failed. Secularism has been discredited by its association with dictatorial nationalism. Islam itself, however, has not been similarly discredited in the realm of politics. Part of its continuing appeal results simply from the fact that Islamists have had relatively few opportunities in government; in an environment of corrupt politics, it is easy for the untried to seem untainted. But the enduring appeal of Islam in the political context cannot be dismissed as mere idealism. Islamists everywhere enjoy a reputation for sincerity and for opposing unjust government. Islamists have repeatedly proven their capacity to mobilize to help the unfortunate—not just earthquake victims or others in crisis, but those suffering under the quiet, constant pressures of poverty.

Islamists also speak a language of truth and values. Like other religious traditions, Islam provides a deeply resonant vocabulary for criticizing government from the standpoint of morality. Muslim scholars, judges, and philosophers have long called for justice and righteousness in the name of Islam. When people in the Muslim world criticize their governments as being "un-Islamic," they are often simply calling those governments unjust, corrupt, and repressive. One of the great strengths of Islam in the political realm lies in the clarity of its moral vision, which holds rulers accountable to justice and the rule of law. The word *Islam*, conventionally translated as "submission," implies no subjugation of one person to any other. The word implies, rather, a recognition of God's ultimate sovereignty—a sovereignty that places all people on equal footing before the divine Majesty. To mistreat one's fellows not only violates their rights but offends God. Muslims serve God alongside other Muslims who are their equals and partners in the creation of the Muslim community.

So criticisms made in Islamic terms possess greater depth and authority than they would if framed in some other rhetoric. Islam captures the universal aspiration to just society and government better than the failed ideologies of socialism and nationalism. But more than that, because it is not simply another ideology but a vibrant faith, Islam can motivate people to act politically while simultaneously transcending politics. A truly Islamic policy is, by implication, not only advantageous but inherently good; un-Islamic behavior is not merely illegal but wrong in the eyes of God.

In a world where the banners of secularism and nominal democracy have been raised and autocratic repression has followed, Islamic government remains the solution that has not yet been tried. If free and fair democratic elections were held all over the Muslim world, many countries would see sizable turnouts of voters favoring Islamist political parties, just as there were in Algeria in 1990 and 1991. The cause would not be sympathy for particular Islamist policies so much as the feeling that nationalism and secularism have not yielded solutions to the problems of the Muslim world.

The likelihood that Islamist parties would get votes, however, does not mean that democratic Muslim states would become Islamist states on the model of Iran, or some alternative vision of a state governed by classical Islamic law or Muslim clerics. Muslims themselves do not all agree about the extent to which Islam should determine how they live. Islam comprises a complex set of contested ideas, values, and beliefs. Some would say that Islam dictates the right way to act in every sphere of human activity. Others would say that in practice, Islam leaves great swaths of individual and communal choice free. Still others might claim that Islam is limited to the sphere of individual faith. Indeed, so great is the diversity among Muslims about these and other matters that some academic writers prefer to speak of "Islams," plural, rather than "Islam," singular. Despite its image in the West, and some egregious examples of intolerance in places like Iran and Saudi Arabia today, Islam has a rich if imperfect tradition of tolerating intra-

Islamic diversity of opinion on matters of religion. Most believing Muslims would say that there is one true Islam and that people disagree about what exactly the right Islam is. Only God knows for sure.

This diversity of views ensures that there is a broad range of ways that Islam and democracy might interact or that Islam might play a role in constitutions and governments. A pure Islamist state based on classical Islamic law is only one of these possibilities. Islam might be the official religion of a state that governed in a basically secular fashion. Islam might provide the basis for family or personal law without infringing on other legal domains. Islam might provide a symbolic basis for general legislation without dictating particular policies. All these are examples of Islamic states that are nonetheless not Islamist. They incorporate Islam and its values into the life of the state but do not insist, as Islamists typically do, that Islam is the only and comprehensive source of law and decision making.

How compatible each of these models is with democracy will depend in part on the definition of democracy one adopts. Democracy may mean simply that the people rule, whether by referendum or by choosing representatives; this structural definition of democracy fits the democracy of Athens and is still serviceable today. A more modern definition requires a range of basic rights to go along with the right to vote and be elected in free elections: broad freedom of speech and association, equality before the law, due process, and more. This liberal democracy includes the panoply of rights that people in Western democracies enjoy.

The range of options for Islamic democracy is thus much greater than the dichotomy of secular state or Islamist state that is sometimes presented as the only set of choices for the contemporary Muslim world. Both Islamists and the autocrats they oppose are heavily invested in arguing that the only options are autocracy or an Islamist state. The Islamists have every reason to present themselves as the sole alternative to the autocratic governments they wish to replace; like candidates everywhere, they have little to gain by emphasizing the chances of some other candidate.

More perversely, the autocrats have discovered that it is also in their interests to depict the Islamists as the only alternative to autocratic rule. Cynically motivated, the autocrats know they are on thin ice with their people, especially during periods when the public is agitated by an issue like the

Palestinian cause. Although some monarchies enjoy the limited legitimacy conferred by tradition, and people who live reasonably well are sometimes willing to support autocratic regimes as the price of stability, autocratic rule generally depends on maintaining political strength by coercion, supported by elites within and foreign powers without. Some Arab rulers control oil re sources and are able to maintain good relations with countries abroad by keeping the oil flowing. Others, poorer in resources, have to make do with convincing foreign powers that they are necessary for maintaining regional stability—again with an eye to keeping oil flowing.

Either way, autocratic governments need friends abroad, especially in the West. But because these governments repress dissent, their best strategy is to persuade potential Western allies that they are better than the alternatives. In this sense, Islamists are a gift from heaven for the autocrats. The West is suspicious of Islamists, whose political ideals are often expressed in anti-Western terms. The anti-Americanism of the Islamic Republic of Iran has left a deep impression in the Western mind, especially in the United States, and Islamists have also tapped into a vein of anti-American feeling connected with American support of Israel. So when autocratic governments tell the West, "No matter what you may think of us, the Islamists would be a lot worse," this message is heard loud and clear in Washington and other Western capitals.

Preserving the conditions that justify repression is good practical policy for the autocrats. If the autocrats were to destroy Islamist opposition completely, then Western countries might begin to feel confident enough in the possibility of secular democracy in the Muslim world to demand or at least to encourage more democratization. The optimal strategy for the autocrats is therefore to eliminate secular democratic dissent, keeping just enough Islamist opposition alive to make Islamism the only alternative without enabling it to become strong enough to overthrow the government. Autocrats also benefit by telling their own citizens, not just the West, that there is no alternative but the Islamists, because secular-minded Muslims—of whom there are no small number, especially among elites—might prefer autocracy to an Islamic state that imposed religious law on them. Some educated Muslim women might prefer an unfree secular autocracy to a relatively democratic Islamic state in which they could vote and work but might, because

of democratically enacted religious regulations, have to wear a head covering and Islamic dress outside their homes. Islamists have, after all, often
made women into a central symbolic focus of their efforts, simultaneously demanding separation of the sexes while insisting that mandatory modesty will
facilitate women's greater participation in public life.

Beyond the Islamists and the autocrats, some ordinary Muslims cannot
yet quite imagine comparatively secular democracy in the Muslim world.
This short-term problem, however, may eventually be resolved. There is
reason to think that even if Islamists come to power, after a few cycles of Islamist government many people in the Muslim world would start to look for
something more secular. That is precisely what has happened recently
in Iran, where twenty years of government by mullahs has produced some
positive changes in the country but also many negative consequences.
The economy is weak, unemployment is high, and the health care system
is a shambles. Corruption is rife, and Iran's regional and global political
strength has declined by most measures. The government has also grossly
violated human rights. The bloom is off the rose, and Iranians have, not surprisingly, been thinking about alternatives. Some would like to see more
moderate government, democratic but still Islamist, while others, perhaps a
majority, are starting to think that increased separation between religion
and state might be desirable. Distinctively Islamic economics, for example,
was imagined in Islamist writings as a form of the free market with a human
face—but it turns out not to have been terribly distinctive or effective in
practice.

There, in a nutshell, is the current problem of government in the Muslim
world. Almost certainly, democratizing the Muslim world would produce
real gains for Islamists in the short and medium term. Untainted by scandal,
and steadfast in challenging autocracy, the Islamists speak the language of
the people. They are not perceived as elitists, and they draw on powerful
ideals of justice and authenticity. In a truly democratic system, they would
have to be given a chance to govern if the people wanted them.

Secular-minded Muslims and most Western governments are justifi-
ably worried that Islamist governments might be undemocratic, oppressive,
and anti-Western. Islamist elected governments might call off democratic
elections, or leave elections in place but pass laws that oppress women or

non-Muslims or political opponents. Like Hezbollah in Lebanon, Islamist groups might partially transform themselves into domestic political parties without renouncing violence against Israel. Care must be taken to guard against these real and dangerous possibilities.

On the other hand, the alternative to democracy in the Muslim world seems to be more autocracy. If there is to be any way out of the impasse, it will have to come from imagining some kind of Islamic democracy. A democracy of Muslims with Islamic content need not be Islamist democracy, governed exclusively by Islamic law. It is far more likely to draw on Islam's values and ideals while simultaneously incorporating democratic principles, legal protections, and institutions. But even Islamist democracy, if it can be imagined, might have some advantages over autocracy. Even in an Islamist democracy, where the people have chosen to be governed solely by Islamic law, leaders would be responsible to an electorate, and the rule of law might conceivably be enforced more consistently than it is by the unelected autocrats who prevail in the Muslim world today.

ISLAM, THE WEST, AND THE QUESTION OF OPPOSITION

There are various reasons for thinking that democracy and Islam cannot coexist. According to one view, held by some Westerners and some Islamists, there is a fundamental opposition of values between Islam and the West, or alternatively between Islam and modernity, or Islam and democracy. This sort of view is sometimes attributed, not altogether fairly, to Samuel Huntington, the scholar of democratic development and author of *The Clash of Civilizations*, which proposed a range of new conflicts to replace the Cold War. Although critics expressed deep skepticism about Huntington's suggestion of unavoidable opposition between Islam and the West, after September 11, Huntington looked prescient. The worst attack on American soil had come from an Islamic source. And the attack had not come from a state in the Muslim world but from non-state terrorists, apparently motivated by religious-political beliefs. That made it look like Islamic "civilization" was the source of the attack on America, rather than Muslim governments.

The historian Bernard Lewis, author and editor of important books like *The Arabs in History* and the *Cambridge History of Islam*, and a member of the same Cold War generation as Huntington, is also occasionally seen as falling into the fundamental opposition camp. In his recent work, especially a book called *What Went Wrong?*, Lewis has emphasized the failure of the Muslim world to make its way forward successfully into modernity. The book provides a dazzling scholarly tour of the later Ottoman Empire, then ends with speculation about how the Muslim world failed to embrace Western ideas as apparently unconnected as classical music and political and economic freedom. Lewis does not subscribe to the inherent incompatibility of Islam and the West, or else he would not imply that the Muslim world still has the option of embracing Western values, but he does hint that at present the Muslim and Western worlds have gone so far down different tracks as to make them profoundly alien to one another.

Are Islam and the West deeply at odds, as Huntington and Lewis would both claim? Has the Muslim world "failed" in its encounter with modernity? Part of the reason that these questions are difficult is that some Islamists agree that the values of Islam and the values of the West are incompatible and that the Muslim world has fallen behind the West. Nor is this opinion new among Muslims. Muslims were starting to talk about having "fallen behind" Europe by the late nineteenth century. An influential Arabic book called *Why the Muslims Have Lagged Behind and Why Others Have Advanced* came out in the 1930s. But the Islamists have a distinctive answer to this question. Islamists argue that the Muslim world has fallen behind because it has neglected the wellspring of its own true value system, namely Islam. Muslims have futilely mimicked the West instead of looking within Islam to find answers for the future.

Those who advocate this strand of Islamist thought call on Muslims to look within themselves and to their own traditions. But another, subtly different tendency coexists with the tendency to oppose Western and Islamic ideas. This second tendency seeks to co-opt Western ideas and transform them into Islamic ideas. Remarkably, revision and incorporation of Western ideas can work alongside the superficial rejection of them. A creative thinker can always claim that he has not really incorporated a Western idea but rather identified a value already implicit within Islam and only coincidentally adopted by the West. The tendencies to rejection and to incorporation maintain a productive tension, and one is rarely found without the other.

Beyond the oppositional views of some Islamists, another factor that makes it hard to approach the question of the relationship between Islam and the West is what Edward Said, in what may be one of the two or three most influential academic books in the last thirty years, dubbed *Orientalism*. Said argued that Westerners who have engaged with the Muslim world have tended to see the East as fundamentally different from the West; as a kind of blank slate on which to inscribe their own beliefs, ideas, and interpretations. According to this view, much of what the West says about or sees in the Eastern other is more a projection of Western fantasy than a reflection of how Muslims or people of the East see themselves. To make matters worse, the political relationship of West to East for most of the last two hundred years has been one of Western domination, through a combination of colonization, indirect rule, gunboat diplomacy, and simple influence. If one connects Western ideas about the East to this political relationship, it is possible to conclude that the West is often trying to make sense of the East in order to control it. The potent combination of fantasy and control typifies Saidian Orientalism at its most blatant.

Generalizing about Western attitudes toward Islam calls for a delicate touch. Western philologists, historians, novelists, painters, adventurers, colonial administrators, diplomats, and politicians have engaged with Islam and Muslims, each with different approaches, strategies, and ideals. But even if one remains agnostic about how fully Said's category of Orientalism captures the range of Western thinking about the Muslim world, the concept of Orientalism cautions any Westerner writing about Islam to avoid reducing Muslims and their beliefs to one essential type. The range, variety, and diversity of the 1.2 billion Muslims in the world is breathtaking, and that extends to views, beliefs, culture, values, family structure—indeed, the whole of human experience. And of course not all Muslims are "Eastern." There are Muslims all over Africa and in Europe and the Americas, in addition to East, South, and Southeast Asia, and the Near and Middle East. Muslims make up the majority of the population in as many as fifty countries, from the tiny to the very populous. What is true of Bahrain may not be true of Morocco or Senegal or Pakistan. It may not even be true of Saudi Arabia, even though Bahrain and Saudi Arabia are near neighbors. And although reliable statistics are difficult to obtain, there seems to be no doubt that Islam is growing quickly, perhaps at a rate as high as 2.13 percent per year, compared with 1.4 percent for the world population generally. In a country like Algeria, half the population is under the age of 20. If today Muslims are somewhere between one in five and one in four of the world's population, by 2025 they may be closer to one in three. When speaking of such numbers and variety, it would be a serious mistake to oversimplify.

But it would also be unnecessarily cautious never to speak of "the Muslim world" at all. Muslim countries share family resemblances connected to the language and values that many Muslims associate with Islam. The meaning of Islam is contested, but it is recognizable in the values and beliefs that many Muslims share. Certain movements and ideas speak to Muslims in diverse circumstances because of the way they draw upon those common values and beliefs.

A further warning that can be read into the concept of Orientalism—one particularly relevant to this book—is to avoid writing and thinking in a way that seeks to dominate or impose values upon the Muslim world. Much Western scholarship about Muslims has undeniably come in connection with various projects of colonial, imperial, or, nowadays, superpower influence. A book that addresses Western policy in the Muslim world can easily fall into a certain tone associated with economic and military dominance. That tone says, "Look, this book will tell you what you need to know about Muslims in order to keep them under control."

The West does need to know more in order to decide how to engage the Muslim world. In the aftermath of September 11, enrollment in courses in Arabic and Persian rose, and academics began to seek the government funding that is sure to be forthcoming for Middle Eastern and Islamic studies. The West feels that it needs to understand the Muslim world better in order to protect itself—and if that means maintaining dominance, then that is no doubt what the West will try to do. But assuming dominance can lead to sloppy thinking. The unspoken belief that Muslims do not act for themselves but are acted upon by the West is not only impolite or politically incorrect: it is actually wrong. Muslims, obviously, think through their realistic options, reflect on their values and interests, and make the best decisions they can make under the circumstances. To speak about Muslims in a tone that implies that Western policy can make decisions *for* Muslims will lead to forgetting that Muslims can and will take decisions of their own, independent of Western policy.

To counsel caution is not to avoid speaking, however. If we left each group or nation to speak only about itself, we would have a world of propaganda, not critical enquiry and discussion. Listening to what people say does not require taking people's own view of themselves and their institutions as correct. As for the danger that proposing Western policy amounts to acquiescing in dominance, there is no neutral position for the West or America to take toward the Muslim world. The West must have *some* policy even if it is one of disengagement and isolationism.

Finally, Orientalist thinking promotes the view that the status quo is inevitable, when in fact we might be able to change it by taking a few chances. Democracy and Islam may not be inherently opposed in the way that some Western democrats and some Islamists insist. Perhaps Islam has a greater capacity for flexibility and accommodation than Westerners tend to believe on the basis of incomplete information and nervous projection. Perhaps democracy, too, provides more possibilities than the simple replication of familiar American or Western European institutions and viewpoints. To see the flexibility on both sides, we need to look not only at abstract ideas, like the ideal of human equality that undergirds both democratic and much Muslim political thought, but to the messy way that ideas play themselves out in real life.

Some idealistic democrats might dismiss Islamic democracy as impossible because they cannot see how Islamic thought could accommodate their ideal theories of true democracy. But in practice, those same idealists might admit that Western democracies do not match their ideals either. Thinking about the inherent incompatibility of democracy and Islam may lead democrats to forget that democracy has to be constructed in the real world, and that there may be more room for play in the joints than they think. On the other side, some Muslims may suspect that democracy can never be compatible with the values they might seek to express in an Islamic state. But maybe that view, too, is overhasty. Perhaps the complexity and flexibility of the Islamic tradition is great enough to accommodate democracy.

ISLAM AND DEMOCRACY AS MOBILE IDEAS

The view that Islam and the West are deeply at odds sees in worldviews, cultures, and civilizations a tendency to define themselves *against* other comprehensive systems. It proposes that these oppositions are the most important, determinative features of who we are as people. On this view, the contact of different cultures or civilizations or worldviews is best understood in terms of conflict, such as the one between communist and democratic-capitalist worldviews, or the eight-hundred-year conflict between Muslims and Christians in medieval Spain, which lasted from the initial Muslim conquest to the completion of the Christian *reconquista*. There is no disputing that sometimes worldviews in contact can clash. But alongside conflict, other options exist. Disparate ideas can also interact to produce new, composite ideas that differ from the original ideas underlying them.

I use the term *ideas* not because the words civilization, culture, worldview, and even ideology are not valuable, but because *idea* carries fewer implications about the way beliefs and values are bound up with identity. The word *idea* also avoids even the hint that the people who hold it are the same. You and I can agree that an idea is important to both of us and still disagree about the details of the idea or its consequences. Ideas can be simple or complex. They can be held deeply or casually, dogmatically or experimentally. To say that one is a Muslim, then, or a democrat, might mean simply that one believes in certain ideas, ideas whose content can still be debated. Of course Islam is not only an idea but also a faith, and democracy is not only an idea but a political practice, yet that does not make the terminology any less useful. Faith includes commitment to ideas, and politics involves putting ideas into practice. To speak about Islam and democracy as ideas, not as civilizations or cultures or worldviews, takes nothing away from their aspirations to truth, their depth, or their effect on human conduct; nor does it imply that democracy and Islam must be reduced to just one idea each.

Islam and democracy are not just any sort of ideas, however. These ideas have spread all over the globe, partly by conquest or domination, but also because different people in different places became convinced they were true and relevant to their lives. These ideas, and others like them, have the proven capacity to appeal to many different kinds of people in many places. Both have staying power, too, albeit in different ways. Islam has thrived uninterruptedly for nearly 1,400 years. Democracy has older roots, going back at least to Athens, four hundred years or so before the Christian Era; it then went into a long latency and did not begin to spread around the world in earnest until the nineteenth century.

There is no commonly accepted term for ideas like these, built to travel all over the world to people of disparate backgrounds who live under different conditions. So let us call them *mobile* ideas. Their mobile character derives from their universality, flexibility, and simplicity.

Start with universality. To travel well, an idea must present itself as relevant and true always and everywhere. If the idea claims to be universally applicable to every person, then it has a chance to convince people of disparate backgrounds that it is relevant to them. Modern democracy generally makes such a claim for itself, because its insistence that everyone have a say in government and equal rights before the law depends on its commitment to universal human equality. Islam also lays claim to universality, for the related reason that it believes God makes the same demands on all people, whom he created equal. As in Christianity, another religion that claims to be appropriate for everybody, there are no gradations or chosen subgroups within Islam.

Of course, many ideas that claim universality convince almost no one outside their original sphere. A mobile idea must also be flexible. It must accommodate itself to a wide variety of situations, cultures, and environments. Islam has amply proven its capacity for this sort of flexibility, maintaining its core beliefs while adapting to the languages, family structures, economic systems, and cultural values of peoples all over the world and over an extended period of time. The different strands of Islam, Sunni and Shi'a, rationalist and mystical, popular and scholarly, further suggest flexibility, since each can present itself as authentically Islamic. Democracy, too, has shown a remarkable capacity for flexibility in the various contexts in which it has been tried and in the development of institutions to fit the particular conditions of countries from India to Sweden to Brazil.

Furthermore, to become a mobile idea, it helps for the idea to be simple, which is to say elegant and easily comprehensible. For an idea to have extremely broad appeal, it must be possible to sum up the basic version of that idea in a sentence or two that almost anyone can understand. Very often this simplicity produces logical elegance as well: once one knows the basic idea, much of the detail can be deduced from it. Simplicity has enormous value in producing mobile ideas because it facilitates spreading the idea to people in widely different contexts. To hold together communities based on the idea, it helps for people to be able to know what they believe and be able to state it simply. Islam has a basic creed that is just one sentence long: There is no god but God, and Muhammad is his Prophet. Democracy, too, may be summed up in brief. Although emphases vary, nearly everyone would agree that democracy involves, as one famous definition has it, choosing leaders and making political decisions on the basis of competition for the people's votes.

The simple elegance of the basic version of the idea does not mean that it cannot have many complicated implications. The initiated can, and no doubt will, engage in endless debate about the finer points. Any idea that appeals to many people will inevitably generate a rich scholarship, both internal, by adherents of the idea, and external, produced by critics and observers. But scholarly complications need not cloud the basic message of a mobile idea, which will maintain its simplicity despite the best efforts of scholars to multiply complications.

Not every idea with many adherents is necessarily mobile. Some, like Judaism, are portable, in the sense that they can be brought to many places and made to work there, but lack a feature such as a claim to universality that might encourage many people to adopt them. Others, like Hinduism, have hundreds of millions of followers yet are so complex in their beliefs that they are difficult to export to noncontiguous cultures except piecemeal. Compare soccer, a kind of athletic mobile idea, with baseball, which exists in the United States and its regions of past cultural and colonial hegemony in Latin America and Asia, or cricket, whose domain strictly follows that of the British Empire. Soccer can be played anywhere, on any surface. Its overall conceptual scheme can be grasped in an instant: two goals, a ball, no hands. Baseball, by contrast, like cricket, cannot be comprehended except with extended study. The pitcher, the batter, the bases, the men in the field: a mess. The slogan "Three strikes and you're out" tells you almost nothing you need to know. The element of simplicity is missing. This does not make baseball or cricket any less wonderful or engaging, any more than the possibility that Judaism and Hinduism are not mobile in my sense reduces their tremendous spiritual richness. That an idea is mobile has no bearing on whether it is good or bad or indifferent; mobility is a shorthand that should help reveal something about what happens when ideas come into contact.

Mobile ideas come into contact the moment a person who espouses one mobile idea hears of another and is moved to figure out the relationship between them. This happens to mobile ideas more than to most others for the simple reason that greater mobility and more adherents increase the likelihood of contact. When mobile ideas meet, they can conflict, but that is hardly the only possibility. People can take on different parts of disparate ideas for themselves, mixing and matching to come up with arrangements that work for them, even if they are not perfectly coherent. A committed socialist may make her living as a day-trading capitalist; someone else may wear a Hermès scarf on her head as a Muslim *hijab*. In his provocative and popular book *The Lexus and the Olive Tree*, Thomas Friedman described a kind of cosmopolitanism in which some people manage to reconcile different ideas in their lives, while others are not able to reconcile these ideas. The ideas from which cosmopolitans pick and choose need not be mobile ideas but often are.

Cosmopolitanism works best for individuals and subcultures, or in limited geographical spaces like cities; it does not work terribly well as a strategy for collective action like government. Cosmopolitanism assumes that people make their own individual, idiosyncratic choices about which parts of which ideas they want to mix and match. This makes it difficult to use cosmopolitan principles to design a political system, which requires some agreement about basic rules. Some techniques of government, like federalism, allow for regional diversity alongside national government. But even in a federal system, some local or semi-local body still has to reach agreement to govern effectively. Cosmopolitanism is also typically a strategy for the rich and free. It is no coincidence that Friedman's title mentions a Lexus, not a Lada. A cosmopolitan needs access to ideas, and the political freedom to express them. Muslim girls in some French schools are not free to wear a *hijab*, Hermès or otherwise. And in some parts of the Muslim world, like Saudi Arabia and Iran, the *hijab* must by law be a dark color. A fleur-de-lis design would not do, so our cosmopolitan Muslim fashionista may not be able to express her particular set of choices.

Another kind of contact between mobile ideas takes place when disparate ideas, juxtaposed almost by accident, spontaneously generate a new hybrid idea. Something like this happens when people who speak different languages—newly captured slaves or military draftees, for example—are thrown together and have to come up with a way to communicate. Their ad hoc communication eventually grows into its own full-fledged creole language. Unlike cosmopolitanism, with its almost irreducible individuality, creolization can produce a common language, culture, idea, or even political system. The creole idea is always becoming something; it is as much a stance or an attitude of openness and spontaneity as it is a single identifiable idea, argument, or belief.

Democracy and Islam might conceivably have produced a creole combination if the West had brought democracy with it to the Muslim world. But the West had no such ambitions, preferring colonial rule, as in French North Africa, or imperial influence, as in the British supervision of the first modern Arab kingdoms; so now, if there is a creole form of government in the Muslim world, it is probably post-socialist autocracy. Creolization is still a real possibility for democracy and Islam in Europe, where millions of Muslims live in democracies and participate in them when and if they are permitted to become citizens. Under these fertile conditions, Muslim-European cultural creolization has already produced thrilling music that combines traditional North African *rai* with rap and techno. But because Muslims are a minority in democratic Europe, the creole that might emerge there is more likely to be a version of Islam that is open to democracy than a system of government that might qualify as Islamic democracy. In the Muslim world, where by definition Muslims are in the majority, one wants to look for a comprehensive system of democratic government infused by Islam, not just an Islam that can coexist with secular democracy; and there has been no accidental or natural juxtaposition of Islam and democracy that would make such a synthesis possible.

So cosmopolitanism and creolization probably are not the best models for the contact between the mobile ideas of Islam and democracy in the Muslim world. Conflict of course remains a possibility, but self-conscious effort has the potential to make democracy and Islam fit together. That kind of self-consciousness means intentionally combining these ideas to produce some distinctively new idea, a creative synthesis of the other two. The new idea of Islamic democracy must be more than just an admixture. It must have its own productive capacity—the ability to appeal to people and solve problems on its own terms. Synthesis requires hard work in figuring how the underlying ideas can function together, and what changes are needed in each in order to make the result meaningful. There are no guarantees or laws of history that make synthesis an inevitable result of the contact between Islam and democracy, but there are also no rules rendering it impossible. The outcome will depend on contingent facts: real people making decisions about ideas in the context of existing policies and institutions.

Syntheses of mobile ideas turn up in unexpected places. Social democracy was born of the self-conscious attempt to synthesize socialism with the democratic idea. Liberal democracy itself is a synthesis of the idea of basic human rights with the idea of collective democratic decision making. That synthesis has been so successful that many definitions of democracy now assume that liberalism is built in. Even Roman Catholicism can be understood historically as a synthesis between the mobile idea of the

Roman imperium and early Christianity, a synthesis that Protestantism self-consciously sought to undo. Nor need the synthesis of mobile ideas always produce positive results—think of National Socialism, the bastard child of ethnic nationalism and "scientific" socialism.

Synthesis is no panacea, and it is not inherently desirable. Each synthesis needs to be evaluated on its own terms. But the possibility for some sort of provisional synthesis between Islam and democracy exists, and it is potentially very promising. At all events, if we assume that, like communism and democracy, Islam and democracy will not prove able to bridge their differences, the prophecy of failure will be self-fulfilling.

———◆———

THE RESILIENCE OF ISLAM

Today, Islam and democracy are very much in contact. Many people in the Muslim world, ordinary and elite, would like to run their countries democratically. There are, furthermore, many good reasons that people should be able to choose their own government, and that it would be in Western interests if Muslim countries were democratic. Why bother, then, to talk about *Islamic* democracy? Why not simply propose that the Muslim world should democratize, and that the West should help, and leave it at that?

The reason, of course, is the persistent power of Islam in the politics of the Muslim world. Yet the prestige of Islam as a source of political language has not been constant. A century ago, an impartial observer might have thought that Islam's influence within its sphere was fading as fast as organized Christianity's in Europe. After almost five hundred years of glory and accomplishment, the Ottoman Empire was on its last legs. The empire formed the institutional center of Islam; its sultan was not only the ruler of the empire but also the caliph: deputy of the Prophet Muhammad, part of a chain stretching back to the beginning of Islam. Shadow of God on Earth and Commander of the Faithful, the caliph purported to direct the affairs of the entire Muslim community, and his legitimacy, which spanned the Sunni Muslim world, depended in part on religious claims.

The modern young men who, starting in the 1860s, sought to reform the empire from within tended to believe that Islam was part of the empire's decline. They associated Islam with an old-world, old-fashioned, and failing way of life. The future lay to the West. In this brief first flowering of democracy in the Muslim world, the Ottoman reformers wanted to transform the empire into a constitutional monarchy, leaving the sultan as a figurehead and running the empire through a basically secular parliament.

The other important voice in the declining Ottoman Empire was that of the Arab nationalists, who, moved by new European ideas, were starting to imagine an Arab nation free from Ottoman control. Arab nationalism sought to locate an identity in Arabic language, culture, and civilization rather than in Islam. The category of Islam included many people, only some of whom were Arab: Ottoman Turks, Balkan Muslims, Persians, and so forth. On the other hand, the nationalists' preferred category—"Arab"—included Christian Arabs, some of whom were theorists of Arab nationalism, and even Arabic-speaking Jews. It very pointedly did not include non-Arab Muslims, like Ottoman Turks. So although Arab nationalists wanted the empire to break apart, while Ottoman reformers wanted to preserve it through rejuvenation, both of the two most vital movements in the dying empire saw Islam as a relic of the past, not an important basis for political ideology or organization. Islam seemed poised to go the way that Christianity did in twentieth-century Western Europe—from a once-powerful organizing system to a mild, private form of worship, taken seriously by only a few. That did not happen, although for a few years in the middle of the twentieth century it once again looked as though it might. Instead Islam, as a basis for political thought and organization, took a curious alternate route.

Around the time that Ottoman reformers and Arab nationalists were beginning to marginalize Islam, a small group of thinkers emerged who argued that it was too soon to consign Islam to the dustbin. Islamic modernists, most famously Jamal al-Din al-Afghani, his student Muhammad Abduh, and his follower Rashid Rida, agreed that Islam as understood and practiced in the Ottoman Empire was failing the Muslims; but instead of blaming Islam, the Islamic modernists blamed traditional Muslim scholars for having allowed the once-vibrant Islamic tradition to ossify. In the Middle Ages, Islamic civilization led the world in science, technology, and philosophy, so Islam could hardly be faulted for the scientific and technological backwardness of Muslim societies. Muslim Córdoba had running water and streetlights when Paris was a sewer. Navigation, mathematics, optics, philosophy, and chemistry had all flourished in the Muslim world and made their way slowly into medieval Europe.

The Islamic modernists concluded that Islam needed to be updated to take account of advances in modern science, technology, and philosophy. They took as precedent the medieval successes of Islamic civilization, which had come in part because Muslims translated and studied Greek science and philosophy, then innovated beyond what they found there. The glories of medieval Islam, in other words, required serious engagement with the best ideas that the rest of the world had to offer. The answer to the problems of the Muslim world was to have another go at such an engagement.

At the same time, the Islamic modernists wanted to revive Islam, so they argued that many ideas in the West were in fact to be found within Islamic tradition. If one went back to the Prophet himself and to his companions, before the traditional scholars decontextualized the authentic and original teachings of Islam, one would discover truths that, coincidentally or not, resembled the ideas of modern Western thinkers.

The political implications of this modernist move were uncertain. Some modernists, envisioning a pan-Islamic politics that would draw on Muslim governmental tradition, called for revival of the caliphate, which the Turks had abolished in a fit of post–World War I secularization. Other modernists moved in the direction of Western liberalism and sought to separate religion and state. One such modernist, 'Ali 'Abd al-Raziq, published a controversial Arabic book arguing that Islam concerned only private life and therefore had nothing whatever to say about politics. This liberal Islamic view was roundly condemned by traditionalists and by some other modernists. It did not catch on in the Muslim world, although some Westerners, equating modernity with liberalism, have never given up arguing that Islam must be privatized to bring the Muslim world into modernity.

The Islamic modernists may have been onto something, but they had only limited success. Traditional scholars, who saw themselves as keepers of the flame, preservers of the traditions that had come down to them in commentaries and dense treatises, resisted the Islamic modernists' approach. Ottoman reformers and Arab nationalists had little need to dress up modern ideas in Islamic garb. They were willing to embrace many Western ideas on their own terms, without attributing Islamic origins to them. One frequently hears Islamic modernism described as a failed intellectual movement.

But if Islamic modernism did not succeed on its own terms, it did unexpectedly provide the material for a different movement within modern Islamic history: the movement known as political Islam, Islamism, or sometimes Islamic fundamentalism. Political Islam continues to attract followers today, despite rumors of its death or failure, and it still matters centrally in the Muslim world. The story of its birth and passage through the twentieth century has been told by others, but it is fascinating and relevant enough to deserve a brief description here.

The most influential student of the Islamic modernists was Hasan al-Banna, an Egyptian born in 1906 and trained in the most modern educational institution in Cairo, then picturesquely known as the House of Sciences. Banna had memorized the Qur'an as a boy but had not attended a religious high school or the seminary mosque of al-Azhar, which was and remains the most important Sunni center of higher Islamic learning. Banna was impressed by the modernists' idea of going back to the Prophet and his companions to find the sources of Islam. Convinced that Islam could provide the answers that were necessary to go forward in the modern world, he did not think those answers were necessarily similar to answers found in the modern West.

Looking back to the Prophet and his companions convinced Banna that Islam was not merely a faith but a comprehensive worldview that covered the whole field of human existence. Islam was "religion and state, book and sword, and a way of life." It provided a blueprint for a just society, organized along Islamic principles. Like the Islamic modernists, Banna thought that the traditional Muslim scholars had failed to preserve the essence of Muhammad's message and had been too willing to go along with whoever held political power. They had allowed Islam to be cabined into the area of religion, without realizing its full potential to express itself politically, legally, socially, and intellectually. Similarly, the medieval books favored by the scholars could for the most part be put aside as digressions from the true Islamic path. The mature Banna's Islam was therefore both political and fundamentalist: political in refusing to be relegated to the sphere of the private or the personal, and fundamentalist in the technical sense that it went back to the most basic, fundamental elements of Islam—the divine message of the Qur'an and the sayings and actions of the Prophet and his followers.

Banna also popularized the use of the word *Islamic* as an adjective. In Arabic, the name of the religion is Islam, and the people who subscribe to its beliefs are Muslims. Though Arabic abounds in adjectives made from nouns, there was little need for the adjective *Islamic*. Banna helped change that by insisting on a description of Islam as a comprehensive worldview that, compared to Western worldviews, was "Islamic," with its own distinctive message and way of life. The adjectival form reflected a new way of thinking, in which Islamism supplanted Islam. *Islamists* are therefore not just Muslims but people who see Islam as a comprehensive political, spiritual, and personal worldview defined in opposition to all that is non-Islamic.

More than an influential thinker, Banna was also a charismatic leader. In 1928 he founded the Muslim Brotherhood, a religious, social, and educational organization that followed Banna's logic and became explicitly political in 1939. It emerged as a sort of organic catchall for personal development, social life, and the promotion of religious and political ideas and action. In particular, the Brotherhood assumed the character of a cohesive, intensely loyal political movement opposed to the British-backed monarchy.

The Brotherhood was not the most important political force in Egypt, but it gave voice to a powerful argument against the existing political order: reliant on the British, the Egyptian government failed to express the ideals of Islamic government and Islamic law. The Brotherhood soon became a thorn in the side of the monarchy. Banna addressed tracts directly to the king, demanding the Islamization of Egyptian life. He compared King Farouk to Pharaoh, an evil denier of God in the Qur'an as much or more than in the Bible. Some Brothers participated in political violence against the monarchy. In 1949, as Farouk clung to power, Banna was assassinated by Egyptian secret police.

Banna's death devastated the Brotherhood; his successor lacked his charisma and clear intellectual vision. But the Brotherhood did have the last laugh on the monarchy when Brotherhood members joined army officers in the coup that deposed Farouk in 1952. The Brotherhood remained affiliated with the new government until 1954, when Gamal Abdul Nasser took power in a coup of his own. Nasser understood that the Brotherhood's message conflicted with his vision of a socialist Egypt. Establishing a pattern that was to be followed by a generation of military dictators, Nasser identified the Brotherhood as a potent threat and banned the organization. Now he, too, became a target of the Brotherhood's disapproval.

Meanwhile the Brotherhood began to spread outside Egypt, and new chapters sprang up in the Muslim world. This process was the single most important institutional element in the diffusion of political Islam. In most places the Brotherhood stayed small and kept a low profile. The death of Banna was fresh in the memory of both the Brothers and the rulers of the countries where they lived. Islamic fundamentalism, in fact, had such a low profile that most people outside the Middle East had never heard of it. In Egypt, where the Brotherhood had started, though, some Brothers took a more radical turn.

The radical faction of the Brothers in Egypt came under the influence of Sayyid Qutb, who, although he was the same age as the executed Banna, had joined the Brotherhood later in life. Qutb was a distinguished literary critic and theorist of education before a midlife turn to Islamism. A talented writer, he embarked on a second career as the most important theorist of radical political Islam. Qutb went further than Banna in his rejection of governments that failed to follow Islamic principles. In a series of influential books and pamphlets, he argued that the world could be divided into two kinds of societies. A society that embodied Islamic values in the realms of law, economics, and politics counted as truly Islamic. A society that fell short in any of these areas belonged to the realm of ignorant barbarism. To communicate this latter idea, Qutb described the un-Islamic society with the word that the Qur'an uses to describe Arabia before Muhammad's prophecy: *jahiliyya*. The Arabic term drips with contempt and a touch of pity. To live in ignorant barbarism, without the Qur'an or Islam, was to be benighted, unlucky, and more than a little immoral.

Qutb's innovation was to apply the idea of ignorant barbarism not only to non-Muslims who had never heard Muhammad's call, but also to states populated by Muslims who had neglected to make their states truly Islamic.

The contempt came in here, but the practical consequences were more important. An imperfect Muslim state might be in need of reform and repair, as Banna had suggested. But a state mired in ignorant barbarism needed to be replaced completely. Its leaders and perhaps its citizens, too, bore the responsibility for neglecting, slighting, and ultimately ignoring the teachings of Islam. Qutb therefore counseled forceful, even violent resistance to un-Islamic government.

Qutb did not hide the fact that he thought his analysis applied to Nasser's Egypt. Not surprisingly, Nasser objected, and Qutb was jailed for a decade, released briefly, then jailed again, and executed in 1966. But he was allowed to write during much of his time in prison, and there he continued to produce the books that have kept his views alive among Islamists. These include a long and often-reprinted commentary on the Qur'an, in which Qutb's worldview is laid out alongside the Qur'anic verses that support it, and a series of essays, called *Milestones*, that forms the core of the radical fundamentalist canon even today.

During the decade and a half between Qutb's execution and the Iranian revolution of 1979, political Islam hit its low point in the Arab world. Chapters of the Brotherhood existed in various places, but they remained relatively quiet. In Egypt the Brotherhood was suppressed. Nationalism, often with a socialist twist and Soviet support, continued to dominate the Arab political scene, and indeed much of the Muslim world. Anwar Sadat, who, succeeding Nasser, began his presidency by briefly showing more sympathy than Nasser had for the Brotherhood, soon reverted to an anti-Islamist position, especially when the Islamists opposed Sadat's peace overtures toward Israel.

During this period from 1966 to 1979, there was still little reason for an impartial observer to think that political Islam was poised for a sudden flowering of support and visibility. But despite the hegemony of nationalism, political Islam never entirely disappeared, even if, after the death of Qutb, it went into suspended animation. The impetus to bring political Islam out of this cryogenic state came not from within the Arab world, but from Iran.

Iran was an unlikely source to rekindle a broader political Islam. Iranian nationalism was at least as secular as Arab nationalism. In fact, the shahs of Iran had pressed secularism even further than had their Arab counterparts. In the 1930s, Reza Shah Pahlavi actually mandated Western attire for women, prohibiting them from leaving their homes while wearing traditional Islamic garb. Young women responded positively, but some older women felt deeply uncomfortable and even refused to leave their homes for fear of appearing in public dressed in a way that made them feel naked.

Iranians were also Shi'i Muslims, not Sunnis. Their form of Islam was anathema to many Sunni Arabs, who were disinclined to listen to Shi'i views of how to run a society. What was more, Shi'i Muslims had a strong tradition of keeping their heads down and letting the government rule unfettered by criticism or resistance. The legacy of years of minority status and oppression at the hands of Sunnis, this quiescence was bred deep in the bone for many Shi'is. It made the flourishing of activist political Islam among Shi'i thinkers all the more unlikely.

But flourish it did. Influenced by their own intellectual traditions, but also indirectly by Banna, Qutb, and the Pakistani activist Abul Ala Maududi, a contemporary who had written in the same Islamist mode, Shi'i clerics began, in the 1960s, to develop their own brand of political Islam. The most famous ideologue remains Ayatollah Ruhollah Khomeini, but there were others of comparable importance in those years, including Ayatollah Muhammad Baqir al-Sadr, an Iraqi Shi'i executed by Saddam Hussein in 1980, and the Iranian intellectual 'Ali Shariati.

In 1979 this brand of Shi'a political Islam entered the world stage; and the role of Islam in politics in the Muslim world would be changed by it permanently. The Iranian Revolution that toppled the shah did not start as a purely Islamic revolution. Communists, socialists, ordinary leftists, and bourgeois Iranians alike were frustrated with Mohammad Reza Shah Pahlavi's corrupt and oppressive regime and with American support for it. All these and more took to the streets in the revolution's first stages. But before long it became clear that the Islamists had the edge at the grass roots and in the revolutionary structure. As the Islamists consolidated power, the other revolutionary factions found themselves excluded. Soon the revolution was an Islamist revolution, with the chance to set up an Islamic government from scratch. Because of its Shi'a character, the state would look very different from the Sunni Muslim state envisioned by Banna and Qutb. In particular, the clergy would play a much greater role, corresponding to the much greater centrality of the imam in Shi'a religious thought. But the state would still be an Islamic state by anyone's yardstick. Political Islam was going to get its day in the sun.

In political ideology as in business, nothing succeeds like success. The moribund Islamist movement in the Arab world began to come alive as Arabs started to think that an Islamic state was a real possibility. Around the same time, people in the Arab world started talking about the failures of Arab nationalism. It had not managed to defeat Israel, nor had it made the Arab states rich or particularly secure. Adding insult to injury, Sadat had broken ranks with the other Arab countries in 1978 and signed a peace deal with Israel. Egypt got back the Sinai Peninsula, which the Israelis had conquered in 1967; but making peace with Israel hardly resonated with the proud tradition of Arab nationalism.

The response to Sadat came not from within the nationalist camp but from political Islam. A small group of Egyptian Islamists, more radical than the Brotherhood and inspired by an updated version of Qutb's philosophy, decided to assassinate Sadat. They reasoned that Sadat was worse than a bad Muslim—he was an outright infidel. Resuscitating a marginal doctrine from Islamic tradition, they declared it their duty to execute the infidel who was ruling their state. Sadat was assassinated in October 1981 by a man who announced he had "killed the Pharaoh."

Now political Islam in the Arab world began to emerge as a serious force. One prominent success was Afghanistan, where non-Afghan Muslims, attracted by the message of political Islam, and supported by the United States, went to fight beside Afghans to liberate Muslim territory from the Soviets. After the war, they went back to their home countries and promoted the ideas they had lived in combat. Since September 11, 2001, much has been written about the Arab Afghans ("Afghans" only in that they had fought in Afghanistan), because one of them was Osama bin Laden. For our purposes, it is enough to say that the Arab Afghans played a key role in propagandizing for political Islam. It did not matter whether they really had fought the Soviets, or how much; reports differ, and one is inclined to be skeptical about the Arabs' military impact. What mattered was that they had impressive stories to tell, that the Soviets had been defeated, and that these Islamists had met each other. Their rhetoric helped form the nucleus of a pan-Islamic movement of the kind Islamists had been talking about since Banna.

A second booster shot for political Islam came in the form of Saudi support. The Saudis were not themselves practitioners of political Islam. Saudi courts apply Islamic law, but the Saudi form of government derives from traditional tribal rule, updated and fitted to monarchy. The Saud family, whose country is named after them, are followers of Wahhabism, a strict form of Islam that has some points in common with political Islam, but which is very far from being the same thing. Both movements believe that the Prophet and his followers are the most important models for crafting a religiously proper life. But that is where they part company. In its Saudi form, Wahhabism is deeply conservative. Two generations ago, the Saudi rulers had to pressure Wahhabi scholars just to allow modern conveniences like cars into the kingdom. By contrast, political Islam is forward-looking and eminently modern in its insistence on science, propaganda, technology, and engagement with the world. Followers of political Islam in the 1980s and 1990s resisted governments and assassinated leaders; Saudi Wahhabism found all this freelancing unnerving. The Saudis thought that the decision to wage jihad lay with the ruler, not the individual believer. And they definitely rejected the idea that small groups could go around declaring rulers to be infidels and killing them. Yet the Saudis became the largest funders of local Muslim Brotherhood chapters and other hard-line Islamists in the eighties and nineties.

Why? One reason was the regional balance of power with Iran. The Saudis knew that the Iranians had gained prestige and influence after their defeat of the U.S.-backed monarchy, and it was in Saudi geostrategic interests to keep the Iranians at bay. The Iranians were exporting their ideas wherever they could—for example, by supporting Shi'i Hezbollah in Lebanon. The Saudis could buy influence of their own by supporting Sunni brands of political Islam, much as the United States supported anticommunist insurgents like the contras in Nicaragua. In the case of Afghanistan, Sunni political Islam and anticommunist insurgency even coincided.

Supporting local Islamists also put the Saudis' finger in every national pie in the Muslim world. It made them major players in places where they might otherwise have been peripheral, like Afghanistan, where the United States was first supportive of the Saudi role, then willing to turn a blind eye once American interest waned. Finally, in broad terms, the Islamists looked like good allies to the Saudis. Banna had been a Saudi sympathizer of sorts. Strict Wahhabi Islam looked as though it might be similar to other kinds of strict Islam. In short, the Saudis made almost the same mistake of confusing Wahhabism with political Islam that might forgivably be made by a casual observer.

With a cohort of self-proclaimed veterans of the Afghan jihad, Saudi financial support, and the example of Iran in mind, political Islam had a good decade in the eighties. When the nineties dawned, political Islam looked like a vibrant force. Since then, however, if measured by political success, it has made little progress. No Arab state officially adopted political Islam in the nineties.

But the failure of violent revolution does not capture the full complexity of the role political Islam plays today. Islamic modernism, and the political Islam that grew from it, introduced a creative, supple, productive capacity into modern Muslim thought. A century ago, it was arguably justified to complain, as the Islamic modernists did, that Islam had fallen into a rut of unthinkingly conservative imitation of past forms. Today no informed critic, internal or external, could say any such thing. To the contrary, Islam today possesses an intellectual vibrancy of which most other great religious traditions can only dream. The ferment in Islam is not always overt or forward-looking, of course. Indeed, one often hears fundamentalists denying the originality of their interpretations, the better to claim that they are simply revealing the true essence of Islam. But ironically or not, it is the very creativity embodied in a century of political Islam that is now allowing political Islam to adopt democratic means and ideals. In its engagement with foreign ideas, even when rejecting them, political Islam has developed a remarkable flexibility.

So perhaps it is not surprising that where democracy has been tentatively tried, Islamist candidates have attracted support. Jordan in the early 1990s is an excellent example. King Hussein ran into economic problems after the Gulf War, as trade with embargoed Iraq slowed. To let off some steam, the king experimented by allowing more open elections for parliament. The local chapter of the Muslim Brotherhood spun off a political party and became a mainstream political force. Eventually Jordan drew back a bit from this democratic experiment, and the Islamist party sat out one set of elections; but the point is that Islamists did well when they were given the chance. Even the Egyptian parliament, hardly a bastion of pluralist democracy, has some members who belong privately to the Brotherhood. Throughout the Arab world, political Islam still exists, and if it has retreated from a strategy of violent overthrow of governments, it is increasingly seeking a greater role in conventional politics.

Meanwhile, outside the Arab world, political Islam has continued to catch on. Several northern Nigerian states have rather haphazardly adopted some elements of *shari'a*, the classical Islamic law that is typically the first plank of the Islamists' electoral platform. The motivation was democratic in the sense that Muslim politicians proposed the adoption of *shari'a* to consolidate popular support. Under the secularist Pervez Musharraf, Islamist political parties won more seats in Pakistani elections than they had in years. In Indonesia, the Islamic movement played an important role in the overthrow of the Suharto dictatorship and the subsequent process of democratization. In Afghanistan, the Taliban, which embodied an extreme yet unsophisticated type of political Islam, took over in the early nineties. The Taliban did not collapse until American bombs sent them fleeing, and if it had not been for the mistake of harboring Osama bin Laden, the Taliban would no doubt be in power still, for all their oppression of women and non-Pashtun Afghans.

This brief history of political Islam suggests that it is always a mistake to count Islam out. Islam looked weak as a political force a hundred years ago and again fifty years ago, yet in each case it stayed alive. Now that the movement of political Islam has in fact been tried in Iran, it is not likely to go into hibernation until other countries, especially Arab countries, have had a chance to try it in one form or another. Political Islam was born in protest against Western-backed Arab governments, and in most places it remains an oppositional movement. That means that people who hate their governments for being unjust and oppressive will be at least loosely sympathetic to Islamist ideas. The primary reason for the resilience of political Islam is that political Islam always depicts itself as aspiring to justice. The rhetoric of justice can be tremendously effective in capturing hearts and minds, especially in states where justice is so obviously lacking.

GOD'S RULE AND THE PEOPLE'S RULE

How, exactly, might Islam and democracy coexist? The sine qua non of democracy is collective self-government through popular elections. If one looks at the medieval classics of Islamic political theory, though, such elections do not figure. Nor have governments in Islamic history, from the earliest period until today, relied on popular elections when choosing their leaders. Yet in recent years, various proposals for Islamic democracy built on consultation, consent of the governed, and political pluralism have emerged. Islamic democrats—from intellectuals like Tunisian exile Rachid Ghannouchi, to politicians like President Mohammad Khatami of Iran, to ordinary Muslim would-be voters—all have subtly different views about the nature of Islamic democracy. But their arguments converge at certain points and can be combined to give an overview of the theory of Islamic democracy.

The central element of all these proposals is a rich conception of the Muslim community, or *umma*. The first Muslim community was organized out of tribes whose pre-Islamic identities derived from intense, complicated structures of tribal solidarity. Tribes had their own poets who sang the tribes' history and glories. They had their own holy men and gods, and their own tribal war cries handed down for generations. The Prophet persuaded the members of these divided tribes to see themselves as united by a belief in God and in Muhammad's prophecy. Adopting Islam meant transcending tribal solidarity to put one's identity as a Muslim and a member of the community of Muslims first. That the Prophet's revolutionary message of community formation succeeded in such an inhospitable environment is testament to its appeal, and to the early Muslims' capacity to imagine themselves in new ways. The coalescence of the Arab tribes under the banner of the Muslim community was as remarkable as it was formidable.

As Islam spread through the Near and Middle East, the idea of the community became ever more capacious, expanding across ethnic, linguistic, and geographical boundaries. The community of the Muslims did not eliminate these other forms of identity nor seek to make them disappear, but presented itself as a point of unification beyond and above other kinds of identity. The community of the Muslims was a community of faith but also a political community, governed during the Prophet's life on the basis of legislative direction provided by God. After Muhammad's death, however, prophecy ceased, leaving questions of who would rule and on what legal basis. In the voluminous and highly speculative literature about the early years of Islam, there is a general consensus that the first rulers of the community adopted the title "Caliph" (Arabic *khalifa*), which means a delegate or a viceroy or a replacement: someone who stands in for someone else. Whether the caliphs were stand-ins for the dead Prophet or delegates of God himself turns out to be a difficult historical question that remains unresolved with respect to the early caliphate. In any case, from the beginning of Muslim history, the caliphs were understood to be selected by people, not God; they were subject to God's law as described in the Qur'an and the sayings of the Prophet; and they were expected to engage in some sort of consultation with the community they governed. These features of early Islamic political theory provide the basis for all modern theories of Islamic democracy.

Early Muslims agreed that the caliph was not to be chosen by God but nominated and then approved by a group of people with the power to "loose and bind." "Loosing" and "binding" are legal metaphors for binding people to allegiance to a government, or absolving people of the responsibility to obey. Once the caliph was nominated, he then had to be approved through an "agreement" (the Arabic word *bay'a* means any contractual agreement, especially a commercial one) in which the binders and loosers formally gave their assent to his ascension to the position of caliph. This bound the community of the Muslims to obey the caliph; but as the concept of "loosing" suggests, the people may in theory have retained the power to displace the caliph if he did not keep his side of the bargain.

Like any historical evidence of ancient constitutional practices, the agreement between the caliph and the people who loose and bind has been subjected to various interpretive strategies over the years. Medieval political theorists tried to make sense of the agreement in ways that would legitimate caliphs and caliphal aspirants who had no intention of letting anyone but themselves have constitutional authority. Many Islamic modernists, however, and some Islamists today, see the roots of modern democracy in the nomination of the caliph and the agreement between the caliph and the binders and loosers. The caliph does not ascend the throne but is selected— or if you will, elected—by a group of people who represent the entire Muslim community. His authority therefore derives, they argue, from the consent of the Muslim people. This is the consent of the governed in capsule form.

The caliph, or any other ruler who might be appointed in the absence of a qualified and effective caliph, has the task of administering Islamic law, not of making it. Islamic law derives ultimately from God, but it is interpreted by the scholars and by the community as a whole through the consensus of the community. The ruler is subject to the law, not above it. The Islamic state is a state of rights and law, not arbitrary or absolute power. In it, the ruler is accountable to God and to the people who have assented to his rule.

And once the ruler is in power, he must follow the Qur'anic command to engage in consultation (*shura*). The nature of this consultation is not specified in any detail in the Qur'an, which leaves a great deal of room for speculation and argument. Indeed, the proceedings of a conference on the subject of *shura* and democracy held at al-Azhar in 1997 fill three thick volumes. But in recent years, Muslim political theorists have argued that *shura* amounts to a robust exchange of political views, expressed through elections that give bite to the opinions of the people. In the process, opinions will differ, but this, too, is anticipated by the disagreement on questions of Islamic law that the community of the Muslims has always tolerated as an inevitable result of human disagreement about what God's word means.

While some critics object that consultation can never be binding, others suggest it is obligatory for the ruler to follow the people's will or lose his post. This is particularly plausible if the ruler is not a caliph but simply a person chosen to lead by virtue of being elected to the job.

It is tempting to undermine this sketch of the "binding and loosing" theory by asking how plausible it is in historical terms, or by assessing the ways that contemporary Muslims have distorted such classical theories in order to rationalize new forms of governance. Historically valuable as such an exercise might be, it would profoundly miss the point—which is that many modern Muslims see in their tradition the seeds of democratic structure. The question is not whether that structure is "really there" in early Muslim history or classical Islamic political theory; that is an interpretive question for Muslims to address. What matters is that potential democratic readings of Islamic tradition are possible, and that Muslims today are reading their tradition that way.

This précis of the theory of Islamic democracy is just the beginning of a full-fledged account of an Islamic democracy, ruled by elected leaders responsible to law and the people. There are various ways in which Islamic democracies might shape the relationship between elections, legislatures, and Islamic governance while remaining true both to some form of democracy and to some form of Islam. All have been suggested by various Muslim thinkers.

One possible Islamic state would guarantee equal rights and freedom of religion to all its citizens, Muslims and non-Muslims alike. What would make such a state Islamic might be simply a declaration that Islam is the state's official religion, and perhaps some commitment to this ideal in the symbolism of flags, oaths of office, prayers of invocation, and state support of mosques. Assume that all these activities were decided by a large majority vote, and that Islamic law did not form the basis for the state's laws. This state would be Islamic in much the same way that Britain is Anglican Christian.

Such a state could surely be counted as a democracy. The existence of an official religion does not necessarily infringe on any basic right. That does not mean that the declaration would have no effect on non-Muslims, who are being told that, in some sense, their state chooses to ally itself with beliefs they do not share. Non-Muslims would likely feel their minority status keenly. They might feel awkward, uncomfortable, or even insecure. But as long as the decision to make Islam the state religion followed a democratic principle of collective self-government, the declaration of Islam as the official religion would be democratically justified. The harm to non-Muslims might be real, but it need not differ from the harm suffered by religious minorities elsewhere, such as British Muslims.

A second possible Islamic democracy might adopt a provision in its constitution announcing that classical Islamic law shall be a source of law for the nation. This is a very popular suggestion among Islamists as a step toward the creation of an Islamic state. Pakistan and Egypt both have versions of such provisions in their constitutions. If the people have in fact chosen this constitutional provision legitimately, then there is a sense in which this is nothing more than a constitutional decision following from electoral politics and expressing values shared by the great majority. In another sense, though, the injection of Islamic law or its values into the state's legal system creates a backdrop for laws that will be passed later. That *shari'a* backdrop brings Islam and traditional or believing Muslims into a potential alliance with the state. Muslims might be able to relate to the laws of the state differently from non-Muslims. Even if we assume that making *shari'a* into a formal source of law means that the people could choose *not* to adopt classical Islamic law whenever they wanted, the constitutional provision still sets the default, making it easier for Muslims than for other people to get laws passed that accord with their preferred values. This places non-Muslims (as well as secular Muslims, sectarian Muslims, and perhaps those who argue that *shari'a* must evolve) at a distinct disadvantage in the political sphere even if they get to vote and participate in elections.

This is a real problem for imagining Islamic democracy, but it is not insurmountable. An Islamic state that acknowledges classical Islamic law as one source of law among several does not embrace Islamic law in its totality. The state can still make sure that basic rights are observed and that everyone is treated equally. As I shall explore in a moment, one does not have to interpret Islam as insisting on second-class citizenship for non-Muslims. So long as the state protects non-Muslims and treats them equally, this state, too, might be compatible with democracy.

A third possible Islamic state might adopt Islamic law as its exclusive legal system. The legislature could accomplish this by enacting, law by law, a code of rules that correspond to Islamic law. There actually is such a code in existence, enacted in the later phases of the Ottoman Empire in an attempt to bring codified order to the classical Islamic law. This code, the Majalla, was used as a model for other codes of law in the Muslim world. In practice, the legislature would have to choose just one interpretation of Islamic law for each of the provisions that it chose. This approach sounds as if it is consistent with democratic practice, since it involves a series of decisions by a democratically elected legislature.

Alternatively, an Islamic democracy might adopt Islamic law across the board by enacting a constitutional provision stating that classical Islamic law shall be the law of the land. Classical Islamic law is more like old English common law than like statute law. Instead of statute books full of hundreds or thousands of codified legal rules, classical Islamic law consists of the opinions of scholars and judges throughout the ages, recorded in everything from books of legal theory, to reports of actual cases and decisions, to handbooks of hypothetical cases. The scholars disagree, and the diversity of opinions on many legal questions is one of the glories of the classical Islamic legal tradition. All these legal sources reflect interpretations of the Qur'an and the sayings and actions of Muhammad and his companions, but the interpretations often differ. Saudi Arabia uses this full-blown system of classical Islamic law except where the law has been supplemented by royal decrees and statutes that govern corporate and tax law as well as oil matters. So when a Saudi judge considers a difficult legal case, he (and it is always he) must make sense of this broad body of knowledge and distill it to its essence for the particular case.

Such a system puts power in the hands of unelected judges, not the people. But the same is true of English or American common law, in which the law cannot be found in just one code or statute book, but must be discovered or invented by judges who look to the body of received opinions to decide the case before them. The common law still governs many legal matters in the United States, from traffic accidents to breaches of contract and even some crimes, without our believing that it upsets our democracy. The reason is that the legislature has voted to adopt the common law, just as the people have chosen to apply Islamic law across the board in our imagined Islamic democracy. So long as there are continuing elections and a changeable constitution, the people could step in and change *that* rule if they wanted to, by changing their constitution. If the people never had a chance to decide whether to follow Islamic law or not, then they lacked democratic choice. Saudi Arabia is not a democracy, because there was never a vote by the people to adopt Islamic law. But if a people democratically enacted a constitution that provided for the use of classical Islamic law, then we might be able to say that this choice was democratic. This is true even though the specific provisions of Islamic law derive from religious tradition. Many laws that are enacted by democracies have their roots in religious ideals and values. Western laws against murder, theft, and adultery (still on the books in many U.S. states) can all be traced to the Ten Commandments.

Once a basic picture of Islamic democracy is in place, it becomes easier to see why Islam and democracy need not be incompatible if both are conceived flexibly. Start with the essences of Islam and democracy, which might appear to be incompatible. *Democracy* literally means the rule of the people. The essence of Islam is often said to lie in *its* basic meaning: submission to God, or more felicitiously, recognition of God's sovereignty. It would seem that either the people or God could be sovereign, but not both. The title of one of the dozens of recent Arabic books on the topic of Islam and democracy nicely captures this problem: *The Rule of God, the Rule of the People.*

The key to resolving the apparent incompatibility is to look more closely at what we mean by sovereignty. Intriguingly, even the U.S. Declaration of Independence does not expressly say that the people are sovereign but rather that all men are created equal and endowed by their Creator with certain unalienable rights. An unalienable right cannot be eliminated even if the people vote to abrogate it. Unalienable rights therefore place a limit on the sovereignty of the people, even in a democracy. If some rights come from God, and the people cannot alienate or override those rights, then isn't God sovereign and not the people? Yet no one would say that the Declaration of Independence is undemocratic.

The bottom line is that even in a democracy the place of sovereignty is complicated. The people may rule with respect to some issues, but other issues are off the table, with the rules coming from some other source, such as a theory of fundamental rights. Although the Constitution, which the people can amend, never mentions unalienable rights or God, the Bill of Rights does speak of certain preexisting rights that are retained by "the people" and must come from somewhere. Referring to the U.S. Constitution does not absolutely prove that the essence of democracy lies somewhere other than in the sovereignty of the people—perhaps the Constitution is undemocratic in some ways—but it does show that some recognizably democratic schemes acknowledge that the people need not be sovereign in the sense of having the last word on every question. That alone opens up some space for us to see how the essences of democracy and Islam might be compatible.

The word *Islam*, for its part, does imply recognition of God's sovereignty. But a Muslim might acknowledge that God is sovereign over everything and also believe, at the same time, that God has left it up to humans to govern themselves on every subject on which he has not provided a definite law or view. Suppose you are a Muslim, and you accept that God said, in the Qur'an, that "there is no coercion in religion," so that religion must be chosen freely. If you believe that, then the people cannot pass a law coercing Jews or Christians to accept Islam. God has spoken, and God is sovereign. The same might be true of the penalty for murder. As a Muslim, you might believe that capital punishment is only permissible for a murderer who has been tried and convicted based on the eyewitness testimony of two reliable men. God has set his limit on the penalty, through his message as interpreted by Islamic law, so the penalty is off the table if there is only one witness, even if we know the accused is guilty. This belief is no different in its structure than what some democrats think about basic rights.

Acknowledging God's sovereignty does not require believing that God has left no room for people to rule themselves. A Muslim can believe that God allows humans to rule themselves however they want so long as they adhere to the basic rules on which he has spoken. If you believe this, and also accept that democracy does not require the absolute sovereignty of the people, then you have the makings of an Islamic democrat. Of course, as a Muslim you might also think that God is sovereign only in the sphere of the personal, not the collective. If you have such a view, you may not feel a need for a distinctively Islamic democracy. It will be enough to be a democrat in public matters and a Muslim in private matters. But Muslims who accept God as sovereign and think that God's sovereignty extends beyond the private sphere can be Islamic democrats in the way just described.

Another possible way for people who accept God's sovereignty to think about democracy is to consider the people as a whole to be entrusted with the collective power and responsibility to interpret and apply God's will on earth. This view does not emphasize a particular *sphere* in which God has left things up to the ruler. Instead, it says that humans need to make sense of how God wants us to govern. It is up to the community of Muslims to perform that task, and they can and must do so collectively. The Iranian writer Abdolkarim Soroush has expressed a view similar to this one.

The appeal of this view for someone who wants Islam and democratic theory to cohere is that the community has tremendous discretion in interpreting Islam and enacting laws that embody its spirit. Democratic decision making can extend to every area of life and law. One limitation of this theory, though, is that it is apparently the Muslim community alone that is entrusted with the task of interpreting and applying God's word. That is all well and good for Muslims, but it excludes non-Muslims. If self-rule consists in figuring out what God wants within the framework of Islam, then non-Muslims will not be full-fledged participants. The answer that minorities in any democracy are excluded when they do not share the fundamental values of the majority may be unsatisfying to someone who thinks that equality is a touchstone of democracy. But perhaps non-Muslims could be permitted to participate in the democratic discussion of God's will, even if they are not full members of the community.

The essences of Islam and democracy can be seen as compatible to the extent that both ideas are flexible. If democracy were restricted to requiring the absolute sovereignty of the people, it would lack the ability to appeal to people and to cultures that do not place humans at the center of the universe. But democracy has flourished even where humanism was not the dominant mode of thinking. Modern Western democracy grew up among pious Christians, many of them staunch Calvinists who emphasized man's sinful and fallen nature, and who themselves grappled with the relationship between democracy and divine sovereignty. Most Americans today probably believe that God, not man, is the measure of all things. It is doubtful whether the majority of Indians place humans at the center of the universe, yet democracy thrives in India. The idea of the rule of the people has been flexible enough to mean that the people or God or nature or nothing is sovereign. On any of these views, the people still govern themselves within the area delineated by their capacities and rights.

Islam has demonstrated a comparable degree of flexibility in its essence. Acknowledging that God is sovereign turns out to mean different things to different people. It has encompassed the idea of free will to some Muslims, while others have thought that a sovereign God must leave nothing to chance or choice. Rationalist Muslim philosophers thought that God was sovereign in the sense that he was the First Mover. Sufi mystics believed that God was sovereign in that God was Truth itself. Islam has been compatible with a number of different systems of government. The flexibility inherent in the essential Muslim idea of acknowledging God's sovereignty enables Islam to be compatible with the essence of democracy if defined flexibly enough.

If the essences of Islam and democracy can be compatible, what about the practical institutional arrangements required by each? In particular, Islam, according to most views, requires that the state not exist in an entirely separate sphere from religion. Can a state that embraces religion be democratic? Britain has no separation of church and state. The queen is Defender of the Faith and head of the Church of England. Anglican bishops sit in the House of Lords, and anyone who wants to change the Book of Common Prayer must go through Parliament to do it. Yet Britain is the cradle of modern democracy. To take another Western European example, in the German state of Bavaria the schools are religious, mostly Catholic, ones, and almost every classroom displays a crucifix. No one seems to think that this makes modern Germany into something other than a democracy.

On the other hand, some people object vociferously to the suggestion that it might be possible to have democracy—especially liberal democracy—without separation of church and state. They argue that to be just to everyone, democracy cannot impose one vision of the good life. Liberal democracy requires government to remain neutral about what values matter most, and to leave that decision up to the individual. If religion and the state do not remain separate, the state will inevitably impose or at least encourage the version of the good life preferred by the official religion.

It *is* necessary for a democracy worthy of the name to respect the individual's right to worship as he or she chooses, and to provide religious liberty for all its inhabitants. But outside the U.S. constitutional structure, individual religious liberty does not necessarily mean that the government will not embrace, endorse, support, or fund one religion in particular. The government can support one particular view of the good life. It can give money to synagogues or ashrams or mosques or all of the above. But so long as the government does not force anyone to adopt religious beliefs that he or she rejects, or perform religious actions that are anathema, it has not violated the basic right to religious liberty. Separation of church and state may be very helpful in maintaining religious liberty, as in the United States, but it is not always necessary for it.

Whether we notice it or not, governments are already endorsing certain visions of the good life all the time. Our government gives medals to heroes who embody the values we admire. It proclaims holidays to celebrate things we care about. Public schools teach students what it means to be polite and honest and sincere, although such values differ from place to place and even family to family. We sponsor some art and not other art, and we use our limited resources to put some books in our public libraries but not others. We say that segregation is wrong because it causes some people to feel excluded. It would be naive to claim that all of these government activities are neutral. They all reflect ideas about the right way to live. They all affect us as citizens, but none of these activities imposes any one set of values on us. We are still free to choose and live as we like. Another way to put it is to say that a democracy could *try* to separate law and morals if it wanted to—although in practice it would be very difficult—but a democracy does not *have* to separate law and morality.

ISLAMIC EQUALITY

Can a state that embraces a single religion really be counted on to recognize the equality of all its citizens, including those who do not belong to the religion that the state has embraced? Democracy requires equality, both equal participation in democratic decision making and equal treatment before the law. So this question is fundamental to the assessment of the plausibility of Islamic democracy, as indeed it would be if one were thinking about the Jewish and democratic state that Israel aspires to be.

In principle, the answer is that a state with an official religion can recognize the equality of all its citizens as long as the religion *itself* embraces equality for everyone. Not every religion recognizes the moral equality of all people. Some religions treat outsiders badly, and others are especially bad about insiders who become outsiders by abandoning the faith. So the question then becomes, in practice, can an Islamic state fully respect the moral equality of non-Muslim citizens? As it turns out, Islam professes a deep commitment to the principle of equality. The logic lies in the structure of Muslim theology: everyone is equal before God. All humans descend from Adam and Eve. As the Qur'an puts it, in a verse that is often quoted to prove Islam's commitment to equality, "O mankind! We created you from male and female, and placed you [into] nations and tribes so that you would know one another." The verse does not use the word *equality*, but it suggests that God created everyone, and that human diversity is meant to be a positive, not a negative, feature of creation.

With respect to equal political participation, there is no principled reason in Islam to suggest that anyone, Muslim or non-Muslim, man or woman, regardless of race or any other characteristic, should not be permitted to participate equally in collective decision making. Some Muslims might argue for special participatory status for Muslims or for men. But aside from Kuwait, where the legislature refused to enact the emir's decree granting women the vote, women have the vote in every Muslim country where there are elections. That includes Iran, with its Islamist constitution; Arab states like Jordan, Egypt, Algeria, Tunisia, and Morocco; and as of 2002 even Bahrain, a Gulf monarchy with traditional ways not unlike Saudi Arabia. As for Muslim women leaders, Benazir Bhutto was elected prime minister of Pakistan (twice); Tansu Ciller served as prime minister of Turkey; in Bangladesh both the current prime minister, Khaleda Zia, and the past prime minister, now leader of the opposition, Sheikh Hasina Wajed, are women; and Indonesia has a woman president, Megawati Sukarnoputri. These women have mixed records in terms of both effectiveness and honesty, but they have been neither better nor worse than male leaders in their countries, and the fact that they were elected should dispel the stereotype that unmitigated sexism prevails everywhere in the Muslim world. There is, admittedly, a saying attributed to the Prophet according to which a nation that makes a woman its ruler will not succeed, and some Muslims have argued that this bars women from serving as heads of state. But this interpretation is not widespread and has not stopped Muslim women from being elected.

Muslim women, then, generally have formal equality of participation. It is true that women's political participation is far more limited than men's, in that women are rarely to be found in parliaments and governments. Women voted in the inaugural Bahraini elections in May 2002, but none of several women candidates were elected. On the other hand, displaying an impulse to affirmative action that would be considered unimaginable in U.S. politics, both Morocco and Pakistan now set aside seats for women in parliamentary elections. In short, the underrepresentation of women is a blot on democracy, to be sure, but unfortunately, it remains a problem in the rest of the democratic world, too.

The same is true for the participation of minority non-Muslims in government, which is not formally banned in any Muslim country, including Iran. And although non-Muslims' actual participation in government is small, that is true of religious and racial minorities in countries we are accustomed to call democratic. What is more, it is rarer today than it once was to hear Islamists argue that women or non-Muslims ought to be barred from political participation. One is more likely to hear a cleric like the Egyptian-born, Qatar-based Shaykh Yusuf al-Qaradawi urging Islamist women to run for office to combat general female immorality. (Qaradawi is a complex, problematic figure. He wrote an influential fatwa declaring Islam and democracy compatible, the scholarly authority of which convinced many Islamists that democracy was a desirable direction for their movement. On September 12, 2001, Qaradawi was one of the first and most important Muslim clerics to condemn the killing of civilians at the World Trade Center as a "heinous crime against Islam." But Qaradawi also advises Hamas and holds that civilians may lawfully be killed in occupied Palestine.)

Equal treatment before the law poses greater challenges for Islamic democracy than equal participation. Classical Islamic law generally does treat men and women equally. Women and men are meant to receive the same punishments for the same misdeeds, and women can own property, which was not always true under Anglo-American common law. But it is also important to acknowledge that classical Islamic law sometimes treats women differently from men, and non-Muslims unequally to Muslims. Beyond these legal inequalities, the law on the books differs from the practical realities of life in many Muslim countries, which often place women at much greater disadvantage than the law itself requires.

The most important instances of formal legal inequality can be described briefly. Under some circumstances, classical Islamic law weighs women's testimony more lightly than the testimony of men. This rule is based on a verse in the Qur'an that calls for the testimony of either two men or a man and two women in attestation of letters of credit: "If one of them shall forget the other shall remind her." Some modern Muslims, feminists and otherwise, have argued that this differentiation is not justified by the text of the Qur'an when taken in context. Some argue that the second woman is not a witness in her own right but serves as a kind of aide-mémoire to the woman who is the witness. There are also other arguments against the classical law's interpretation of the verse. Without entering into the debate about the "correct" reading of the Qur'anic verse, one can recognize both that classical Islamic law does interpret the verse to weigh women's testimony differently in some cases and that some modern Muslims disagree with that interpretation. It is also worth noting that classical Jewish law (*halakha*) bars women's testimony altogether under most circumstances.

Women's share of inheritance in classical Islamic law is also less than that of men, typically by half. Again, the comparison to classical Jewish law provides context; in Jewish law, women normally do not inherit at all unless there are no male heirs. And of course, in Anglo-American common law until the modern era, the firstborn male inherited, to the exclusion of anyone else. Once again, modern Muslims offer a variety of apologias for and arguments against women's unequal treatment in inheritance law. Not all Muslims think that classical Islamic law ought to prevail on this point. But some do. For those who think that to be truly Islamic a state must apply classical Islamic law, there is no denying that this provision institutionalizes inequality on the basis of sex.

The law of divorce also places women at a relative disadvantage. Under classical Islam, women cannot easily initiate divorce nor compel their husbands to grant it unless a prenuptial agreement so specifies. If they do manage to compel divorce, they may lose the right to a lump-sum alimony payment to which they would otherwise be entitled. Efforts under way by Muslim women activists to improve these arrangements, but they have met with real resistance, not only from scholars but from men who for extralegal reasons would like to preserve male prerogatives in the context of family law.

These are real and troubling examples of unequal treatment of women under classical Islamic law, and advocates of sex equality have their work cut out for them in seeking reform. Of course, imperfect democracy can still exist where sex equality before the law is incomplete. After all, such is the case in the United States, where women gained the vote late in constitutional history and are still fighting for equality in other legal areas. Israel sanctions unequal treatment of women in the religious courts on which it confers sole jurisdiction over marriage and divorce. So it is not necessary to write off the possibility of Islamic democracy just because women are not yet fully equal under Islamic law. Furthermore, it is not the case that a government that guaranteed full sex equality before the law would automatically be considered "un-Islamic" by the majority of Muslims.

The point is not to claim that women in Saudi Arabia, say, are treated equally. They cannot drive or move about without male supervision, and their subordinate status is enforced by both law and culture. A state applying strict Islamic law as it is currently interpreted in much of the Muslim world would never be a perfect place for women. Conditions for women in much of the Muslim world remain profoundly unequal, as indeed they do for the vast majority of women in the world, especially outside Western Europe and North America. It would be misleading or even dishonest to deny that Islamists frequently speak in terms of the natural subordination of women, even as they claim that Islam can unleash women's full potential in the private and public spheres. I wish only to suggest that Islamic law itself is less unequal in its treatment of women than is imagined by many in the West and the Muslim world alike, and that unequal treatment of women, while reprehensible, should not be seen as an insurmountable barrier to democracy. If it were, there would today be no democracies at all, because the equality of the sexes remains unaccomplished everywhere.

The question of the veil and covering becomes relevant here. As a symbolic matter, the clothes that women wear have become one of the focal points for those who argue that Islam and democracy are incompatible. This is true among Westerners who believe in incompatibility and among some Islamists. Both groups argue that a society is only Islamic if women go about garbed in head scarves or in even more concealing clothing, like the full-body-and-face-covering burka or chador. Both also argue that a democratic society is one in which women are free to wear anything they choose.

The emphasis on clothing, however, obscures more than it clarifies. It is true that women's clothing is a central symbol of the culture of Islamism. Head scarves and long, loose-fitting clothing serve as emblems of Islamism when they are proudly worn by Islamists in places like Turkey and Indonesia, and when they are legally coerced by Islamist regimes, as in Iran. But there are many Muslims who think that Islam requires only that everyone dress modestly, men and women alike. Such a requirement is certainly compatible with democracy. Indeed, most democracies have laws governing who can wear what and where, including different standards for men and women. Perhaps democracy might even be consistent with rather strict rules for dress, so long as they are roughly equal in treatment of men and women. And Islam is, or can be, consistent with restrictions that do not go so far as to demand that women wear a head scarf or chador. Obviously I do not mean to endorse compulsory covering, or for that matter the compulsory uncovering of the head that one finds in French schools or in the Turkish Assembly, where secularists prevented the seating of an elected delegate who wore a head scarf. Rather, while acknowledging the tremendous symbolic importance of dress, I want to maintain that our natural focus on clothing should not mislead us into portraying Islam as so unequal that it cannot be democratic.

Beyond the equality of women, equality for non-Muslims in an Islamic state also raises some difficult challenges. If everyone in the political sphere speaks in terms of Islamic values, that may in practice exclude non-Muslims to a degree. But the same problem would arise in a state that defines itself as "Jewish and democratic," as Israel does; in Britain, where the Church of England is the official church; or even in the United States, where the Supreme Court implicitly excluded atheists when it said not so very long ago, "We are a religious people, whose institutions presuppose a Supreme Being."

One sometimes hears the argument that non-Muslims can never be equal participants in the Islamic state because Islam does not recognize a distinction between the Islamic state and the community (*umma*) of the Muslims. Yet in the Prophet's lifetime, the Muslim community at Medina coexisted with non-Muslims in a statelike arrangement embodied in a compact that still survives. Subsequent Islamic states were also home to non-Muslims who participated in government and public life, sometimes in important positions. Samuel ibn Naghrela, the Jewish politician-poet-philosopher known in Hebrew as Samuel the Prince, rose to the viziership of medieval Granada. Furthermore, from early in Muslim history there were competing Muslim states, suggesting a difference between the state and the community of Muslims. Today some Islamists still dream of a single pan-Islamic state, but most are more modest and realistic in their aims, hoping only for a number of Islamic states covering different geographical areas.

The Islamic state, then, no more overlaps with the community of the Muslims than, say, the state of Israel overlaps with Jews, or the Federal Republic of Germany overlaps with German ethnicity. Israel has a law of return that gives Jews automatic citizenship if they want it. Germany has a similar law for ethnic Germans, and indeed there are many ethnic Turks born in Germany to guest-worker parents who cannot easily become German citizens.

As for equality of treatment before the law, the Islamic state can treat non-Muslims as well as it treats Muslims. Islamic states traditionally required Jews, Christians, and other non-pagans deemed "peoples of the book" to pay a special tax and wear distinctive dress; legally, the state accorded them special status as "protected persons." Churches and synagogues had to be modest in size relative to mosques. The enforcement of these rules varied historically from rigorous to lax, and treatment of non-Muslims ranged from highly tolerant to repressive and even violent. There is an extensive literature arguing about whether this protected status must amount to second-class citizenship—a question that might plausibly be answered either way. But even if these discriminatory taxing and zoning requirements were put in place—and they need not be adopted by an Islamic state that is not fully Islamist—the Islamic state faces no theoretical barrier to treating its non-Muslim citizens equally. And today's Islamists, influenced perhaps by mobile democracy, do not generally propose to treat non-Muslims unequally, at least not in their published writings or official pronouncements. Some Islamic democrats, such as Rachid Ghannouchi, argue that Islam no longer requires that non-Muslims be treated as "protected persons." Instead they are to be accorded full citizenship rights, just like their Muslim fellows.

ISLAMIC LIBERTY

Not every definition of democracy requires all the individual liberties found in the constitutions of the United States and Western Europe, but most democracies today embody some version of liberalism. Would this be true of Islamic democracy? One challenge to the very idea of Islamic democracy is the claim that liberal democracy restricts the sphere of government to the public realm, while Islam thinks it necessary to extend government into the private sphere as well. Yet the divide between public and private, even in liberal democratic states, is more permeable than the challenge assumes; and in Islam there is a greater distinction between the private and public realms than many people, Muslim and non-Muslim, believe.

Just about every democracy in the world regulates personal relationships to a striking degree, deciding how you can get married, and whom you can marry; what counts as a good reason for getting a divorce, and how the divorce will divide assets. What is more, no democracy, however liberal, has ever adopted the pure liberal view that the state must refrain from regulating conduct that does no harm to anyone except the actor. The law in most democracies tells you to wear a seat belt or a crash helmet. It tells you where and when you can drink or buy alcohol. It prohibits drugs, including drugs that a person might take without bothering anyone. Equipped with a warrant, the state can tap your phones or burst into your house and search every nook and cranny. The tax man sees every detail of your finances, and if you are audited, just about nothing is private. In short, even liberal democracies do not strictly respect the public/private distinction.

For its part, Islam does not insist on the erasure of the public/private distinction. The Qur'an says that there shall be no coercion in religion. Classical Islamic law and most modern Muslims think this means that in theory, neither government nor anyone else can coerce you in matters of private belief. On the other hand, it would be difficult for a Muslim to abjure his religion publicly in an Islamic state that had laws against apostasy. This problem poses a real challenge to what Westerners consider freedom of religion and speech; a related problem arises where there are blasphemy laws on the books that make it a crime to insult Islam or the Prophet. The reason this problem arises is that to many Muslims apostasy and blasphemy are public acts that the state should be able to regulate, not private matters of faith that are restricted to the individual realm. This may also explain why the Saudi and Iranian governments think it acceptable to coerce people to attend prayers when the Qur'an bans coercion in religion. The difference between the prevalent Western and Muslim views on this subject derives not from any rejection of the public/private distinction, but from the different places each tradition draws the line.

Classical Islamic law also enforces the right to privacy in the home. The Qur'an instructs its listeners, "O you who believe! Enter not houses other than your own, until you have asked permission and greeted those in them." The earliest Muslim reporters of hadith, traditions associated with the Prophet, understood this injunction in terms of privacy. The most important hadith collectors report the following explanation of the Qur'anic statement: "Sahl bin Sa'd (may Allah be pleased with him) reported: The Messenger of Allah, peace be upon him, said, 'Seeking permission to enter has been proscribed in order to restrain the eyes.'" The evocative language "to restrain the eyes" suggests the existence of a realm of privacy into which no one may enter without permission.

Of course classical Islamic law, like other religious law, extends to all sorts of personal and private areas of human behavior. It prescribes the right way to wash one's hands, keep oneself clean, and so forth. But the existence of this kind of detailed law respecting personal matters does not mean that the Islamic *state* must pass laws requiring these sorts of details or that it is anyone's business but one's own. Although Islamic law requires daily prayer and fasting during Ramadan, that does not mean that a state must enforce these laws in order to be legitimately Islamic. The reason is that Islamic law does not specify punishments for failing to perform many of these religious obligations, and the government does not have the responsibility of ensuring that all religious laws are carried out. It is enough for the state to enforce Islamic civil and criminal law. The framework of "Islamic law" thus includes both personal religious obligations and also laws governing interpersonal relations, but an Islamic state can be Islamic even if it does not enforce all of the personal religious obligations that are imposed on individuals by Islamic law. Islamic law draws a basic distinction between duties toward God and duties toward other human beings. Even if this distinction does not map exactly onto the distinction between the private and the public spheres, most duties toward God do not need to be enforced by a state that would be considered "Islamic" by just about all Muslims.

Almost all Islamists want to apply Islamic law in many areas of life. But there is widespread misunderstanding, even in the Muslim world, about the scope of classical Islamic law. In the criminal law, for example, only a handful of crimes count as part of the required system of Islamic law. These crimes, called *hudud*, are famous in the West because of the harsh punishments associated with them: in theory, the convicted thief would lose his hand; the murderer and the apostate their heads; the adulterers their lives. Punishments are comparably harsh for those who falsely accuse others of these crimes. What is rarely added is that these punishments can only be meted out after proof of a standard that is extraordinarily difficult to reach. Unless there is a freely given confession, there must be two eyewitnesses to the crime, men of proven good character. For adultery there must be *four* eyewitnesses to the act itself, a circumstance by its nature very unusual indeed.

In the view of most Islamists, *hudud* crimes must be on the books for a state to be Islamic. But it is likely that almost no one will be punished under these laws if the laws are applied correctly, because the standard of proof is too high to meet. Judges who wanted to could almost always find a way to acquit. Historically, in fact, these punishments were only rarely enforced and, even then, were restricted to the most egregious cases of murder and the like.

In the few cases and places where such punishments have been applied in the modern Muslim world, there are usually political motivations involved that fall outside the strict ambit of Islamic law. In Afghanistan under the Taliban, extreme punishments were often not even the ones specified in Islamic law but were rather Pashtun customs masquerading as "Islamic." In northern Nigeria, where Islamic law is being introduced today, the threat of such punishments functions as a symbol of the new order, to Islamists and non-Muslim opponents alike. Everyone involved gets some benefit out of drawing attention to the possible stoning of an adulteress. It is free publicity for Islamists, and a good rallying point for opponents. It would be a horrible tragedy if anyone should be unlucky enough to be executed for adultery there, but an Islamic system need not execute anyone for adultery under normal circumstances. There is almost always some legal way out. The existence of *hudud* punishments is therefore not incompatible with democracy, unless we think that capital punishment makes a country undemocratic.

Beyond the fact that these laws need never be applied in practice in an Islamic state, it is important to realize that the *hudud* punishments cover just a small number of crimes, and therefore leave room for just about every further law one could imagine to be made. The rest of the criminal laws can be determined by the government, according to criteria that the government specifies. That is the way the law always operated in Muslim countries in the past: a small number of legal matters were regulated under the *hudud* or other *shari'a* principles, but most practical matters were regulated by the government, not by classical Islamic law. An Islamic democracy could, in other words, decide on just about every criminal law by democratic means, and specify the punishments too.

Islamists do not think that Islamic law must govern family relations for everyone who lives in an Islamic state, just the Muslims. According to the Islamists, other religious groups, like Christians and Jews, should be governed by their own religious laws when it comes to family law. Beginning in the earliest years of the Muslim polity, Muslim rulers reached accommodations with minority religious groups that allowed those groups self-regulation in the area of communal affairs, including family law. This formed the model that all Islamic states have used, up to and including the present. In India, for example, when the Muslim Mughal Empire ruled, the majority of the population were Hindus. They were never forcibly converted to Islam, and their personal life and laws operated according to Hindu tradition. This was also the model under the Ottoman Empire. In fact, the Ottomans gave even broader autonomy to minority religious communities, allowing them not only to regulate their own family law but to collect their own taxes and run their own educational system.

It is instructive that modern Israel operates on precisely this Muslim-invented model of family law allocated by religion. When it came into being in 1948, Israel simply kept the Ottoman family law model that had prevailed even after the British mandate took Palestine from the Ottoman Empire. This system has its problems. It assumes that everyone fits into a religious group of one kind or another, making things hard on atheists and religious individualists; these people cannot legally marry or divorce as they would wish, since the law does not provide for nonreligious civil marriage to occur within Israel. An Israeli Jew who does not want an Orthodox rabbi to officiate at her wedding flies to Cyprus (the Israeli's Las Vegas) and gets married there in a civil ceremony that Israeli law recognizes via a loophole. This sounds like a serious restriction on religious freedom, but if you want to get married in New York State, you must be married by a judge, the clerk at city hall, a member of the clergy, or a judicially endorsed contract as specified in the state's Domestic Relations Law. If you want to get married on your own, in a field of daisies, with no government sanction, you may not. It is a class-C misdemeanor in New York to purport to perform a wedding without legal authorization.

Assigning legal power over marriage and divorce to religious authorities also requires the state to choose among denominations, and makes it hard for people who want to marry across religions. Many Catholic and Protestant churches around the world permit such weddings nowadays; Islam permits Muslim men to marry women who are not Muslims, though not the other way around. The overwhelming majority of Orthodox and Conservative rabbis will not officiate at such ceremonies, nor will many (perhaps most) Reform rabbis.

The constraints on personal choice that emerge in the realm of family law are unfortunate, but not necessarily undemocratic. After all, liberal democratic states also restrict who can marry whom. Only the most liberal Western European countries and now Vermont permit same-sex couples to form a partnership akin to marriage; the origin and continuing basis for restricting marriage to the union of a man and a woman is plainly religious, even in a country like the United States, which has constitutional separation of church and state. The ban on same-sex marriage may someday look discriminatory to a majority of Americans, as it does today to some. But like the allocation of marriage to religious authorities, this problem can be addressed within the democratic framework.

The Universality of Mobile Ideas

B efore turning to particular Muslim countries and their prospects for democracy, I want to turn back to the larger framework—the contact of mobile ideas. I said earlier that one of the features that make ideas mobile is their universality. Democracy holds itself out as a system that can and should be the model for people everywhere, because people are everywhere the same and of equal value. Similarly, Islam claims to be universal, because it holds that God has a single message for all human beings, all of whom are equal in God's eyes.

One might look at democracy and Islam and think that their mutual claims to universality are a recipe for disaster. If democracy claims to work for everyone, and so does Islam, then surely they will end up competing for adherents. As a result, each will end up arguing that the other is wrong. If these were more modest ideas, claiming only to work in some times and places, then maybe they could avoid clashing by settling on a compromise.

I want to argue to the contrary that the claims to universality made by both democracy and Islam can actually form the basis for a potential synthesis between them. The reason lies in the fact that each of the two claims to universality depends on the basic equality and similarity of all human beings. Democracy only makes sense as a universal solution if one believes that people everywhere are equal. The basic insight of democracy is the fundamental, equal right of everyone to have the same final say in collective decisions. If democracy is a bad idea in a given situation, it is usually because in that situation some people know better than others. Few families use democracy to make collective family decisions, because most adults think they know better than children and that their voices should count for more. Similarly, people who think democracy should not be applied universally to every country, and that only some countries can flourish under democratic government, generally believe that not everyone is equally well qualified for self-rule: some people know better than others what is good for the community, and a certain degree of wisdom or education or judgment is necessary to participate in government.

Interestingly, Islam, too, only makes sense as a universal solution because, according to Islam, every human is equal before God. In this sense, Islam is a radically egalitarian worldview. Just as the Qur'an emphasizes time and again that Muhammad was a human being, not a divine one, mainstream Islam today rejects the notion of priests as intercessors between man and God. Perhaps even more strikingly, the Muslim world differs from Europe and South Asia in that it has never adopted a system of fixed feudal classes or castes. The medieval records are full of tales of poor boys who learn to write beautiful poetry in refined calligraphy and are elevated to positions of power and influence as a result of their initiative and talent.

When Islam spread through the world, the Arabs who spread it did not generally claim religiously superior status to the new converts. After all, the Arabs were converts to Islam, too. The Arab conquerors, like any conquerors, set up political structures designed initially to consolidate their colonial power over the Persians—but they did not and could not do so in the name of Islam. And when non-Arabs came to dominate the political scene, as they eventually did, they were able to use Islam as the glue of their rule as easily as had the Arabs.

Of course, class as a social phenomenon exists in the Muslim world, as it seems to exist everywhere. People are rich or poor, educated or not, from "good" families or less distinguished ones. Some people claim the title "sayyid" as descendants of the Prophet Muhammad. The Muslim world is no egalitarian utopia. But the central *idea* of Islam—recognition of God's absolute sovereignty—has the effect of leveling everyone else. This is the notion of the equality of people on identical footing before God that so powerfully struck Malcolm X on his pilgrimage to Mecca, where he saw pilgrims of every race marching and praying together in the same simple white garments.

Put a little differently, Islam aspires to spread because Muslims believe that Islam is equally applicable to everyone, regardless of race or geography. There is no idea of a "chosen people" in Islam. In fact, Muhammad undercut the Jewish idea of chosenness by describing Moses as just one in a long line of prophets whom God sent to various peoples. Paul had expanded the notion of chosenness to include anyone who accepts Christ. For Muhammad, though, the notion of chosenness was not expanded but repudiated. Muslims are not specially chosen by God for anything. Muslims are just people who recognize God's sovereignty and follow God's rules. Muslims, it might be said, choose themselves by acknowledging Muhammad's prophecy and acting accordingly.

If both democracy and Islam are universal because they rely on a principle of basic human equality, then we have a potentially rich common starting point for developing the relationship between the two ideas. A commitment to equality can be used to remind democrats that they need to take seriously Muslims' ideas about how a good life should be lived. That does not mean that everyone's ideas will be equally correct or appealing. But certainly democrats should be prepared to consider the worth of any idea that commits itself to human equality. On the other side, Muslims' commitment to human equality can be used to argue for systems of government that recognize that same equality. No self-respecting Muslim would deny that all people are equal. If that is true, then why should any Muslim embrace a form of government that seems to be based on some premise other than equality?

Of course, universality also has a practical side. To be universal, one must be flexible, too. Democrats must be able to convince people with different family structures, economic arrangements, and social values that democracy will work for them. The way to do that is to showcase the openness of democracy, by pointing out that there are many different choices that the people collectively can make once they are democratically empowered. To persuade Brazilians to be democrats, one must be able to tell them that democracy will give them the option of voting for land reform, even though many democratic countries protect property rights very tightly.

Brazilians will need to be told that democracy can work in a fantastically multiracial society, one with some distinctive ethnic groups in it. But when urging democracy in Ukraine, the arguments will be rather different. One may have to emphasize the possibility that democracy can be used to choose a strong leader and to create a central defense. The arguments in Kuwait or Algeria will be different still.

The same need for flexibility is true of Islam, in an interesting way. To persuade Indonesians to become Muslims, Islam flexibly showed its compatibility with the preservation of traditional languages, family structures, and systems of rule. When Islam recruited in Central Asia, the languages, family structures, and systems of government were different yet again. Persian pre-Islamic political theory, literature, and culture were highly sophisticated and developed, and Islam was open to all of these to an extraordinary degree when it was making its first forays into the Persian-speaking world. There has been a great range of forms of government among Muslims, and the reason is that Islam had to be open to all of these to have any chance at achieving universality.

The ideas of democracy and Islam may seem far apart, then, but perhaps they are not as far apart as we might think. Committed to equality, and blessed by flexibility, these two universal ideas may potentially be good partners in the search for a provisional synthesis. It would be a great shame if the ease of condemning Islamic states as imperfect were to pose a bar to supporting Islamic democracy. It would also be shortsighted. Western democracies have long been riddled with inequalities along the axes of race, sex, and citizenship. Yet we still tend to think that democracy is the best thing going. We must not perversely oppose democracy in the Muslim world just because Islamic democracy is fraught with difficulties and perils. If they want it, Muslims deserve their own shot at democracy. They deserve a chance to make democracy work for them.

PART TWO

Varieties of Islamic Democracy

DEMOCRATIZATION AND MUSLIM REALITY: AN OVERVIEW

I n principle, I have argued, Islamic democracy is possible. But is it likely in practice? What are the political and historical conditions in the Muslim world that might enable democracy to emerge? There is no single answer to this question. The Muslim world is extraordinarily diverse, possessed of different languages, different cultures, and different social and economic conditions. Malaysia, Saudi Arabia, and Senegal are far apart not just on the map but in every way. All they have in common is Islam, though the Islam practiced in each place is distinct from the others. The great anthropologist Clifford Geertz became famous by comparing Morocco and Indonesia: two Muslim countries that differed in almost every imaginable respect but nonetheless had something in common because of Islam.

This diversity matters enormously for theories about democratization, which start with case studies and try valiantly to generalize from them. The best theories depend heavily on local circumstances, whether political, economic, linguistic, ideological, or cultural. Because democracy theorists agree that specifics matter, Islam will play a different part in each place, and democratization will proceed—if it proceeds at all—differently each place we look. On the other hand, in a world where activists use satellite television, the Internet, mobile phones, and text-messaging, Islamic democrats in one country can learn fast what their counterparts elsewhere are doing.

The toughest and most fascinating case for thinking about Islamic democracy is Iran, the only Muslim country that is almost totally Shi'i Muslim. (The majority of Muslims are Sunni; Iraq has a slight Shi'i majority, as does Bahrain. Elsewhere Shi'is are minorities, as in Lebanon and Pakistan.) Iranians speak Persian and boast a four-thousand-year-old civilization that developed sophisticated political theory—not to mention culture, literature, history, and science—long before Iran became Muslim. Since the advent of Islam, Iranians have often defined themselves in contrast to Arabs, Arabic language, and Arab culture; Arabs do the same vis-à-vis Iranians. Iran therefore is a special and complicated case, and also crucially important for thinking about Islamic democracy because within Iran there are theorists of Islamic democracy and an actual Islamic democracy movement. Its activists are locked in a deep and bitter struggle with opponents who want to preserve the autocratic religious structures of the revolutionary state.

Turkey, another non-Arab country, is remarkable in the Muslim world both for its modern history of militantly secularist autocracy and for the moderately stable, vestigially authoritarian democracy that has emerged from this history. Turkey has already been through one democratic government formed by an Islamic party, and it is now experimenting with a second. Under Turkey's unique constitution, the military, which functions as guardian of the secular character of the state, pushed out the first Islamic party after just a year, but nonetheless moderate Islamists were recently again elected to run the Turkish political system. The unique history of official promotion of secularism in Turkey makes it an example that cannot easily be imitated elsewhere, yet Turkey offers a model of a democracy in which Islamic parties play a continuing role, and so Turkey has something important to offer for an account of real-world Islamic democracy.

Several other very populous non-Arab Muslim countries are worth discussing. One is Indonesia, where Islamists played a key role in the democracy movement that eventually replaced Suharto. A pro-democracy Muslim cleric, Abdurrahman Wahid, became the first prime minister of democratic Indonesia. Old and blind, Wahid governed poorly by most accounts and was eventually eased from office by quasi-democratic means. But despite some grumbling, he relinquished power peacefully, and his party, Nahdlatul Ulama, followed his lead and returned to ordinary politics. Thus Indonesia suggests that Islamic parties can contribute to democratization, take power, and give up that power without violence where appropriate. Pakistan is another example of a non-Arab Muslim state that has had brief periods of democracy, in the context of a state with Islamic features. Carved out of colonial India to give a homeland to South Asian Muslims, Pakistan has never managed to hold on to democracy for long, but it does display some aspects of how Islamic democracy might be imagined. Bangladesh, by contrast, itself once part of Pakistan, has managed to emerge from military autocracy to tentative democracy despite its profound poverty. Since 1991, there have been two democratic changes of power there.

It is in the Arab world that the prospects of democratization, Islamic or otherwise, currently seem bleakest, while the need for something like Islamic democracy seems greatest. Dividing Arab states into monarchies and autocracies, oil producers and non–oil producers, provides a rubric for discussing the prospects for democratization in each of these contexts. Different strategies apply to different categories, but in all cases there is progress to be made. Ironically, monarchies now pose the greatest hope for gradual democratization; in presidential dictatorships, though, the transition to democracy will be harder to achieve by gradual means. If a country produces a great deal of oil, that makes it still harder for outside countries to exert influence in favor of democratization; but even oil producers, who have greater leverage over the West, are susceptible to some kinds of carrots and some kinds of sticks.

There is no single protocol for producing democracy in the Muslim world, because democratization is not a single, unified phenomenon. In most Muslim countries, elections are not meaningful, either because the elected body has little power or because the elections are not free. Consider the most recent presidential election in Tunisia, where $99^{44}/_{100}$ percent of the vote, a number apparently inspired by old Ivory Soap ads, went to one candidate. Where elections have become meaningless, it is possible that the best route to increased democratization is to free up these elections immediately, so that more people can run for office and so the elected legislature or president can have more meaningful legitimate power. Freeing elections is unlikely to have enough impact on its own to change the political structure in productive ways, unless new political parties are allowed to emerge and new ideas can be expressed. The way to make that happen is to increase basic individual rights, so people can make controversial political arguments and form new political associations. One important effect of increasing individual rights in this way is that multiple points of view will have the chance to emerge, so that Islamist political parties are not the only organized parties when elections are held.

There are a few places in the Persian Gulf where elections have not been held at all. Saudi Arabia is the glaring example; the other is the United Arab Emirates. These countries can and should begin their experiments with democracy by introducing elections for the consultative assemblies that are presently appointed. The assemblies could grow into legislatures, and eventually the ruling families could transform themselves into constitutional monarchies. Elections, like those in Bahrain in spring and autumn 2002, are needed to begin this process, because unless they occur, increasing individual rights will allow people's frustrations to build without any form of release. People will criticize the monarchy, especially in Islamist terms, and the potential for violent revolution might expand faster than it can be contained. In general, democratization is better achieved through gradual processes than through violent revolution. Allowing elections would be a good way for monarchies like Saudi Arabia to signal that they are interested in what their citizens have to say.

The consequence of allowing elections, though, is that a monarch or autocrat must be prepared to deal with the government that the people elect. Starting in 1989, King Hussein allowed the first real elections in Jordan in many years. These relatively open elections led to the rise of Islamists, who did well in 1989, before political parties had been made legal, and again in 1993. At first the monarchy worked with the Islamists, who joined the cabinet. This looked like a successful beginning to the democratization process. Some even said that the king had brilliantly co-opted the Islamists by bringing them into the governing structure in a democratic fashion. But eventually King Hussein became frustrated with the Islamists and began to limit their capacity to act and speak freely. The Islamists' political positions often differed from those the king supported, especially regarding Israel. King Hussein signed a peace deal with Israel that the Islamists opposed, and eventually it started to appear that the parliament had little actual say in how important decisions in Jordan were made. When the 1997 elections rolled around, the Islamists decided to boycott them. The result was a significant step backward for democratization in Jordan. Public confidence in the democratization process had stalled.

There are also places where neither meaningful elections nor rights are on the horizon unless the government is replaced. Saddam Hussein would never permit the democratization of Iraq; nor will Muammar Qadhafi change his tune after years as a dictator. If there is to be democracy in Iraq or Libya, it will have to be a completely different process that produces it. Only foreign invasion, assassination, or natural death can bring down a Saddam or a Qadhafi. Then whoever takes over, perhaps the United Nations or even the United States, will face the extraordinary task of implementing democratic government. This is not just a theoretical possibility but a potential growth market for Islamic democracy. After the United States retaliated for the September 11 attacks by destroying the Taliban government in Afghanistan, the new interim government there got the job of rebuilding the country and creating a democratic state where none had existed before.

Afghanistan is now in the very early stages of a process designed to produce Islamic democracy from the ground up. No one doubts that the new government of Afghanistan will be in some important sense Islamic. Afghanistan was always an Islamic state. Its earliest constitution, adopted in 1923, declared Islam the state religion, even as it promised "protection" to Jews and Hindus. In fact, Afghanistan was one of the first independent Islamic states admitted to the League of Nations in 1934, when most of the Muslim world was under colonial or mandatory control. Islam, not Afghan nationalism, was the fuel that fed the Afghans' successful resistance against the Soviets.

At the same time, there is enormous pressure on the Afghans—and the United States—to make the new Afghanistan a democracy. In today's climate, because the United States eliminated the existing government, it is perceived as having a duty to make sure that what replaces the old government is something better. The *loya jirga* of June 2002, under the sponsorship of the United Nations and the protection of the United States and Germany, began the democratic process in Afghanistan. Members were elected locally and spoke freely while Afghans listened on the radio. This astonishingly democratic event was not always edifying, with warlords jockeying for seats up front, participating in backroom deals, and condoning the intimidation of some of the more outspoken delegates, but it certainly counted as nascent democracy, and it followed directly from U.S. intervention.

By contrast, in Kuwait, where the U.S. restored the emir to power after kicking out Iraq in 1991, the emir continued his autocratic rule and gave little new power to his elected consultative assembly. No political parties are allowed, and women may not vote. Times have changed, though. From the case of Afghanistan one can deduce that some Muslim countries, including Iraq, are going to have to build democracy from the ground up in the wake of a change of regime. In that context, individual rights should probably come first, while the first government helps build the basic structure of the state. Then, when the state is built, elections can follow.

In other words, there is no single formula that would work in every Muslim country. Islam itself differs in its practice and form across the Muslim world, even though Islam aspires to universality. Similarly, democracy claims universality, but it too will have to operate differently in various Muslim countries. It follows that the process of democratization will look very different in Muslim countries that differ so much from each other. In each case, the ideas of Islam and democracy are coming into contact, and that contact is already having notable effects. Sometimes that contact looks promising, elsewhere it appears more threatening, but everywhere government and citizens are keenly aware of it. The way that contact works itself out will have enormous consequences for Muslims and the rest of the world.

We are not going to see perfect democracy emerge overnight anywhere in the Muslim world. There are no guarantees that Islamic democracy is around the corner. On the other hand, possibilities do exist, many of them rich, interesting, and surprising. Skepticism is appropriate, but so is creativity. If we can look at the countries of the Muslim world with fresh eyes, perhaps the likelihood of Islamic democracy will begin to approach the pressing need for it.

Iran: Islamic Democracy in the Balance

A decade ago, Iran seemed a powerful counterexample to the possibility of Islamic democracy. In its first fifteen years, Iran was the very archetype of an undemocratic Islamic state, offering putative evidence that the rise of Islamists elsewhere would spell the downfall of any hope for democracy. Now the idea, if not the complete practice, of democracy has come to the Islamic Republic of Iran. The results have been fascinating and complex, and the outcome of the interaction is still uncertain; but Iran now provides some indication of how democracy can tentatively begin to make itself felt in a thoroughly Islamic environment.

In 1979 young Iranians took to the streets. They chanted "Death to America" and burned American flags. Students occupied the U.S. Embassy in Tehran, and, with the acquiescence of the new government, took hostages: diplomats, Marines, and office workers from the embassy. Most of this occurred in the name of a newly resurgent Islam, committed to replacing the secularist, corrupt regime of Mohammad Reza Shah Pahlavi with a government that would be truly Islamic. Although the government that emerged from the Iranian revolution was called an Islamic *Republic*, a name that implied that some sort of democratic self-rule would coexist alongside Islam, it quickly became clear that democracy was far from the minds of the mullahs who took power under the leadership of Ayatollah

Ruhollah Khomeini. One autocrat—the shah—seemed to have been replaced by another autocrat—the ayatollah.

The centrality of the religious leader in Iranian Shi'ism went back to the split between Sunni and Shi'i Muslims, which took place in the years following the Prophet Muhammad's death. Muhammad left no son, nor had he ever described succession to the caliphate as a family matter. After his death, some Muslims supported Abu Bakr for the caliphate, and others supported the Prophet's cousin and son-in-law 'Ali. In the event, Abu Bakr became caliph; after his death, the caliphate passed to 'Umar and then to 'Uthman. When 'Uthman was assassinated, 'Ali became caliph, but his caliphate was never firmly established. His supporters fought a war against Mu'awiya, the governor of Syria; ultimately Mu'awiya broke with 'Ali and became the founder of the Umayyad dynasty that claimed the caliphate for itself. 'Ali's supporters were known as *shi'at 'Ali*, the party of 'Ali, and the word *Shi'a* comes from that term.

The party of 'Ali now argued that the Prophet had always intended 'Ali to inherit his mantle; Abu Bakr, 'Umar, and 'Uthman had not been legitimate, full-fledged successors to the Prophet. Rejecting the title caliph, which by now was being used by the Umayyads, the Shi'is adopted the term imam to describe 'Ali and his successors. After 'Ali, the imamate passed from father to son until the eleventh imam, Hasan al-'Askari, who died without an heir. Some Shi'is concluded that Hasan actually did have a son, but that the son had been mystically hidden and would someday return. "Twelver" Shi'is, from whom Iranian Shi'is descend, anticipated the eventual return of the Hidden Twelfth Imam; during his absence or occultation, the highest authorities were the ayatollahs, the most qualified jurists recognized in the Shi'a hierarchy of scholarly qualifications.

Khomeini, building on the structure of the imamate and the importance of the ayatollahs, developed a radical and original theory of government based on the nineteenth-century Shi'a political doctrine of "the authority of the jurist" (*wilayat al-faqih* in Arabic, *velayat-e faqih* in Persian). Khomeini's version of the doctrine held that the best-qualified jurist, who had the best-possible access to the true content of Islamic law and tradition, ought to have the last word in all matters of governance. Khomeini went beyond classical Shi'a thought in raising the best of the living ayatollahs—himself, as it turned out—to the status of Supreme Leader. The logic of this move resonated with the Shi'a tradition of venerating the imam, but it also transformed that tradition by making a religious authority into a political, not just a spiritual leader.

The ideology of Iranian Shi'ism thus had much to do with Ayatollah Khomeini's political thought, and, as a result, with the reception of democratic ideas in Iran. Khomeini's elevation of the office of ayatollah almost, but not quite, to the level of imam, gave the ayatollah more power to propose novel interpretations of Islamic law than earlier Shi'a tradition had allowed. This power was extended to other aspects of leadership as well. Enacted under Khomeini's guidance, then amended days after his death in 1989, the Iranian constitution gave the Supreme Leader tremendous power. It provided for an Islamic Consultative Assembly and for an elected president. All legislation proposed by the assembly had to be approved by a twelve-member Council of Guardians, at least six of whom were required to be jurists, assigned the task of assuring that legislation corresponded to the constitution and to Islamic law. Foreign policy was ultimately vested in the Supreme Leader, whom the constitution gave the power to approve decisions by the Supreme Council for National Security. For the first fifteen years of the republic, this structure could not even remotely have been called democratic. Candidates for assembly and president were handpicked, and the Supreme Leader maintained strict control.

In 1997, with Khomeini long dead and the war with Iraq over for nearly a decade, the picture of Iranian government began to get more complicated. The idea of democracy had begun to return to Iran, which was no longer as closed as it once had been. The mullahs, some motivated by a sincere hope for reform, others by the imperative of enhancing the legitimacy of their rule, decided it was time for a limited experiment with democracy Islamic style. The Supreme Leader and the Council of Guardians allowed a number of candidates to run for the presidency. All were vetted by the Council and the Supreme Leader in what was not at all an open election. Most of the candidates were trained clerics themselves. One candidate, Mohammad Khatami, was identified through his reputation and public statements and writings as more moderate than the others. To the surprise of many outside observers, the presidential election was run without credible accounts of fraud. Khatami was elected president with an astonishing 70 percent of the vote. Reformers organized into a pro-Khatami faction won a large majority in February 2000 elections for the assembly. In 2001, presidential elections were held again, and this time Khatami received more than 78 percent of the vote. In both 1997 and 2001, election turnout exceeded 35 million voters, better than 80 percent of those eligible. That is an impressive figure, both because it is so high—showing that people badly wanted to vote—and because it is so low—showing that people were not coerced to vote. These margins of victory communicated a clear message to the hard-liners: Khatami was and is the people's candidate.

Better read than most politicians in any country, President Khatami has written admiringly and thoughtfully about democratic political theory and principles of toleration. He is, to be sure, still a supporter of the Islamic Republic and its constitution, and he is a mullah by training. But he is a mullah within a tradition of intellectually broad and liberal mullahs who have sought, over the last century, to integrate Islamic law and philosophy with the best that Western thought has to offer. By his own account, Khatami is an Islamic democrat who embraces the synthesis of democracy and Islamic belief. Steeped in the classics of democracy and Islam, he has tried to articulate an explanation of the compatibility of both; and as a mullah and an elected president at once, he embodies the hope that synthesis is possible in practice as well as in theory. Certainly Khatami's books suggest that he takes seriously the goal of reconciling democratic and Islamic values. He writes of the importance of civil society and dialogue, and of the Islamic commitment to liberty.

Khatami's power is limited by the Iranian constitution as it has been applied under the mullahs. The Supreme Leader, Ayatollah 'Ali Khamene'i, frequently intervenes to block reform and maintain the status quo. During Khatami's time in office, his supporters have often been stopped from speaking and writing freely. As many as sixty newspapers run by moderates who back him have been closed; newspaper editors have been punished and tortured; outspoken moderate governors and assembly members have been jailed, both with and without trial. Although Khatami himself has retained his position, backed by the hard-liners' realization that a man elected twice with more than 70 percent of the vote should not be molested directly, the hard-liners have had few qualms about grossly violating the human rights of anyone else who disagrees with them. As a result of Khatami's apparent impotence, many Western Iran-watchers have despaired of him, and no doubt many initially enthusiastic Iranians have also become disillusioned.

Yet the many Iranians who supported Khatami in two elections have done more than show up at the polls. Just a little more than two decades after the revolution, in autumn 2001, young people again took to the streets in Tehran. After soccer matches, those exemplars of secular international culture, the fans protested against the mullahs. According to some reports, the protesters shouted, "Long live freedom." Some even expressed support for Reza Pahlavi, the exiled son and heir of the very shah against whom their elders had revolted. Perhaps even more shocking, there were reports of a chant that ran exactly counter to the chant of the 1979 revolution: "We love America!" In the wake of the September 11 attacks on the United States, young Iranians were among the only people in the Muslim world who spontaneously showed sympathy for American suffering.

One reason for this sea change since 1979 is surely that during the intervening decades, the United States has implacably opposed the Iranian government. Young Iranians associate the U.S. with freedom and democracy, as do young Muslims everywhere. The young people of Iran hate their undemocratic government as much as young Muslims elsewhere hate theirs. But nearly every other undemocratic regime in the Muslim world has benefited from U.S. government support at one time or another since 1979, including Iraq, which the U.S. supported in its war against Iran. The greatest cause of the difference in attitudes is that in the case of Iran, today's young people know that the U.S. is not behind their government. Where the U.S. supports autocrats, anti-American sentiment has only grown as a new generation of Muslims begin to suspect that the values represented by the U.S. will never be applied to them. Where the U.S. opposes autocrats, on the other hand, the people can forgive past wrongs because they see American interests aligned with their own.

Support for this hypothesis may be gleaned from the sources of the Iranian anti-Americanism of 1979. In the years before the 1979 revolution, the West generally and the United States in particular were broadly understood to be the prime supporters of the shah's regime. When young Iranians chanted "Death to America" and took American hostages, there was no great mystery about why they hated the U.S. With Great Britain, the U.S. had funded and arranged the "countercoup" of 1953 in which the democratically elected prime minister, Mohammed Mossadegh, had been displaced and the autocratic rule of the shah affirmed. This was public knowledge; the events were even described in a candid book on the topic written by the CIA man who ran the operation. The U.S. was deeply, one might almost have thought irrevocably, associated with the shah's repression of dissidents and his push for secularization and modernization. Today, however, young people in Iran do not remember the shah's depredations, and they do not especially focus on how the U.S. supported a government that repressed them. Instead, young people are focused on repression perpetrated not by the secular shah but by the religious mullahs. America now seems to be a beacon of hope and democracy. All this goodwill was purchased at the low cost of declining to support an autocratic government.

How should one characterize the encounter of Islam and democracy occurring in Iran today? Will the hard-line mullahs who deny the compatibility of Islam and democracy crush the reformers? Are the Khatami-inspired reformers within the Iranian elite capable of effecting a synthesis that would provide for real democracy within the framework of an Islamic state, accomplishing democratization without revolution? Or will more secularly inclined young people, disenchanted with religion (or at least its political uses), lead a new, democratic revolution in which religion will be relegated to the private sphere?

To ask these questions is to enter a treacherous sphere of political and intellectual debate in which all positions are held with equal tenacity and no one can prove that his or her position is definitively correct. But this debate cannot be ignored, because Iran is the one place in the Muslim world where a revolutionary movement put an Islamic state into power. It is the one place in the Muslim world where an Islamic government has had twenty years in which to run the state its way. And Iran is also undeniably one of the few countries in the Muslim world where a homegrown democracy movement is now engaged in a struggle to reform the Islamic state from within.

The best way to begin to answer these questions about the encounter of mobile ideas in Iran is to consider the structure of the Islamic Republic and its relation to the previous century of Iranian political history. According to one influential view, the Islamic Republic should be understood as the latest iteration in a constitutional process that got its start in 1906 with the drafting of the first written Iranian constitution. That constitution began a negotiation of the role of religion and democracy in Iranian political life that has continued fitfully ever since.

This school of thought, skeptical of the possibilities of Islamic democracy, tends to see the 1979 revolution as a deviation from a process of secularization that began with the introduction of constitutional monarchy in 1906. The shah and his father before him may have been autocrats, but they knew that the future of Iran depended on secularization and contact with the West. They improved education, liberalized the position of women in society, and drove Iran into relative prosperity in the modern world. Opinions are divided within this school of thought on whether the overthrow of Mossadegh saved Iran from tilting toward communism or represented a deviation from democratic development. But there is broad agreement that the Islamic revolution was a disaster for modern Iran.

Under the shah, the country was run by a cadre of well-trained Ph.D.'s and civil servants. Some, even many, may have been corrupt, but at least they knew their jobs. By contrast, after the revolution, the country came to be run by mullahs whose training was in religious law, not practical affairs. No one can say quite how this happened, since before the revolution Khomeini had never suggested that mullahs should run the economy and the health care system and the rest of the practical administration. But happen it did, and with dire consequences. Unprepared to perform the bureaucratic tasks of government or the entrepreneurial function of operating the businesses that the state took over, the mullahs ran the country into the ground. Nothing in Iran works as it did twenty years ago. People who return to see the place for the first time since then are horrified to see the infrastructure, far and away the most advanced in the Middle East before the revolution, degraded to well below its capacity. The U.S. embargo has not helped matters, but there has long been trade with Europe, and much of the damage is clearly self-inflicted. Iranian foreign policy has been spotty and often ineffective; the economy has declined while the population has grown.

Of course, not everything in the Islamic Republic has changed for the worse since the revolution. Women now make up nearly 60 percent of university entrants. Critics of the mullahs say, with some justice, that this increase results from the rise in women's education under the shah, but the truth is that the Islamic Republic has taken women's education seriously. Women are broadly present in the workforce, much more so than during the shah's regime. Again, some of this results from the fact that so many men died during the long war with Iraq; but it is an undeniable fact that under the Islamic Republic, women participate in the public sphere, *hijab* and all. Indeed, one hears the quasi-feminist argument that in a traditionally sexist society, Islamic dress can actually free women to participate in public space without being conceptualized as sex objects. Obviously this issue is extremely complex and sensitive. But even if one would like to say that society ought to change so that women need not cover themselves to be taken seriously, the argument cannot be dismissed out of hand as absurd. Wealth is also more evenly distributed in Iran today than it was before the revolution. Some mullahs have gained ground at the expense of older elites, but there has also been land reform and some redistribution of business wealth. Corruption is pervasive, but perhaps even now it has not reached the levels it had before the revolution.

Nonetheless, the years of the republic are widely understood to have produced a decline that has left many people fed up with government by mullahs. It is not just inefficiency that has got people frustrated but also the continuing supervision of the religious police in matters of clothing, music, and cultural style. The whole country is a bit like a Catholic school or yeshiva in which nuns or rabbis walk around checking hemlines and necklines and Walkmen, except more extreme, since too much hair spilling from a head scarf or a flash of makeup or nail polish can get you into serious trouble. This stuff is silly enough in high school, but it borders on the absurd when adults are being regulated and the punishments sanctioned by the state. No modern government can continue this policy without alienating its citizens over the long term.

The skeptics of reform conclude from this evidence that the latest encounter of Islam and democracy cannot lead to a successful synthesis. After all, the reign of the Islamic Republic has not been democratic. The Supreme Leader has made—and still makes—most of the important decisions for the country, and the assembly has often been a rubber stamp, kept in check by the Council of Guardians. Even today, the regular suppression of free speech and association in Iran, perpetrated by the hard-liners, makes it impossible to say that democracy is likely to expand in the next few years. The moderates who are elected have run for office at the sufferance of the hard-liners who control access to the ballot. For every step forward toward democracy, there seem to have been several steps back.

When they are feeling optimistic, the skeptics say that the mullahs may be able to hold on a bit longer, but ultimately the long-term process of secularization will get back on track, and the people will rise. On this view, the Islamic Republic represents a profound deviation from the history of modernization and secularization in twentieth-century Iran, and anyone who thinks that Iran should be an Islamic state fails to realize that no mullah, however moderate, is a good mullah when he is in government. Since the proper course for the future must be greater secularization, a mullah cannot be the right person to restart the modernization process stalled since the revolution.

The skeptics therefore think that the moderate reformers are dupes or worse, and that Khatami is the hard-liners' best friend. A moderate, liberal face for the Iranian regime, he is presentable abroad, and at home his existence gives some slight hope that the system can be reformed from within. By allowing Khatami to serve as president, the hard-liners lost nothing, since Khatami does not control the budget or the army or foreign policy or the courts. His supporters can be repressed when convenient. Yet he is still a mullah, still operating within the legal, logical, and constitutional structures that sustain the regime. Opponents' energies are dissipated in hoping that Khatami will bring about democratic reform, when in reality he just buys time and space for the hard-liners. According to this theory, either Khatami is naively hoping to achieve some good on his own, or else, more cynically, he knows exactly what is going on and accepts the use of his identity and persona as a moderate figurehead for reasons of greed, vanity, or secret sympathy with the hard-liners.

But those who would deny the compatibility of an Islamic state and a modern democracy in Iran also must confront some arguments running the opposite way. For one thing, the skeptics' secularizing, modernizing heroes, the shah and his father, were hardly democratic. Modernization and secularization were pursued by fiat and edict, not at the ballot box. Iran's one apparent chance at democratization, Mossadegh's election, happened fifty years ago and was thwarted by the Western countries who supported the shah. A simple opposition between Islam on the one side and democratization on the other drastically oversimplifies Iranian history. Indeed, it would be a mistake to associate democracy with either secularization or religion. There can be secularizing autocrats and religious autocrats, secularist democrats and religious democrats.

Unlike those critics who see twentieth-century Iranian history as a process of modernization and secularization tragically reversed by the Islamic Republic, other observers see the last century of Iranian history as a complicated interplay between democracy, autocracy, secularization, and religion. On this view, the 1906 constitution began a gradual movement toward democracy. The Islamic Republic that was declared in 1979 was framed in terms that sought to reconcile democracy and religion. After all, the revolutionaries declared a republic, not an imamate, and a republic is, by its definition and logic, a "thing of the public," a state devoted to serving the public's needs. The constitution of 1979 established an assembly and some separation of powers. Although it declared that Islam would provide the values of the republic, the constitution envisioned real democratic input into the process of governance. Things went awry, and the autocratic impulse swamped the democratic impulse. Now, since 1997, there are religious democrats, people like Khatami, who seek to put religious democracy back on the right track. Books of political theory are notoriously different from politics in action, but it turns out to be rather difficult to show that President Khatami has himself taken actions that differ deeply from his expressed preference for free speech. In office, Khatami's power is limited, and he may justly be criticized for passivity in the face of repression, but he seems to have exercised what power he does have in the direction of promoting the values of democratic Islam. Frustrated with the obstacles placed in the way of reform, Khatami has recently spoken out against the Council of Guardians' vetoes of his attempts to introduce greater supervision of the courts. Perhaps he has not yet squandered the public support that attached to him as an advocate of reform.

The skeptics have an easy answer to this point: *of course* Khatami looks good to lovers of democracy. He is playing good cop to the hard-liners' bad cop. Even if Khatami himself prefers democracy, though, he has not taken the drastic steps necessary to bring it about. He has not led his people into the streets to call for the ouster of the Supreme Leader. He has not appeared in courts or at prisons to free his moderate supporters when the regime puts them on trial or in jail. He is, by any account, working within the system, so if the system is undemocratic, then so is Khatami, for acquiescing to it.

This objection raises a deeper problem for making sense out of the current state of affairs in Iran. Some observers think that Khatami and his followers learned one crucial lesson from the revolution: revolutions are extreme, bloody, and do untold harm even when their intentions are good. Iran needs gradual democratization, not another upheaval on the scale of the Islamic revolution. Gradual democratization means the preservation of the basic constitutional structure of the Islamic Republic, at least for now. It means bringing more democracy into the Islamic realm, not eliminating the Islamic Republic altogether.

So the question arises: Will this vision of gradual democratization of the Islamic Republic work? Is it working right now? To those who see Islam and democracy as fundamentally opposed, this vision of gradual democratization is pure fantasy. The only route to democracy is to achieve a drastic change in the structure of the Iranian state—to depose the mullahs and replace the Islamic Republic with something secular and democratic. It seems likely that Khatami's various failures in office have led to the growth of this view inside Iran. On the other hand, to those who believe that Islam and democracy can be synthesized in Iran, the Islamic Republic now represents a unique and extraordinary opportunity for Islamic democracy to emerge. Such an Islamic democracy would not only begin to solve the problems that Iran faces today without violent upheaval, but would also represent a model for other places in the Muslim world to emulate. A true Islamic democracy in Iran would influence the Muslim world as much as the Islamic revolution influenced it twenty years ago.

How would the Islamic Republic get from where it is now to a state of true Islamic democracy? Elections lie at the heart of the process. Before the election of Khatami in 1997, there was literally no basis for any leader in the republic to claim any sort of democratic legitimacy. By permitting a free election, even one where the candidates were carefully vetted and hand-picked, the hard-liners created the option for the public to confer democratic legitimacy on one candidate. The hard-liners may never have realized what they were doing, and in fact may have been surprised by the extent and depth of the support for Khatami. But the moment that the public has cast its ballots for one candidate rather than others, it has pushed the thin edge of the wedge of democracy into an otherwise autocratic system. Three national elections really have occurred in Iran. Although not everyone who wanted to run for office was permitted to run, there were candidates, Khatami among them, who did not enjoy the support of the hard-liners, and who won by large margins.

Once the public has spoken in this way, the hard-liners may become limited in what they can do. To depose Khatami or bar him from running again would directly and explicitly contradict the wishes of a large super-majority of the Iranian people. The hard-liners have not been prepared to do that. Of course, they have been more than willing to attack Khatami's supporters physically and legally, but the reason they are able to do so is that those supporters, whether newspaper editors or local governors, do not enjoy the same public imprimatur that results from national elections.

The point is that free or relatively free elections *themselves* can create the baseline for democratic legitimacy that can then spread. In Iran today, the hard-liners are trying to limit the spread of such legitimacy and to repress voices of reform. For his part, Khatami has been cautious and realistic about what authority his election has in fact conferred on him. He has not taken big risks with his legitimacy, perhaps because he fears that if the hard-liners discredit him, the experiment with democracy could be brought to an end. More elections for a broader range of candidates, though, would enhance democratization in Iran very definitively.

But will it happen? Those frustrated with the slow pace of reform in Iran fear that it may not, and that the hard-liners can maintain their position indefinitely. They therefore counsel implacable opposition to the regime.

This school of thought persuaded President Bush in his January 2002 State of the Union address to describe Iran as one of three members of an "axis of evil," along with Iraq and North Korea. In June of the same year, Bush made a further policy statement declaring in essence that the United States would not engage with moderates in the Iranian government but would reach out directly to ordinary Iranians who sought to oppose their government. This was music to the ears of those who doubt that reform in Iran can ever be accomplished within the structure of the Islamic Republic. In support of their contention, they pointed to a shipment of arms sent by the Iranian government to the Palestinian Authority, intercepted by Israel in early 2002—powerful evidence of the "Palestinization" of an Iranian foreign policy that also includes financial support for Lebanese Hezbollah and the Palestinian organization Islamic Jihad.

Those who think that Iran has the capacity to reform itself from within, however, were for the most part disappointed by Bush's statements. As they saw it, the average moderate Iranian would hear the expression "axis of evil" and immediately start to wonder whether the United States was going to invade Iran. This might alienate those Iranians who, for the first time in twenty years, were beginning to feel something like sympathy for the U.S. More to the point, Bush's formulation would also embolden hard-liners within Iran who believe that the U.S. could never be anything but hostile to an Islamic state. The theory of implacable opposition between Islam and democracy exists within Iran as well as outside. Hard-line Muslims who agree that democracy and Islam are incompatible regularly tell moderate Islamic democrats that they are deceiving themselves into thinking that the West will ever accept Islamic democracy. The West, say the hard-liners, believes that its interests and those of Muslims are inevitably opposed. The apparent confirmation of this view by the Bush statements then becomes an excuse for further repression of moderates within Iran.

The potential tragedy of this way of thinking is not just that it may turn out to be correct, but that it may be self-fulfilling. Absolutist thinkers on both sides influence not only the tenor of the argument, but actual policies. Not even the most optimistic observers of the Iranian political scene could claim that Iran is on an inevitable march to democracy, Islamic or otherwise. By any account, the hard-liners still control most of the government, and they continue to repress and suppress democratic voices. The repression has been especially bad in 2001–02. Iran is still very far from being a free or democratic country. But those observers who do take Khatami and the reformers seriously have a set of arguments that deserve to be heard. The most important homegrown democracy movement in the Muslim world arose in an Islamic state, and that state has now twice seen the election of a confirmed Islamic democrat. The absolutists who deny that these facts may be harbingers of synthesis have the capacity to prove themselves right by driving both moderate Iranians and the United States into opposition. All that moderates on either side can ever say is that there exists a *possibility* of something better and less oppositional. But without the claim of possibility, we are guaranteed to lose.

Turkey: The Outlier

Turkish politics today offers a fascinating perspective on the possibility of Islamic democracy. Turkey has, along with post-1991 Bangladesh, the most fully functioning democracy of any majority-Muslim state in the world. The Grand National Assembly is elected in relatively free elections, which have occurred regularly since 1983. The assembly elects the president, who in turn names a prime minister to form a government. Almost all of Turkey's 66 million citizens are Muslims. On its face, the progress of democratization in Turkey in the last twenty years would seem to prove that there can be democracy in a Muslim country.

Yet the relationship between Islam and democracy in Turkey remains troubled, haunted by a legacy of Turkish politics that rejected both. Although there is a functioning system of electoral politics, and the assembly in summer 2002 enacted laws broadening civil liberties, two groups outside the secular elites who have traditionally dominated the Turkish establishment remain vulnerable to exclusion or even to human rights violations. These are the Islamists, among the most moderate in the Muslim world, and the Kurds, whose traditional homeland of Kurdistan was divided among Turkey, Iran, and Iraq in the years after World War I, and who have been seeking to restore it ever since.

It is easy to explain, though not to justify, the treatment of the supporters of Kurdish independence, who are either freedom fighters or terrorists, depending on how you look at it. Those Kurds who did not wish to disappear into Turkish society have pursued the various routes open to independence-seeking peoples, ranging from negotiation and politics to rebellion and terrorism. The Turkish government, for its part, has sought to make the Kurdish problem go away, harassing individual Kurds whom it suspects of sympathy to the independence movement, jailing and torturing leaders, and mounting military action against Kurdish rebels when it can find them. For years the Turkish government called the Kurds "mountain Turks" and banned their languages. It's an ugly business, although by most accounts it has improved in recent years, since the Turkish government caught and tried the leader of the PKK (the Kurdistan Workers' Party), the largest Kurdish separatist group. The violence may be coming to an end; the PKK recently renounced violence and claimed it would turn to peaceful politics. Allowing education and radio broadcasts in Kurdish was among the reforms passed in 2002, albeit amid great controversy.

But if the marginalization of Kurds from Turkish political life can be explained as a garden-variety instance of conflict between a nationalist state and a separatist independence movement, understanding the sometimes harsh treatment of Turkey's suit-and-tie Islamists by a basically democratic government requires some background on the place of Islam in modern Turkish history. This history will reveal why Turkey is such an important case for Islamic democracy: a developing democracy, it is both the home of the most forward-looking group of Islamic democrats in the world, and the country in which Islamic democracy is most widely dismissed as a contradiction.

The salient fact about Turkey for purposes of an account of democracy and Islam today is that it went through a period in which the government set out to remove Islam from public life. This was a shocking, even bizarre thing for a country like Turkey to do. Modern Turkey arose from the ruins of the Ottoman Empire after that empire joined the Austro-Hungarian Empire on the losing side of World War I. The Ottoman Empire had lasted some five hundred years, longer than any other empire in Muslim history, and it extended to three continents. On the European side, it ranged over Greece, Yugoslavia, and Bulgaria and reached all the way to Hungary. On the Asian side, it crossed Anatolia—modern Turkey—and extended to Iran, covering

Iraq, Syria, Lebanon, and Palestine. In Africa, the Ottoman Empire included Egypt and eventually extended across the whole of North Africa.

The Ottoman Empire was definitively and proudly Muslim, governed by principles of Islamic law and bound together by Ottoman ideology that relied on Islam. From the fifteenth century, Istanbul was the hub from which the spokes of Islam spread outward. So one can imagine how radical it was to turn the new Turkish Republic away from Islam and in the direction of the West. As Islam declined in the late years of the empire, the newly vibrant nations of Europe seemed to be uniting not around religion but around national identity. Before defeat in World War I reduced the Ottoman Empire to country size, the young men who sought to revive their state looked to nationalism, not religion, as the unifying force. The Young Turks who became the power behind the sultan in 1908 took their name from a new, nationalist idea of what united the people who lived on the Anatolian Peninsula. Turkish ethnicity was to be the beginning point for the construction of a nation.

Those residents of the Anatolian Peninsula who were not prepared to think of themselves as Turks were made to feel unwelcome during the war years that followed. Hundreds of thousands of Armenians living near the hostile Russian border were killed in what today would be called genocide. (The Turkish government and many Turks vociferously disagree with this characterization, although almost no one today questions the enormous numbers of Armenian dead.) Through the 1920s, hundreds of thousands of ethnic Greeks were killed or forced to flee Anatolia, while ethnic Turks who lived in Greece were fleeing Greek nationalists there.

Out of the wreckage of the war, General Mustafa Kemal emerged as the dominant military figure. Almost alone among the Ottoman generals, Kemal had a great victory in the war to his credit, having commanded the Ottoman troops at Gallipoli. Open about his desire to replace the sultan with a nationalist government of his own, Kemal formed the Grand National Assembly in 1920 and was elected its president. In 1923, Kemal declared the Republic of Turkey, and modern Turkey came into being.

Kemal's ideology raised the incipient nationalism of the Young Turks to the level of obsession. Kemal presented himself as the embodiment of the Turkish people. He took the new name Ataturk, "Father of the Turks." Ataturk's program of nationalist ideology was essentially unprecedented. It strove to replace the social bonds that held together the complex and pluralist Ottoman society with bonds that would tie the individual to the Turkish nation. He abolished the Ottoman *millet* system, the tradition of Islamic pluralism under which each religious community had responsibility for its own affairs. People were discouraged from thinking of themselves as Muslims or Jews or Christians: now everyone was a Turk, full stop, who would speak, think, and live Turkish.

But elevating Turkishness to the central and exclusive social identity was only one part of the Kemalist reforms, which also sought to turn the Turkish people away from the Muslim East and toward the West, associated with progress, modernity, and secularization—though not, notably, democratization. With a pen stroke, Ataturk abolished the Islamic legal system and replaced it with secular legal codes modeled on European laws. Religious institutions were disbanded or brought under strict state control. Secularism became the law of the state. Ataturk banned the fez, the conical red hat that was the distinguishing fashion accessory for men of the late Ottoman period, and required men to wear European headgear or none at all. He banned the veil and traditional dress for women as well.

Most idiosyncratically, Ataturk decreed that Turkish would no longer be written in the Ottoman alphabet, which was based on the Arabic alphabet. He instituted, in its place, the Roman alphabet, altered by the addition of a variety of diacritical marks to make it correspond to the sounds of Turkish. It is doubtful whether any ruler in history ever before switched an entire system of writing from one borrowed alphabet to another in the space of a few months (although King Sejong ordered the creation of an alphabet from scratch in fifteenth-century Korea). Ataturk's decree was justified on the theory that it would be easier to read Turkish in the Roman alphabet than in the Arabic alphabet, a questionable justification still repeated in modern Turkey. But the main reason was that Ataturk believed that a language written in Roman characters would seem more Western and would turn Turks away from the Muslim world and their Muslim past. It would certainly have been possible to refine or improve or simplify the Arabic-based Turkish script instead of replacing it altogether, and one wonders if the Roman alphabet did much to encourage a turn to the West; but changing the alphabet did cut off the great majority of Turks from their own history by rendering it literally illegible to them.

Both nationalism and the turn to the West corresponded to an intense secularism and the repression of organized Islam. Even after Ataturk's death, this mix continued to provide the basic flavor of the Turkish national ethos. The Turkish constitution of 1982 declares in its preamble that Turkey is a secular democratic state that remains "loyal to the nationalism of Ataturk." One still sees Ataturk's statue in Turkey today, a decade after Stalin's statues disappeared from the former Soviet Union. The former mayor of Jerusalem, Teddy Kollek, used to delight in saying that after socialism and communism were gone, Zionism was "the one ism" that survived the turbulent twentieth century. But Kollek overstated his case: Kemalism, in some form, remains a viable and vital "ism," and the preamble to the Turkish constitution stands as a testimony to it.

Notwithstanding the strength of Kemalism, the Turkish government has been shaky in the modern era, and there were military coups in 1960, 1971, and 1980. Yet throughout this history the military has understood itself, and is understood by many Turks, as the protector of the secular character of the Turkish state. When democratically elected Islamic parties begin to succeed in Turkish politics, there always exists the possibility that the Turkish military will intervene to remove the Islamists from office.

To advocates of the Turkish system, the military operates as a safety valve to make democracy work in the Muslim world. These advocates think that relying on the military to keep the state secular represents a solution to the "paradox" that in democratic elections some people will choose to vote for Islamic parties. If you believe, as many advocates of the Turkish system do, that Islamic politics is incompatible with democracy, then this paradox amounts to a major problem with democratization in the Muslim world.

This "paradox" has existed in Turkey as long as there have been free elections because some parties have always organized themselves on the basis of Islam. The Islamic political parties in Turkey have been very moderate in comparison with Islamist organizations elsewhere in the Muslim world. They have never advocated violence or the imposition of the more extreme versions of classical Islamic law. All have advocated democracy.

But Islamic parties in Turkey do call for a renewal of the Islamic values of justice and equality, and they call especially for Islamic religious values to play a greater role in Turkish life. It also happens that a sizable number of Turks have been sympathetic to these Islamic parties each time they have come onto the political scene.

The Turkish system relies on the military to resolve this paradox in a very blunt way: by limiting the shelf life of the Islamic parties, and forcing them to disband once they start to succeed. If necessary, the army is supposed to remove the Islamic parties from power. Democracy is thus "preserved" by barring Islamic parties from participating in politics. The threat of Islam is staved off at the expense of stopping people from voting for the Islamic parties that they prefer. This model sees democracy, still a relatively recent arrival in Turkey, as needing protection from the resurgent Islam that has sprung up again in the country despite seventy-five years of official discouragement.

This is not just theory, but reality. The most recent version of military intervention against an Islamic party occurred just a few years ago. In December 1995, Turkey held national elections. One of the parties that competed was an Islamic party headed by Necmettin Erbakan, a mechanical engineer educated in Germany and a figure in Turkish politics since the 1970s. He became attracted to Islamic politics as early as 1970, when he founded an Islamic party that was banned by the military a year later. Erbakan refounded the party in 1972 under a new name; in 1980 he was a leader in Islamically inspired protests that led to military intervention, and his party was banned yet again. Undeterred, Erbakan refounded his party in 1983 as the Welfare Party.

Erbakan and his Welfare Party had a reputation for being free of corruption. In the 1995 elections the Welfare Party drew 21.4 percent of the total vote. The rest of the parties split the vote, so that no one party had a majority. At first, the other parties forged a coalition that excluded the Welfare Party, but when that coalition faltered, Erbakan entered a coalition with the True Path Party of Tansu Ciller, a former prime minister who had always been strongly secularist. They agreed that they would alternate as prime minister, with Erbakan having the first turn.

From the beginning of Erbakan's time in office in 1996, secular Turks and Western allies of Turkey looked skeptically on him. In one chapter of his thoughtful book on U.S. foreign policy toward Islamists, Fawaz Gerges charts the ambivalence of U.S. policy toward Erbakan's government. On the one hand, the United States wanted to signal that it supported the democratically elected government in Turkey; on the other, it wanted to distance itself as much as possible from Erbakan and what it worried might be his policies. In fact, the conventional wisdom was that Erbakan could not change Turkey's foreign policy very drastically even if he wanted to do so. His party was in a coalition government, and Turkey's basic strategic interests were aligned against its neighbors Syria and Iran and with the United States. But nearly everything Erbakan did worried Turkey's American allies. Erbakan's largely symbolic visit to Libya, in which Qadhafi reprimanded him like a schoolboy in front of the press, nonetheless sent shivers down American spines. The worry was that Turkey under Erbakan would become increasingly Islamic in its politics and alliances.

Meanwhile, Turkish secular elites were worried, too. They could not point to many particular policies of Erbakan's that were inherently troubling. He closed casinos, which worried some secularists but could hardly be considered a major move in the direction of Islamization of society or politics. But still, seventy years of ideologically secularist politics made it very hard to accept the idea that the prime minister of Turkey came from an Islamic political party.

The military therefore unsubtly moved to bring Erbakan's brief tenure in office to an end. Tansu Ciller asked early for her turn as prime minister. Then, through the exercise of military pressure, what most observers have called a "soft coup" took place. There was no violence, but Erbakan was forced to resign. Instead of Ciller's taking office, a new coalition government was formed between Ciller's party and a third party. The president of Turkey announced that he was giving an opportunity to the leader of that third party, a man called Mesut Yilmaz, to form a new coalition government without the Welfare Party in it, and Yilmaz did so.

As if to prove that this was no mere power shuffle in a complicated parliamentary system, the Constitutional Court then formally banned Erbakan's Welfare Party. The Welfare Party now joined the ranks of its two predecessor parties that had been banned by the government. The party was immediately re-formed for a fourth time, this time as the Virtue Party (itself later banned), but the process was not quite over. Erbakan was put on trial for "inciting hatred and animosity among people on the basis of racial, religious, and social discrimination" in a 1994 speech.

In the speech, made in a heavily Kurdish city in southeastern Turkey, Erbakan had criticized discrimination against Kurds. According to the court, his crime consisted of the following statement: "If you say, 'I am a Turk, brave and hardworking,' it is only normal that some other people will come up and say, 'I am a Kurd. I am braver and harder-working than you.'" The court found that in making that statement, Erbakan had incited hatred based on discrimination between Kurds and other Turks. The charge was made and sustained on appeal under a provision of the Turkish Penal Code known as Article 312, which is often used to jail and silence human rights leaders and other dissidents. Erbakan was convicted and sentenced to a year in prison, of which he served four months. As further punishment, he was banned from politics for life, although the political ban was later partially lifted in a political side deal.

Now the process was complete, and by the lights of the supporters of the Turkish system, it had "worked." The military had stepped in to preserve Turkey from the dangers of Islamic democracy. The European Union, which Turkey desperately wants to join, made polite noises about how a country should ban political parties only in extreme circumstances, but it was clear that the Europeans were relieved not to have an Islamic government seeking to join their club. The United States held its peace. Most Western governments breathed a sigh of relief that the specter of Islamic democracy had been avoided once more.

The cycle, however, may begin again. Today, the latest new political party to attract the very same Islamically inclined voters is the Justice and Development Party, which finished first in the November 2002 elections. The party is headed by former Istanbul mayor Recep Tayyep Erdogan, himself once preposterously convicted under the same Article 312 for reciting a poem found in many Turkish schoolbooks that includes a comparison between minarets and swords. Before the election, the party's opponents arranged to have an electoral commission ban Erdogan from politics, just as Erbakan had been banned. Meanwhile, Justice and Development, having learned from Virtue's experience, publicly denies that it has any Islamic character at all. But its supporters understand that both the party's social conservatism and its reputation for honesty are connected to its Islamic character; and the party's opponents stand ready to try to suppress it as Islamic if they can. Distorted by the threat of military intervention, the next encounter of Islam and democracy in Turkey may produce a synthesis more like crypto-Islamic democracy than like Islamic democracy proper.

One does not need to be an admirer of Necmettin Erbakan or his putative successor to think that there is something unsatisfying about the Turkish model for dealing with Islamic politics. Those people who speak warmly of the Turkish military as the protector of democracy in Turkey are in fact choosing secularism over democracy, just like the Algerian autocrats. Those who admit that the Turkish system is designed to protect the country's secularism against Islamic politics regardless of the democratic consequences are at least making an accurate observation. But the price of protecting secularism the Turkish way is selectively sacrificing democracy.

Turkish secular democracy means that the people can vote for any candidate they want, unless their candidate believes in Islamic values. That kind of limitation recalls the Iranian model, in which the public can vote for any candidate provided that candidate *does* espouse Islamic values. In both cases, authorities who are not responsible to the public limit the range of democratic options that the public may exercise. The Supreme Leader in Iran and the military in Turkey both have the capacity to shape electoral outcomes by standing in the way of any candidates whom they do not like. Both limit individual rights, like free speech, to do it. The Turkish military acts in the name of secularism, while the Supreme Leader acts in the name of Islam.

It would be grossly unfair to make Turkey appear to be as undemocratic as Iran. Each time the Turkish military has intervened in Turkish politics in recent years, it has subsequently yielded power back to relatively more democratic governments. By contrast, the hard-liners in the Islamic Republic have not yet yielded meaningful power to democratic government, and they may never do so. Turkey may be a place where you can go to jail for saying that Turks and Kurds both feel ethnic pride, but Turkey is still far freer than Iran. People are, for the most part, free to practice Islam in secular Turkey.

It is just that they cannot freely bring their Islamic values to bear in picking their government.

This radical form of the separation of church and state, backed by the authority of the military, goes well beyond the separation in, say, the United States. If Erdogan wanted to found the Justice and Development Party in the United States, he could do it, even if its principles were identifiably Islamic. If—to extend the hypothetical scenario—Erdogan became president and his party controlled Congress, President Erdogan could announce that Islamic values were important to him. He could tell interviewers that he prayed about important decisions, and he could replace Billy Graham, a regular feature of every inauguration since President Nixon's, with the imam of his choice.

Of course, unless the Constitution were amended, there would be a range of laws that the Justice and Development Party could not enact. Under current American constitutional law, the party could not enact laws designed to support mosques or Islamic education in particular. It could not make Islamic law into the law of the state, or make the government pay for public-service announcements touting the virtues of an Islamic lifestyle. But Erdogan could run for office on a platform of amending the Constitution to make the United States an Islamic country, and if he had the votes, then, under Article V of the Constitution, he could do it. The military would not intervene, or, at least, under the Constitution it would not be allowed to intervene. Separation of church and state is subject to amendment, like the rest of the Constitution.

The hypothetical American president Erdogan is meant to demonstrate a subtlety of genuine constitutional democracy. Even when some democratic options are taken off the table, it generally remains possible to advocate for changes that would put these matters back on the table. It also remains possible to organize a political party around any deeply held set of beliefs that are in principle compatible with democracy.

This again gives rise to the question of what to do about parties that advocate undemocratic systems of government. In Europe, the experience of Nazism has led many countries to be willing to ban political parties that are racist or that advocate undemocratic beliefs. In the United States, the rules tend to be more forgiving. Before being banned, a party would probably have to advocate the immediate violent overthrow of the U.S. government and then actually act on its ideals. It seems reasonable for democracies to do what it takes to prevent being overthrown violently. But what about parties that propose fundamental changes by democratic means?

Most theorists of democracy would be willing to concede that one could perhaps justly ban a party that advocated putting an end to democracy. But the Islamic parties in Turkey have not made this argument. Erbakan certainly never opposed democracy, and gave no special hint of undemocratic tendencies in his brief tenure as prime minister—at least not by Turkish standards. It is an open question what a democracy should do when it is faced with a party that *says* it is democratic but in fact looks suspiciously undemocratic. Supporters of the Turkish model always insist that the Turkish Islamic parties speak a democratic language without believing in democracy. But they have little evidence to show for this assertion. They are mostly relying on the mistaken belief that Islamic parties are *inherently* undemocratic.

That supporters of the Turkish way assume that Islam and democracy are incompatible has led Turkish secularists to stand in the way of democratic values in Turkey. The same unfounded assumption has led the West to stand by and even approve of this undemocratic impulse. Perhaps more disturbingly, the assumption that democracy and Islam are incompatible has led observers of Turkey to miss a tremendously important, salient fact about Turkish politics: Turkey has an active Islamic democratic movement. Islamic democrats in Turkey are not hard-liners who run for office on a platform of imposing *shari'a* on everyone. They do not call for repression of civil liberties in Turkey. Instead, Turkish Islamic politics is mainstream. Its leaders are modernist Muslims, not traditionalists or fundamentalists. Turkey provides a living, breathing example of what Islamic democracy can look like. When an Islamic democrat became prime minister of Turkey, the sky did not fall. Democracy was not abolished—at least not by the Islamic parties.

The example of Turkey does not demonstrate that every broadly popular Islamic movement will be democratic. Turkey has a special character because of its history of secularism. But Turkey also does not prove that a history of government-enforced secularism necessarily produces moderate Islam. After all, the only other Muslim country to have experienced a process of secularization on the magnitude of Turkey was Iran. In Iran, coercive secularization ultimately had the opposite effect: it produced a radicalized Islamism that was the antithesis of moderation. No one who aims to promote moderate Islam would be well advised to undertake a policy of coercive secularization in the Muslim world. Ataturk's approach cannot and should not be repeated.

But the observation that Turkey has produced a moderate politics of Islamic democracy does have relevance for democratization in other parts of the Muslim world. If it can happen in Turkey, it can happen elsewhere. Conditions will be different, the players will be different, and the institutions, history, and beliefs will differ. Ironically, if the secular elites should decide to suppress Islamic democracy in Turkey again, that would make it more likely, not less, that undemocratic Islamism will spread to other Muslim countries. Turkey can provide a model for how moderate Islamic parties can act in the democratic sphere. Or Turkey can send a message to Islamists that even if they are democratic, they will be suppressed in the name of democracy. That would represent a lost opportunity for democratization in a world where people take Islam seriously.

Turkey poses a perfect test of the possibility of Islamic democracy. Despite being suppressed and marginalized for eighty years, Islam in Turkey has shown its characteristic resilience. Democracy, for its part, has advanced steadily if irregularly, driven by its inherent attractions and its connection to Turkish national self-interest. The more truly democratic Turkey becomes, the more Islamic it is likely to be. Turkey therefore may become an Islamic democracy simply by permitting its citizens to choose the candidates they wish, without upheaval or violence. If this happens, the lessons for the rest of the world would be profound. The Turks will have moved beyond Mustafa Kemal's legacy of opposing Islam and the West, and will have created a synthesis that makes the compatibility of Islam and democracy into a reality.

————◆◆◆————

ISLAM AND DEMOCRACY IN
SOUTH AND SOUTHEAST ASIA:
MOBILITY AND POSSIBILITY

More than half of the world's Muslims live in South and Southeast Asia. Indonesia is home to some 180 million Muslims, who make up 87 percent of its people. Pakistan has nearly 150 million citizens, almost all Muslims. Add another 110 million or so Muslims in India, the same number in Bangladesh, perhaps 11.5 million Muslim Malays in Malaysia, and around 6 million Muslims total in the Philippines, Burma/Myanmar, and Cambodia, and one has an extraordinary number of very diverse people living across a vast geographical area, all of whom profess some version of Islam.

The presence of Islam across so wide a swath of territory suggests its flexibility and its capacity to accommodate local languages, customs, family structures, and values. Democracy has demonstrated its mobility in South and Southeast Asia as well, with India its most prominent and remarkable success. The encounter between Islam and democracy has therefore been especially rich and interesting in these regions. In Malaysia, for example, where Muslim Malays outnumber the ethnic Chinese non-Muslims who long dominated the country's economy, there have been regular, basically free elections every five years since independence in 1957. Essentially the same ruling coalition has remained in power all that time, but Islamic parties participate in the elections, and Islamic political ideas have gradually become to some extent mainstream. As a result, Malaysia has produced some interesting experimental innovations by juxtaposing Islamic and democratic institutions, such as the adaptation of the classical Islamic market supervisor as a kind of government ombudsman. One Islamic party, running on an anticorruption platform, has emerged as the largest opposition party in parliament.

But the stability and extraordinary economic growth of Malaysia have not been accompanied by impressive gains in basic civil liberties. To the contrary, in recent years free speech and association, never strongly protected, have been further curtailed. The capstone in this process of jailing dissidents under the draconian Internal Security Act was the arrest and show trial of Anwar Ibrahim, erstwhile deputy prime minister and protégé of Prime Minister Mahathir Mohamad. A modernist-Islamist politician and former youth-movement leader who rose rapidly as the government sought to co-opt the Islamists during the period of economic growth, Ibrahim disagreed publicly with his mentor about fiscal policy when Malaysia ran into tough economic times. Once Ibrahim began to appear as a potential challenger, the prime minister's embrace turned to more of a stranglehold. Mohamad contrived to have Ibrahim convicted of sodomy and thrown in prison, where he remains. This nasty turn suggests that in Malaysia complete democracy is still some ways off; still, when and if Ibrahim is released, it is likely that Islamic politics will become even more closely fused with democratic opposition.

With its economic success and correspondingly high profile as a Muslim success story, Malaysia offers a partial model for one sort of Islamic democracy. Another, more secularized model may be glimpsed in Bangladesh, which since its 1991 elections has emerged as a remarkably free democracy notwithstanding its extreme economic underdevelopment. The constitution makes Islam the official religion but also guarantees freedom of religion to minorities, who are mainly Hindu. The Islamist Jamaat-e-Islami party was long banned because of its pro-Pakistani sympathies, but it now participates in elections and even managed to win 16 seats in the 300-member parliament in 2001 elections. That was enough to get a couple of cabinet positions when it joined the coalition government of the conservative Nationalist Party, although Prime Minister Khaleda Zia insisted that Bangladesh would not become an Islamic state.

Bangladesh faces enormous challenges. Government institutions, including parliament, are still very weak. A recent study rated Bangladesh as the most corrupt country in the world. Dire poverty and national debt remain the country's most serious problems, with law and order not far behind. There has been occasional anti-Hindu violence, some of it perpetrated by Islamists. The nascent democracy is still very fragile. But the bottom line is that Bangladesh is struggling to become a Muslim democracy, evidence that it can be done even under the most difficult conditions.

Intriguing as the prospects of Islamic democracy in Malaysia and Bangladesh may be, the more important Asian stories for an assessment of the future of Islamic democracy belong to the two largest Muslim countries in the world: Indonesia and Pakistan. The former gives grounds for guarded optimism; the latter inspires frustration. The stories are profoundly different, but juxtaposed, they reveal how unpredictable—and how fruitful—the encounter of Islam and democracy can be.

Islam did not enter Indonesia by conquest, but first reached the island of Java in the twelfth century by means of Muslim traders who plied the Indian Ocean, engaging in the lucrative spice trade. The traders came from Iran, India, and as far away as the Arab side of the Persian Gulf. They explained their religion to the coastal people whom they met, and the religion proved attractive. Some coastal rulers adopted Islam; later they defeated inland kings and spread Islam further through the country. By the mid-1500s, Islam had spread over much of the Indonesian archipelago, largely replacing a well-developed Hindu-Buddhist religious tradition.

Indonesian Islam, especially that of Java, is famous for its relaxed style. Many Indonesian Muslims have continued to follow customs and practices that predate the spread of Islam, incorporating them into their own version of Muslim practice and identity. Other Indonesian Muslims practice a stricter Islam, but they, too, have been tolerant of religious difference through most of modern Indonesian history. Indonesian Islam thus perfectly exemplifies the kind of flexibility that an idea must have to spread.

Democracy, unlike Islam, came to Indonesia very recently. Indonesia was Holland's most important colony, and the Dutch clung to it for a long time, so that Indonesia achieved independence only in 1949. The country was conceived as a democracy, in which citizens would vote for a constituent assembly to write a constitution and institute democratic government. Two Muslim parties, one appealing to modernist Muslims and the other to more traditional Muslims, participated in elections in 1955, along with nationalist, communist, and Christian parties. But in 1958, President Ahmad Sukarno capitalized on an impasse in the constituent assembly to call off the constitution-making exercise, then instituted what became a secular, socialist dictatorship that lasted until 1965. In 1965–66, the year of living dangerously, Sukarno gave way to a new dictator, Suharto, who came to power with American assistance and the support of a range of Indonesian groups, including both modernist and traditional Muslims. In the terrible transition, some members of Islamic parties participated in massacres of Indonesians who were thought to be communists or communist sympathizers.

Over the next thirty-two years, Suharto ruled Indonesia with a sophisticated combination of ideology and power politics. Suharto initially marginalized organized Islam, preferring a self-conscious syncretism that was associated with the unorthodox Islam of Java. But later in his regime, when secularists drew away from him, he turned toward Muslims, both Islamist and more traditional, in order to shore up his support. The Muslim parties, for their part, cooperated, with Islamists in particular taking advantage of government funding for their education programs. Traditionalist Muslims kept up a cautious critique of the regime, then turned on Suharto and participated in his ouster. This extraordinary dance between Suharto and Indonesian Muslim groups is detailed in Robert Hefner's fascinating book *Civil Islam*.

Suharto's rule came to an end in 1998, after widespread violence made it clear that he no longer had the support of the military nor of any other major constituency in Indonesian society. There were free elections in 1999, and Abdurrahman Wahid, a Muslim cleric, became the first democratically elected leader of Indonesia. Wahid was blind and partly paralyzed by a stroke by the time of his election. But he had been, for many years, the leader of the largest traditional Muslim party in Indonesia, the Nahdlatul Ulama. His election signaled that many Indonesians saw Islam and democracy as fully compatible.

Wahid's own views were grounded in Islam, but were also deeply democratic. He was a founder of an organization called the Forum for Democracy and argued publicly that Indonesia did not need to institute Islamic law. Wahid advocated a pluralist state, not an Islamic one, and in 1994, before becoming president, he actually visited Israel and embraced the idea of relations between Israel and Muslim states.

In the event, Wahid's presidency was brief and unsuccessful. During his term, the Indonesian province of East Timor voted for independence, after which militias that had the support of the Indonesian military embarked on a campaign of terror and murder in the region. Sporadic Muslim-Christian violence has been recurrent. Wahid's illness made him ineffective, and he was ultimately eased from power by Megawati Sukarnoputri, his vice president, who is now the president of Indonesia. Wahid grumbled but went peacefully.

Today the situation in Indonesia is mixed. Corruption can still be found throughout the country, and Megawati is depicted by some as insufficiently active in rooting it out. The young democracy still cannot claim to be fully stabilized. The economy is shaky. Terrorist cells are said to operate with relative ease, and may have found support from local Islamist extremists in the al-Qaeda mold. The military remains for the moment the major institutional force in the country, and the same officers who perpetrated human rights abuses great enough for the United States to cut ties with the Indonesian military in 1998 remain in place. The Bush administration renewed contact with the military in 2002, but more out of the necessities of the war on terror than because of any real confidence that change had occurred.

On the other hand, Indonesia looks much more promising than it did five years ago. Notwithstanding the terrible Bali nightclub bombing of autumn 2002, fledgling democracy unquestionably exists. The violence in East Timor, with its spillover effects on Muslim-Christian relations, has for the most part disappeared. Violence between government and separatist forces in Aceh province continues, although prospects for peace through negotiation are on the horizon. New constitutional amendments require the military and police to give up the assembly seats allocated to them. And when a small fundamentalist party introduced legislation in August 2002 mandating the broad imposition of *shari'a*, the proposal did not even make it to the floor of the assembly for a vote. Islamist democracy is for now out of the question, although pluralist democracy informed by Islam remains a possibility.

The details of Indonesian politics and the transition from autocracy to democracy are so complex that anyone who has not spent a lifetime studying Indonesia should approach them with great caution. What can be said, however, is that Islamic organizations in Indonesia played an important role in bringing about greater democracy there, and that those Muslim parties continue to participate in Indonesian politics in mostly peaceful ways. Indonesia is now struggling to become a full-fledged democracy—and it is doing so with the participation of its 180 million Muslims. Indonesia is not an Islamic state, but it shows how a flexible Islam can participate in democratic development and democratic politics. It shows that a Muslim population may choose secular government after voting for Islamic parties. Distinctive as Indonesia and its Islam are, they disprove some myths about Islamic democracy and reveal that the possibilities are very broad.

Pakistan: The Islamic State
and the Struggle for Stability

akistan was conceived specifically as a state for Muslims, and also as a democracy: the first and only state of its kind. Whether Pakistan was to be an Islamic state, not only a state for Muslims, was unresolved when Pakistan was established in 1947 and has remained so. Meanwhile, democracy in Pakistan continues to be maddeningly elusive. The story of the interaction between Islam and democracy in Pakistan reveals much about the various types of Islamic democracies that might be proposed in various Muslim countries, because nearly every possibility has been proposed for Pakistan. At the same time, Pakistan stands as a testament to the challenges of achieving democracy. Pakistan is unique in the Muslim world in many ways: in its problems, its importance, and its potential promise. It has much to teach the rest of the Muslim world, but before it can do that it must break free of its own tendency to short-circuit every time its productive energy starts to rise.

In the years leading up to and following World War II, the British reluctantly realized that they had no choice but to leave India, the jewel in the imperial crown. The British would not have reached this conclusion without a great deal of pressure from the Indian independence movement, and especially the Congress Party, under the moral leadership of Gandhi and the political leadership of Jawaharlal Nehru. For years, the official line of the Congress Party envisioned a single, multireligious, multiethnic state in India, in which Hindus would be the great majority and Muslims the largest minority.

Not all Indians thought this solution satisfactory. Hindus and Muslims on the Indian subcontinent had a history full of difficulties and tensions along with periods of peaceful coexistence. The Muslim Mughals who ruled India from the sixteenth century until shortly before the British arrived had varied from the enlightened and tolerant to the despotic, depending on time and place; and not surprisingly, Muslims were typically at the top of the hierarchy during this period. The Mughals never forcibly converted the Hindu population, although in some areas low-caste Hindus converted to Islam in large numbers, in part to avoid the misery of being at the bottom of the caste system. Hindus inevitably resented being ruled by non-Hindus, but that was just one, precolonial source of tension. The already strained relations between Muslims and Hindus were made much worse by the British colonial strategy of divide and rule, which sometimes involved playing off Muslim and Hindu interests against one another to distract attention from British domination.

As Indian independence approached, some Muslims, especially those associated with the Muslim League and inspired by the poet-theorist Mohammed Iqbal, began to think that they needed two states side by side, one Hindu and one Muslim, to avoid being marginalized or worse by rising Hindu nationalism. Thus was born the idea of Pakistan, whose name was dreamed up by young Muslims studying at Cambridge in the 1930s—*p* for the Punjab, *a* for the Afghan border, *k* for Kashmir, *s* for Sind, and "stan" for Baluchistan. The word *stan* also means "country," and *pak* means "pure" in Urdu—hence "Pakistan" means the land of the pure. There is some debate about whether Mohammed Ali Jinnah, the head of the Muslim League and the prime mover in the founding of Pakistan, fully expected that a two-state solution would actually materialize. He certainly did not anticipate the violence that accompanied partition and the recrimination that followed it. The British, though, were ultimately convinced that the Muslims needed a state of their own, and on August 15, 1947, both India and Pakistan became states in their own right.

As the acronym that makes up its name suggests, Pakistan was a gerrymander of various majority-Muslim areas of India, cobbled together to form a state with a large Muslim majority. In its original form, Pakistan was not even one contiguous piece of land. It was composed of West Pakistan, now Pakistan proper, and East Pakistan, which became the separate country of Bangladesh after bloody fighting in 1971–72. West Pakistan comprised various ethnic groups with their own languages; the common language of the educated classes in West Pakistan was Urdu, which began its life as a language that evolved from the communicative needs of different groups thrown together in the Mughal armies, and became the language spoken by educated Muslims on the Indian subcontinent. East Pakistan was part of the old imperial province of Bengal, which had been split up to put as many of its Muslims as possible in Pakistan and as many Hindus as possible in India. East Pakistanis spoke Bengali, an ancient language with its own rich literary heritage unrelated to Urdu. Separated by hundreds of miles of Indian territory, the two Pakistans did not even share a language—not an auspicious beginning for a new country.

Pakistan was conceived on the theory that South Asian Muslims shared some feature that made them suitable for having a nation of their own. That feature was not language or ethnicity or geography or culture, but religion. From the beginning, though, there was debate about whether the state would be Islamic or secular. Many of the Western-educated Muslim thinkers and politicians who were in the vanguard of early Pakistani politics favored secular government. Jinnah was a secularist by inclination, for whom Islam was a political unifier more than a religious one. This vision faced the formidable challenge that the only thing uniting Pakistanis into their newly invented identity was the fact that all were Muslims. As a result, there were always voices calling for the creation of Pakistan as an Islamic Republic. Ultimately, after much constitutional struggle and uncertainty, these voices prevailed. The constitution of 1956 called Pakistan an Islamic Republic, and the country remains today the Islamic Republic of Pakistan.

Even among these pro-Islamic voices, there was always a range of visions for how Islamic the Islamic Republic would actually be. On one extreme was Abul Ala Maududi, whose writings influenced and were influenced in turn by early Islamists such as Hasan al-Banna and Sayyid Qutb of the Muslim Brotherhood. Maududi was skeptical of the quasi-secular concept of a nation-state for Muslims, preferring a state devoted to and ruled by Islamic law. Maududi had a highly circumscribed view of democracy in such a state: he argued that there could be a legislature, but that it must be composed of scholars, who would vote on the correct interpretation of Islamic law. Government officials would have to be religiously observant Muslims in good standing. Maududi was not above hinting that he himself was one of the few men alive qualified to lead Pakistan. This was mostly fantasy—Maududi never commanded broad political support for his position—but he did have followers throughout his life. He founded the Jamaat-e-Islami, a Muslim party that still exists. Another Islamist party, the Jamaat Ulema-e-Islami, or JUI, more traditional in orientation, was formed originally in the seminaries of Deoband in India and is still a player in Pakistani politics; both parties have now joined an alliance known as the Mutahhida Majlis-e Amal (MMA), which came in third in the October 2002 elections.

Further along the spectrum of advocates of an Islamic Pakistan were those who thought that a Pakistani nation-state could both be democratic and reflect Islamic values without fully embracing classical Islamic law—an early formulation of Islamic democracy as synthesis. After independence, there were intermittent elections for a constituent assembly to draft a constitution. On October 22, 1953, *The New York Times*, observing the deliberations of the assembly, caught the mood of the moment when it called Pakistan "a stable and progressive Muslim nation, a staunch ally of the free West and a bastion of democracy in Asia." The draft constitution proposed an interesting approach to the institutionalization of Islamic democracy. The elected assembly would have the right to pass laws, and then the Supreme Court would decide whether these laws were consistent with Islam. Islamic values would therefore serve as a kind of constitutional grounding for the state, interpreted through judicial review. Over time, the Supreme Court, not a religious body, would have developed a body of precedents on the question of what Islamic values meant in practice. It is possible that this approach would not have worked, since Islamists could have challenged the right of the Supreme Court to decide questions of Islamic law. That criticism has been heard on a few occasions in India, where the Supreme Court must sometimes decide cases that affect Islamic family law. But perhaps in Pakistan, a Muslim state, things would have been different, especially if the practice of the Supreme Court's reviewing legislation had begun in the 1950s.

But the constitution that the assembly drafted never became law. In 1954, on the brink of ratification, the governor-general disbanded the assembly and canceled the draft constitution. The Supreme Court, acknowledging the governor-general's power, upheld the decision. Shortly thereafter, in 1958, Pakistan came under the dictatorship of General Ayub Khan. The pattern for the country's roller-coaster history of high democratic aspirations and disappointing failures had been set. Khan's rule brought some economic growth to West Pakistan, and some basic liberties were enforced. Khan was no Islamist, and the constitution he imposed in 1962 did not even call Islam the official religion of Pakistan. Perhaps needless to say, Khan's rule was also not a step in the direction of democracy.

Ayub Khan, a dictator with few friends, fell in 1969, and a hopeful moment in Pakistani history followed. Under General Yahya Khan, who took over from Ayub Khan, free and basically fair elections were held for the first time. In East Pakistan, a majority supported the Awami League, a party that favored autonomy for East Pakistan. But the military did not agree, nor did it relinquish power, and in 1971–72, after Indian military intervention, East Pakistan broke away and became Bangladesh.

In the wake of this disaster, the socialist-populist Zulfikar Bhutto, whose party had done well in the Punjab, part of West Pakistan, ascended to the prime ministership. Bhutto himself thought that Pakistan should operate on secular, not Islamic principles, a view still shared by a cadre of Pakistani intellectuals. But in general, secularism was more prevalent in East Pakistan than West, so after the East split off to become Bangladesh, secularism in Pakistan became even more liminal. Bhutto, seeking a catchall legitimating ideology, adopted the slogan "Islamic socialism." When corruption and his authoritarian rule resulted in a loss of popular support, he made concessions to the Islamists as well as to the military, from which he never really broke free. He was deposed in 1977 by General Mohammed Zia ul-Haq, subjected to a dubious murder trial, and hanged.

Zia, who although backed by the United States could make no pretense to democratic legitimacy, set out to Islamize Pakistani law and government in order to provide some basis for his rule. Under Zia, the Islamic provisions of the constitution took the form they have now. Before 1985 the constitution, changed since Ayub Khan's day as a concession to Islamists, simply declared that "Islam shall be the State religion of Pakistan," rendering Pakistan nominally Islamic. In 1985, Zia added

> and the Injunctions of Islam as laid down in the Holy Quran and Sunnah shall be the supreme law and source of guidance for legislation to be administered through laws enacted by the Parliament and Provincial Assemblies, and for policy making by the Government.

In making Islamic law supreme and either a source or *the* source of guidance for legislation, this new language went well beyond calling Islam the official religion. It shifted Pakistan into a different category of Islamic state, one in which the Islamic character was meant to have legislative teeth. In practice, however, as applied, this language did not mean that Pakistani courts started administering classical Islamic law. In fact, much of existing Pakistani law remained intact. But the door was opened for harsh blasphemy laws and the imposition of some severe *hudud* punishments; and Islamists who sought to change other laws now had a powerful symbolic-constitutional basis on which to rest their arguments.

There has still never been a properly democratic transfer of power from one government to another in Pakistan. After Zia died in a plane crash in 1988, there was another hopeful moment for democracy. Elections were held, and Zulfikar Bhutto's daughter Benazir won in a relatively free election. This was cause for rejoicing in the West. Benazir promised to be a perfect democrat. Elegant and well-spoken, educated at Harvard and Oxford, she was the first woman to be elected prime minister of an important Muslim country. Even her look, with an elegant silk scarf allowing plenty of well-coiffed hair to show, seemed to signal a successful synthesis of Western-style women's liberation and Islamic tradition.

Unfortunately, Benazir was a disappointment to democrats in Pakistan and the West alike. Young and inexperienced, she was dogged by charges of corruption, attaching especially to her husband, a businessman first jailed in Pakistan and eventually charged with money laundering by Swiss prosecutors. Benazir was dismissed from office by the president shortly after being elected. New elections were held in 1990, and victory went to Mian Nawaz Sharif, a rival politician who had risen to prominence under Zia's patronage and had strong connections to the military. Nawaz Sharif served as prime minister for several years but ran into trouble when Pakistan's president dismissed him for attempting to curtail presidential power. In a surprising turn, the Supreme Court ordered his reinstatement. The military then stepped in to require the resignation of both the president and Nawaz Sharif.

This led to the 1993 elections, yet another hopeful moment. Benazir's Pakistan People's Party (PPP) did not win a majority of seats in the election, but she formed a coalition government and returned to power. The second time was not a charm. Still plagued by corruption charges, and unable to rule effectively, Benazir was dismissed again in 1996. Nawaz Sharif again took power, only to be plagued by corruption charges himself and deposed by General Pervez Musharraf in 1999. Nawaz Sharif had tried to fend off Musharraf by denying his plane permission to land, which would have led to a bumpy end for Musharraf. But Musharraf countermanded the prime minister's orders and landed at a military air base, after which Nawaz Sharif ended up in jail.

Musharraf promised—and delivered—general elections from which both Benazir and Nawaz Sharif were barred. But Pakistanis are not holding their breath after Musharraf bought himself five years in office through a questionable referendum in spring 2002. The constitutional changes that Musharraf unilaterally announced later that summer were even less promising, aimed as they were at consolidating presidential power at the expense of the assembly and the prime minister. Musharraf seems sincerely to want to put his country back on the right footing, but his distrust of Pakistan's politicians—many of whom really are corrupt—makes it hard to see how he can move Pakistan back to democracy.

The ups and downs of democracy in Pakistan since 1988 have the formulaic character, the melodramatic tone, and the limited cast of a daytime television drama. If the spectacle were not so tragic and real, it would almost be comic. Sadly for Pakistanis, the plot twists cannot be explained away as a dream. Why has democracy done so poorly in Pakistan? Is Islam somehow at fault, given that neighboring majority-Hindu India has managed to preserve its democracy for half a century?

The artificiality of Pakistan as a country surely is part of the answer. That Pakistan was cobbled together out of various provinces of the British Empire in India has made the country unstable almost by definition. (In fact, around the world, many countries that got their shape through the vagaries of colonial and postcolonial border-drawing have had a hard time making democracy work.) The turmoil of the months surrounding Pakistani and Indian independence—with millions of Muslims fleeing India in favor of Pakistan, a comparable number of Hindus fleeing Pakistan for India, and hundreds of thousands of Hindus and Muslims killing one another in the process—only made matters worse. The vast number of new residents who had to be integrated into the new Pakistan, traumatized by flight and death, have existed in tense engagement with the earlier inhabitants ever since.

Beyond this, Pakistan was and remains a relatively poor country, in which a small number of well-off landlords own much of the land, and have stayed influential and rich since independence. The literacy rate hovers just above 50 percent for men and 30 percent for women, and the economy, which grew at 2.6 percent in 2001 and perhaps 3 percent in 2002, is barely keeping pace with a population growing at around 2.8 percent each year. The military, which is the only really strong institution in Pakistan, eats up 40 percent of the national budget. Finally, there was the problem of the division between West and East Pakistan, which led to the breakup of the country.

So Islam cannot fairly be blamed for Pakistan's difficulty in achieving stability and democratic rule. The hundred million Muslims who remain in India participate in democratic Indian politics. Secularists and socialists have contributed to the failure of democracy in Pakistan as much as Islamist politicians. The corruption that plagues Pakistani politics is not particularly associated with Islam or Islamic politics; if anything, Islamists have often raised their voices against corruption in Pakistan. The Islamists have participated in national elections whenever these have been held. In the October 2002 elections, the consolidated Islamist MMA won 45 out of 342 seats, well behind the Musharraf-friendly Pakistan Muslim League and Benazir's PPP, but far ahead of the other contenders. These results need to be interpreted cautiously, because turnout was low in an election from which Benazir and

Nawaz Sharif were banned. But it is clear that there is grassroots support for Islamist politics expressed democratically.

Elections aside, the Islamists' influence in Pakistan is difficult to gauge from outside the country. The legacy of Zia's Islamization program is that the army in general, and the Directorate for Inter-Services Intelligence, or ISI, in particular, came to be dominated by Islamist sympathizers. In the 1980s and 1990s, the ISI more or less took control of Pakistan's policy in Afghanistan. This began with the explicit agreement and financial backing of the United States, which used Pakistan as a staging area from which to support the mujahidin who fought the Soviets in Afghanistan; then, in the 1990s, the ISI functioned as the major supporter of the Taliban, who came to rule Afghanistan with the backing of Pakistan and the tacit consent of the United States. When the United States decided to displace the Taliban after the September 11 attacks, and General Musharraf insisted that the ISI abandon the Taliban, the ISI was not pleased. Its officers may have colluded in the escape of Taliban or even al-Qaeda leaders, and they may not have completely stopped their support of Kashmiri terrorists.

Yet despite some recalcitrance, the ISI essentially did comply with Musharraf's orders. It did not directly support the Taliban against the U.S.-backed Northern Alliance. Basic military discipline applied, more than some observers had expected, and there was no obvious or public flouting of Musharraf's new policy. As Musharraf responds to American pressure to crack down on radicals and terrorists, the Islamists' influence within the Pakistani government and military may well be on the wane.

Outside government, Islamists are a ubiquitous part of contemporary Pakistani life. Their thousands of madrasas are well attended, primarily because they offer affordable education even for the very poor. The Islamists offer a vision of morally grounded life to young people, educated and uneducated, who are looking for an authentic identity in a world that is increasingly complex and fragmented. Islam also offers a powerful condemnation of the widespread corruption in Pakistani society. Islamists have a powerful ethical base from which to criticize drug and alcohol abuse, as well as other forms of depressive or antisocial behavior that have grown in Pakistan in recent years. It remains to be seen whether the steady growth of Islamist organizations outside the realm of politics, in the sphere of civic organizations, will have staying power in the political sphere, where Islamist success is new. It seems likely that Islamist politics in Pakistan is on the rise.

Is Islamic revolution in Pakistan possible? The question merits close attention from the broader world for the pragmatic reason that Pakistan has nuclear capability. Those who fear or welcome the rise of Islamists like to imagine what would happen if Pakistan's "Islamic bomb" were to fall into the hands of a revolutionary Islamist state, but such an eventuality appears unlikely right now. The Islamists do not seem to have the depth of influence necessary for a revolution, and anyway, elections seem to be serving their interests well.

Yet the real tensions are as dangerous as the fantastical ones. The perpetual Pakistan-India conflict over Kashmir is a nearly mythical grudge match in which both sides have nuclear weapons. Kashmiri separatists, backed by Pakistan, are accused of terrorist attacks in India, including an attack on the Indian parliament, and Pakistan accuses India of oppressing and killing Kashmiri Muslims. The conflict is depicted in religious terms by Islamists within Pakistan: Hindu India against Muslim Pakistan for control over majority-Muslim Kashmir. Like most such conflicts, the Kashmir struggle is enormously complicated. High tensions, coupled with the nuclear capabilities on both sides, make South Asia a dangerous place, if not, as President Bill Clinton once put it, the most dangerous spot in the world.

So for those people, Muslims and non-Muslims, who consider Islam a spark plug that might ignite the conflict, Islamist ideology and rhetoric in Pakistan bear careful watching. There is no question that there are Islamists in Pakistan who would like to escalate the conflict. But they are not the only ones fomenting hatred. Many Pakistani secularists, in the army for example, have similar views. And on the Indian side, there are ethnonationalist Hindus and more secular nationalists who must also shoulder responsibility for keeping the conflict alive.

Islam in Pakistan right now is neither a force for democratization nor a force against it; it is merely one ingredient in a volatile mix. In the long run, though, Islam will be crucial to any move toward a more democratic Pakistan. Pakistan is still an Islamic Republic, a state organized around the idea of Muslim identity. Any democracy that is to emerge in Pakistan will have to possess at least some aspects that are identifiably Islamic, and will likely be couched in the rhetoric of Islam. Islamist parties are going to have an important continuing role.

It is in this future that the special promise of Pakistan comes into play. From the country's earliest days, politicians, intellectuals, and religious thinkers have argued about how an Islamic democracy should work. They have drafted and amended constitutions in ways that reflect engagement with Islamic ideas and values. And in part because freedom of speech in Pakistan has periodically been well protected (less so in the Zia era), Pakistanis have years of experience in debating the relationship between Islam and democracy. What is new ground for debate in much of the Muslim world is more familiar to Pakistanis.

Pakistan can thus become a leader in the movement toward Islamic democracy, if only it can move in the direction of democracy itself. The challenge for Pakistan is not so much to make democracy and Islam coexist; after years of discussion, Pakistanis mostly agree that these ideas can and should work together. The impediment to Islamic democracy is not Islam, but anti-democratic forces in Pakistani government and society. The challenge for Pakistan is to make the transition to democracy work this time. There are no guarantees, and the track record is not promising. But despite General Musharraf's early missteps, another of Pakistan's hopeful moments has arrived.

General Musharraf has the support of the United States in the form of hundreds of millions of dollars in aid and military cooperation, and he will need to preserve this lifeline to his government. He has, in word if not yet in deed, committed himself to making the transition to democracy. On his watch, Pakistan is experimenting with a new federalism that is designed to devolve power away from the disconnected politicians who operate on the national stage and toward local figures who might be more responsive to people's actual concerns. There are risks associated with the strategy, particularly the danger that increased local control will empower petty quasi-feudal landlords who are no more interested in serving the people than are the national politicians. But the experiment still seems worth making. What

Musharraf must now do is facilitate the growth of political institutions strong enough to make democracy work. If he can—if he is willing to try— then Pakistan stands poised to show the world that Islamic democracy is not the same as Islamist democracy, that Muslims from across the religious and political spectrum can draw on Islamic values to build a country capable of transcending ethnic differences and embodying the democratic values to which Pakistan is, in theory, committed.

———◆•◉•◆———

THE DIVERSITY OF THE ARABS

Arab and Muslim history, culture, and politics are deeply inter-
twined. The Prophet Muhammad was an Arab, whose message,
the Qur'an, was revealed to him in Arabic, the only language
that he and his hearers knew. In Muhammad's day, the Arabic
language was restricted to the Arabian Peninsula, and the term *Arab* re-
ferred to a person who lived there. But as the united tribes of the Arabian
Peninsula conquered Syria, the Lebanon, Palestine, and Iraq to create the
Muslim East, and North Africa and Spain to form the Muslim West, they
brought the Arabic language and Islam with them. Most of the peoples in
these countries who adopted Islam also adopted Arabic. While there were a
few exceptions, like the Berbers in Morocco and Algeria, the other peoples
of the region took Arabic names, married Arabs, and, in short, became what
the modern world calls Arab. By contrast, when Islam spread beyond the
boundaries of North Africa and Iraq, people became Muslims without
adopting Arab language and identity. Persia became Muslim but preserved
its language and its philosophy, literature, and culture. Turkic peoples kept
their languages; Afghans theirs. Sub-Saharan Africans who became Muslim also typically maintained their own languages and traditions. Farther
afield in Indonesia and Malaysia, and as far away as the Philippines, Islam
reached many people without transforming them into Arabs, either.

The idea that 280 million Arabs constitute one ethnic group is therefore slightly misleading. The Arabs stretch from Morocco to Iraq and possess very different cultures. Although educated Arabs all know some classical Arabic, and almost all Arabs can understand the modified classical Arabic, known as modern standard, that is spoken on the radio and television, ordinary Arabic speakers communicate in local variants of the language that differ strongly from place to place. A Moroccan and an Iraqi cannot speak easily to each other in their respective dialects; they would need to speak modern standard Arabic to have more than a rudimentary conversation. As a result of geographical distance, distinctive histories, and local cultures that never completely abandoned their pre-Islamic folkways, Arabs are a strikingly diverse group of people who are nonetheless designated by a single word.

Westerners who think it is possible to identify some distinctive Arab "mentality" are therefore oversimplifying, as were Arab nationalists who sought to unify the Arabs around a central identity as an Arab nation, bound by a common language and aspiring to common goals. Perhaps unifying Arabs through nationalism was no more quixotic than Garibaldi's idea of unifying the city-states and regions of Italy into one Italian nation. But Arab nationalists faced a problem that the Italians did not, at least not in the same form: the problem of Western imperialism. After World War I, France and England split the Arab world into distinct states. Those states have proved surprisingly durable, even when their borders were drawn more or less arbitrarily, and even (maybe especially) after Europeans were driven out or departed. Today Egyptians think proudly of themselves as Egyptians, Iraqis as Iraqis, Moroccans as Moroccans, Algerians as Algerians, and so forth.

The dream of unifying the Arab world through Arab nationalism faded in the 1960s, as has the idea of a single pan-Islamic state since then. The Arab states seem to be here to stay. What complicates matters is that these states have further differences, along two main axes. One axis is the political system: monarchy or dictatorship. Jordan, Morocco, Saudi Arabia, and the smaller Gulf states are monarchies. Each of these places has its own history of how the monarchy came to power. The Hashemite Jordanian royal family descend from Sharif Husayn of Mecca, who sided with the British against the Ottomans in World War I and was rewarded with four separate kingdoms: Arabia, Transjordan, Syria, and Iraq. Of these kingdoms, Jordan alone remains. Husayn's son Faysal, the king of Syria, was deposed by the French, so the British made him king of Iraq; his son was later deposed in a military coup. The Arabian monarchy, which Husayn briefly held, was replaced by 'Abdulaziz Ibn Sa'ud, who led a rebellion against the Hashemites with the help of the Wahhabi religious ideology, then named the country for himself and his family.

Ibn Sa'ud died in 1953, but his sons still reign in Arabia. The word *Saudi* in the name Saudi Arabia is an adjective, referring to the Arabia that belongs to the House of Saud. Saudi legitimacy still depends, to a great extent, on the Wahhabism that brought Ibn Sa'ud to power. A form of purist Islam, Wahhabism came into existence in Arabia as early as the 1780s. Its eponymous founder, Muhammad Ibn 'Abdul-Wahhab, called for reform of Muslim religious practices and beliefs and preached a return to the pure way of the Prophet and his companions. Wahhabism has always had a tendency to look backward to an idealized version of the Prophet's practices. That poses a challenge for the Saudi monarchy whenever it wishes to modernize. To maintain its legitimacy, it must carefully tend to its relationship with Wahhabi scholars. Those scholars, in turn, police the monarchy's political choices and stand ready to offer criticism.

The Moroccan monarchy has deeper roots in Morocco than other Arab monarchies have in their countries. The present king, Muhammad VI, is descended from a family whose members have been sultans of Morocco for five hundred years. Muhammad's grandfather took the title of king only in 1967, but the royal family's legitimacy depends on very old feelings of loyalty to it. Alone among the Arab monarchies, the Moroccan monarchy managed to associate itself with anticolonialism when the French conveniently exiled Muhammad V, only to restore him when Moroccans resisted the dictator whom the French put in his place.

The Gulf emirates, for their part, are mostly run by the descendants of tribesmen who conquered the coastal cities of the Persian Gulf (to Arabs, the Arabian Gulf) in the nineteenth and twentieth centuries. These coastal cities were no great prizes. Ruling them meant little more than exacting some tribute from traders and maintaining warm relations with the British, who considered the Gulf part of a sphere of influence reaching from Egypt to their imperial outpost in India. Then came oil. Beginning in the 1950s, these sleepy Gulf principalities were transformed into some of the richest spots in the world. The ancestors of today's Gulf monarchs had conquered better than they knew. Their descendants subsist in surreal desert paradises like Dubai, where one can go hunting and falconing on the dunes in the morning and cavort in a world-class water park in the afternoon. The populations of the Gulf states are small and made up mostly of workers who come from outside to do the managerial and menial work of running an oil-producing country. The old families spread the wealth around enough to keep each other reasonably happy. People quietly criticize the emirs, but they remain the only game in town.

It was not always so, but in the Arab countries where there is no monarchy, there is mostly dictatorship. In Lebanon between 1943 and 1975, there were periods of democratic politics, admittedly interspersed with civil strife and foreign intervention. Heterogeneous, cosmopolitan Lebanon is peopled by Christians, Sunni and Shi'a Muslims, and Druze. Its democracy sought to accommodate this diversity in a multireligious power-sharing arrangement. But this democracy, never stable for long, proved too delicate to survive the entry of the Palestine Liberation Organization into Lebanese politics after it was violently ejected from Jordan by King Hussein in September 1970. By 1975, Lebanon was deep in Christian-Muslim civil war. Wars of various sorts continued into the 1990s; Israel invaded to drive out the PLO, then stayed in southern Lebanon for nearly two decades. Syria now exercises much of the real power in Lebanon, through the presence of an estimated thirty thousand troops. Although the Lebanese president is elected by the National Assembly, and some progress has been made toward renewing meaningful democracy, Syria exercises an implicit veto over the decision.

Most other Arab dictatorships follow a relatively common pattern: young officers, inspired by Arab nationalism, took power in coups in the 1950s and 1960s, and either they or their successors have remained in power ever since. This paradigm describes Egypt, Syria, Iraq, and Libya. Tunisia and Algeria are subtly different; there, anticolonialist movements developed into quasi-military dictatorships. Yemen, which wraps along the bottom of the Arabian Peninsula, also has a peculiar history. The British stayed until the 1960s, then the country split into a Marxist dictatorship—the only pure one in the Arab world—and a more conventional non-Marxist dictatorship. The two have recently been united and taken a shot at democracy, with mixed results. After initial elections, the president seems headed for old-fashioned dictatorship.

Dictatorships preside over the bulk of the population of the Arab world. They ban political parties and free speech, and they often jail people without trial or on trumped-up charges. During the Cold War, most of these countries leaned toward the Soviet Union. Under Anwar Sadat, Egypt turned away from the Soviets, toward the United States, and made peace with Israel; since Sadat's assassination by Islamists in 1981, his successor, Hosni Mubarak, who was sitting beside him when he was shot, has been a cautious man. He remains an ally of the United States, watches closely over the Islamists, and keeps his distance from Israel. During the Cold War, Iraq was always willing to follow the prevailing winds, turning one day to the United States, the next to the Soviets. When the United States went to war against Iraq in 1990, there were plenty of American-made weapons in Saddam's arsenal.

Like the monarchies, the dictatorships can be arrayed along a second axis that divides the Arab world, that of oil. By the accidents of geography and geology, the ancient shales beneath the earth either appeared or didn't, either took the right pressure or didn't, and either produced epic quantities of rich crude oil or did not. Where the oil is, economic conditions are by and large good. That is not to say that the oil-producing Arab countries are as economically healthy as they ought to be. Oil has remained the only economic driver almost everywhere except relatively oil-poor Dubai, where the emir has put into motion a plan for diversifying the economy. No Arab oil producer has sunk as far as Nigeria, where tremendous oil profits, siphoned off by corrupt politicians, have not appreciably bettered the lives of the country's vast, mostly poor, population. The Arab countries that do not have oil, however, are relatively poor. Not as poor as China; not as poor as Bangladesh or sub-Saharan Africa; but poor enough. The poor Arab countries are sufficiently well-off to be able to see their richer neighbors on television, but poor enough to realize from what they see that there is a massive wealth gap between them and their neighbors. That juxtaposition of wealth and poverty carries a message for Islamists and democrats alike, one worth keeping in mind as we survey the complicated interaction of Islam, democracy, monarchy, dictatorship, and oil in the Arab states.

———————◆———————

Monarchies with Oil:
The Rentier State in Action

O f the Arab monarchies, Saudi Arabia and the Gulf states have oil; Jordan and Morocco do not. Of the dictatorships, Libya and Iraq have oil aplenty; Algeria has oil and gas besides; Egypt, Syria, Yemen, and Tunisia have a little oil, but far less than the others. This division along the oil axis matters for almost every aspect of thinking about these countries. It matters for their internal politics; it matters for how they treat each other; and it matters for their relations with the rest of the world. Oil therefore matters for purposes of democratization, because it helps explain how power is kept and shared and what stakes rulers and their foreign allies have in maintaining the status quo.

Oil certainly matters profoundly for American policy toward individual Arab countries. It also matters for understanding the way that Islam and politics interact in the Arab and Muslim worlds more generally. For example, the Saudi monarchy put some of its oil money into promoting various Islamist groups throughout the Arab world, and so it has influence far and wide; yet almost at the same time, it has become a target of Islamist anger for agreeing to allow American troops to remain on Saudi soil. Why are the troops there? Largely because Saudi Arabia wants to protect its oil from greedy neighbors like Saddam Hussein, and the United States is happy to oblige in order to maintain a presence in oil country. A classic book on

Saudi foreign policy has the expressive name *Saudi Arabia: The Ceaseless Quest for Security.*

Since the Gulf War, when the U.S. troops came to stay, some Islamists have developed the view that their presence represents a violation of the holiness of Arabia. This charge, a staple of Osama bin Laden's rhetoric, combines anticolonialist politics with religion. The U.S. troops of course never set foot in Mecca, the holiest city in Islam, from which non-Muslims have long been barred. In fact they rarely leave their bases, and one could travel over most of Saudi Arabia without ever knowing the troops were there. So the Islamists are not charging that the troops are defiling Arabia by their conduct. Rather, their violation is symbolic, even though other non-Muslims are permitted to visit and work in Saudi Arabia.

There is clearly a connection between the Islamist argument for the holiness of Arabia and the anti-imperialist idea that the United States is an occupying power that is propping up the Saudi regime in exchange for its collusion. Although the American troops in Saudi Arabia have not directly assisted the Saudis in controlling demonstrations against the regime—which have been few and small in any case—their presence clearly bolsters the monarchy. There is therefore, in the Islamists' view, an imperialist element to the role of the U.S. troops in Saudi Arabia. The Islamists frame the anti-imperialist critique in religious terms, and some of them have acted on that critique in ways that are almost unimaginably violent.

Oil affects everything in Saudi Arabia, from Islam to politics. Where there is both oil and a monarchy, it will be difficult for any outside force to demand democratization and get real results, and it will be even harder for inside forces to achieve any real change. The reason has to do with the way that the Saudi monarchy, like its Gulf counterparts, uses oil in preserving its power. Simply put, the Gulf monarchies sell oil to foreign countries who need it, and use the revenues to buy the silence of their critics and to buy protection against those they cannot silence. The oil-thirsty Western states have no reason to upset this cozy arrangement, so long as the oil flows at a good price.

Political scientists consider oil-producing monarchies "rentier states" because they collect the rent—in the form of payments for their oil—from foreigners, instead of generating revenue by taxing their own citizens. If the government of France wants to build roads or increase the president's salary or support the French film industry, it has to raise taxes to do it. The taxes come from the French people. The same is true even in a non-democratic regime like Syria, which since the fall of the Soviet Union can no longer rely on significant foreign aid. This means that there is a direct connection between the state and the citizens. Even if there is taxation without representation, the government still has to worry about what the people will do if taxes are too high or services too few. By contrast, the oil monarchy is collecting the money it needs to stay alive from people *outside* the country. There is no fiscal connection between the government and the people. The government has only to keep its people in line so that they do not overthrow it and start collecting the oil rents themselves.

A monarchy that does not need to tax its own people has a certain superficial advantage for the citizens, who are not asked to support the typically lavish lifestyles of the extended royal family or to pay taxes for new roads, either. Because the monarch must buy the acquiescence of his people, the people will get some small share of the wealth. The average citizen of a Gulf state does reasonably well, and a salaried worker of any means will often have enough to pay the much lower salaries of the Filipinas and Bangladeshis who do his domestic work. Of course, there might be squabbles over distribution of the wealth among princes or between influential families or even between various social classes within an emirate, but every country has distributional problems to solve, regardless of whether it supports itself by taxes or some other mechanism. The problem with rentier states arises if you think either that people should have a say in governing themselves—the basic democratic idea—or else that government should distribute nationally owned wealth on a fair basis, which the rentier state assuredly does not. Order is purchased at the price of forgoing participation in government, and state assets are held closely by the ruling elites.

As it happens, the only two groups troubled by the arrangement in the oil monarchies are the democrats and the Islamists. Democrats object, of course, to the concentration of power in the hands of the few. At the structural level, democrats realize that a government that does not have to tax its people also lacks most incentives to respond to the people's desires. Democratization is far more likely if the government needs the people's agreement to collect the money necessary for government. In England, for example, Parliament historically gained influence relative to the monarchy because it acquired the power of the purse: the king had to go to Parliament to raise taxes, and Parliament was, in some sense, a representative of the people. The more the king needed, the more power the people had. This led to the development of a mutually dependent relationship, in which the monarchy gradually became accustomed to needing consent from Parliament to do what it wanted. Over time, and not without some revolutionary activity, this led to Britain's becoming first a constitutional monarchy, then a proper democracy. By contrast, a rentier state has the capacity to avoid relying on the people for money. The mutualistic process never develops, and the government becomes accustomed to doing what it wants. Rentier states therefore pose particular problems for democratic development.

For their part, Islamists are troubled by what they see as the immorality of the monarchies' way of life. In their view, the monarchs take God's oil bounty and spend it on lavish living, often in the West, while their Muslim brothers elsewhere suffer in poverty. This is essentially a moral response to the monarchies, framed in religious terms. Marxism, which was popular among the educated young in the Arab world before Islamism began to take its place, has also left its mark on this Islamist critique of the squandering of wealth. The Marxist critique of wealth fits easily into Islamic terms; the proof of Marxist influence is that many of the same sorts of people in Muslim countries were making a similar argument in Marxist terms for a couple of decades before the critique turned Islamist.

The Islamists' criticism of the oil monarchies is therefore partly a critique of the unjust distribution of wealth and power. A few people are monopolizing wealth and power that should be shared more broadly. This injustice is, the Islamists say, un-Islamic. The logic of this terminology is not mere fundamentalism; it is a matter of sincere belief and effective political rhetoric. Everyone in the Muslim world would agree that Islam in general and Islamic law in particular demand justice. So when a government behaves unjustly, it is possible to call that injustice "un-Islamic." The effect of this language must not be underestimated. By calling injustice un-Islamic, the Islamists hark back to a long tradition of political criticism made by independent-minded Muslim scholars.

They believe what they say, but the Islamists also know that their audiences will hear their criticisms more clearly if they frame them in religious terms. Using an Islamic language for criticism makes it harder for the oil monarchies to retaliate, because the monarchs themselves all profess to be good Muslims. Unlike Iran, where much of the government is made up of mullahs, the Sunni oil monarchies are governed by Muslim laypeople, susceptible to admonishment in religious terms if, for example, their courts deliver corrupt verdicts. Even Muslims who are not qualified scholars can lay claim to this critical tradition. Osama bin Laden, for example, had no religious or scholarly qualifications whatever, even though his followers called him *shaykh*, a term traditionally reserved for scholars, and he issued what he presumptuously called fatwas, even though such formal opinions of Islamic law may in principle only be issued by a qualified scholar known as a mufti. The Islamists have learned that by cloaking themselves in the language and titles of Muslim scholars they can partake of the legitimacy that has long attached itself to the scholars' critiques of government.

By using religious language to criticize the oil monarchies, the Islamists are criticizing not only unjust distributions of wealth and power, but the very structure of the rentier state, in which the people cannot easily hold government responsible. The Islamists are suggesting that government should be held responsible to Islamic law and that the people should be the ones who hold government to that standard. The long tradition of Muslim scholars who criticized unjust government was part of the way power and authority were managed and arranged in the classical Muslim world. In principle, the job of government under Sunni Islam was to make certain that Islamic law was followed, to keep the peace, and to manage foreign affairs. If the government failed to enforce the law evenhandedly, or acted unjustly toward the people, then the scholars had the unofficial job of pointing out the injustice. People listened to and respected the scholars, because the scholars were repositories of Islam and Islamic law. That gave the scholars an independent source of authority to criticize government. They deserved respect because they knew Islam and the law, not because they held official posts in government.

In other words, in the classical Islamic state, the scholars were to some extent supposed to be independent of the government. Scholars, even famous ones, would decline invitations to be judges because they did not want to be associated with government. Of course in practice, the scholars' independence was rarely absolute—once criticized, the government could retaliate or try to intimidate a freethinking scholar into silence. But at the same time, the scholars generally enjoyed enough respect from the public that the government could not totally suppress them without undercutting its own claim to be legitimate. The government, after all, needed the people to have basic respect for it so that they paid their taxes and did not rebel. Scholars therefore played the key role in keeping government responsible to the people, by invoking the language of religious law to criticize government when it went too far in the direction of injustice.

In the rentier state, though, where the monarchy does not have to care very deeply about what the people think of it, it can buy the guns and the men to keep itself in place. It can build up an apparatus of secret intelligence services to intimidate and threaten people to obey. It can, if it wants, create a semi-totalitarian state where freedoms are severely limited. What is more, it can bribe, co-opt, or intimidate many of the traditionally trained Muslim scholars who would otherwise have the job of criticizing it. So long as the oil flows, it can make citizens accept repressive measures as a trade-off for a comfortable standard of living.

So when Islamists criticize the government, they are implicitly telling the monarchy, "It doesn't matter how rich you are—we can't be bought." That message appeals to ordinary people who know about the tradition of religious criticism of the government. It allows Islamists to cloak themselves in the mantle of the scholars even when they lack the training to be scholarly themselves. It is the reason that the oil monarchies fear the Islamists, and try to co-opt them to their causes.

Rentier states have trouble making the transition to democracy: because oil monarchies have banned all political parties, there is not much in the way of nonreligious criticism. Yet there are some glimmers of hope for democratization. In February 2002, the emirate of Bahrain announced the creation of an elected assembly, and elections were successfully held in May and October of that year. Several prominent Saudi princes, including the outspoken Prince Talal, have called openly for such elections in Saudi Arabia. What are we to make of these developments?

The rentier oil monarchies are still able to repress internal dissent, but they need protection from their potentially hostile neighbors because they have an asset worth stealing. This was one lesson of the Gulf War: Kuwait's oil attracted Saddam, who had plenty of oil of his own, because Kuwait was essentially undefended. Saudi Arabia joined the United States and the rest of the Gulf War alliance against Iraq because the Saudis knew that they could be next. The need for foreign protection is one of the few points of leverage that the United States has over the Gulf oil monarchies. They need American protection; if they perceive that the West will protect them more assiduously if they show signs of democratization, they will likely respond. Make no mistake: they will not actually cede power to their people—then they might lose the rentier structure that keeps them in place. But they might create structures of democratization simply in order not to lose their place as valued Western allies, and those structures might in turn help bring about actual democracy.

The West has not been very good about applying such pressure, not as long as the oil still flows. The Saudis, for example, drew much closer to the United States after the Shah of Iran was deposed by the Islamic revolution. Once the close alliance between the United States and Iran collapsed, the U.S. needed another big oil-producing partner, and the Saudis needed an ally to help keep them safe from Iran (and later Iraq). But if Iran, for example, were to become more democratic and less anti-Israel, and thus drew closer to the U.S., Saudi Arabia would have to respond to keep itself, not Iran, as a partner and ally to the West. The September 11 attacks created a rift between the U.S. and Saudi Arabia in particular, as Osama bin Laden apparently hoped it would. American officials were skeptical about whether the Saudis had sufficiently monitored the hard-liners whom they were funding. The U.S. government therefore took the war on terrorism as an occasion to tell the oil monarchies, and especially Saudi Arabia, that the policy of funding Islamists of all kinds around the Muslim world had backfired. Meanwhile, after September 11, many Americans were in no mood to make fine distinctions between the Saudi government and the Saudi Islamist dissidents who attacked the United States—and there was some indication that al-Qaeda had received funding even from within the royal family.

All this meant that the Saudis had to take action to repair relations with the United States. The first big step in that direction was Saudi crown prince Abdullah's proposed Middle East peace plan of March 2002. The plan itself was simple and unoriginal: if Israel withdraws to pre-1967 borders, the Arab world will recognize Israel and aim to achieve "full normalization" of relations with it. A comparable deal was discussed in Israeli-Palestinian talks at Taba in 2000, but the Saudis reportedly discouraged Yasser Arafat and the Palestinians from agreeing to it. After the September 11 attacks, however, the Saudis had a greater incentive to appear moderate on Israel and, therefore, a more desirable ally for the United States.

It is possible to interpret the Saudi royal voices calling for an elected assembly as being connected with the Saudi peace plan. Like the peace plan, the talk of democracy hints that Saudi Arabia and the United States are not so different, not so far apart. Even if the mention of democracy is just a smoke screen or an attention-getting device on the part of a few Saudi royals, it still indicates that democracy in the Muslim world is in the air—and that the royals know it.

The smaller Gulf monarchies are all subtly jockeying for closer relations to Western countries so as to stimulate trade and diversify their economies beyond oil. Dubai, for example, which has less oil than the others, has done a good job of attracting banking and tourism. The introduction of an elected assembly and greater freedom of speech in Bahrain is also probably calculated to maneuver Bahrain toward the United States and the West. An elected assembly is one badge of Westernization and modernization. It puts Bahrain in the headlines as an emblem of progress—and that is good for Bahrain. One can expect other oil monarchies to think about doing the same. Qatar has gotten excellent publicity out of giving a home to al-Jazeera, the first unregulated TV channel in the Arab world. Qatar still has no elected assembly, and speech in the country remains regulated. But the presence of al-Jazeera (since 1996) means great international prominence for Qatar and a reputation for comparatively liberal policies.

Is al-Jazeera a harbinger of democracy? In its first few years, Middle East specialists regarded it with fascination and some excitement. The channel exposed people with satellite dishes all over the Arab world to a range of opinions on a wide variety of issues. You could find feminists debating Islamists, and talk shows alongside cooking shows. There seemed little doubt that al-Jazeera would be a vector of modernity and democracy wherever it was seen. Driven by market forces, it was, after all, an actor in the free marketplace of ideas.

Most Americans heard of al-Jazeera only when it became the medium of choice for Osama bin Laden to release his videotaped message to the world after September 11. Bin Laden picked al-Jazeera because it is free of government regulation—and so would show his tapes, which were news—and because it reached a broad Arab audience. Al-Jazeera also got reporters into Kabul under the Taliban, probably because the Taliban wanted to reach a broad Arab audience, too. But bin Laden and the Taliban were not the ideal brand associations from the perspective of American public opinion. Soon Fouad Ajami published an article in *The New York Times Magazine* criticizing al-Jazeera as bad for the United States, and arguing that al-Jazeera was fomenting intolerance, not tolerance: it was implicitly taking sides in the conflict between the U.S. and the Taliban—and not the American side. It was beaming video clips of Israeli soldiers harming Palestinians in the West Bank and Gaza on a daily basis. The footage was, Ajami argued with some justification, contributing to a hardening of attitudes toward Israel among great swaths of the Arab public.

Even as al-Jazeera is having a negative impact on America's short-term interests in the Middle East, from the point of view of democracy, it still looks very promising. If a free press is to spread in the Arab world, one can hardly expect it not to reflect the preferences and views of its staff and viewership, especially in times of crisis. American journalism reflects pro-American bias when it comes to reporting on war or national disaster, which reflects a press corps made up of Americans who both care about their country and are attuned to U.S. public opinion and ratings. It would be strange if the American press reported the deaths of 3,000 American civilians or eight U.S. soldiers dispassionately. What we want is accuracy and the chance to criticize the press if they get things wrong or overdo their partisanship.

The key measure for judging al-Jazeera should be accuracy, the same as it is in the United States. As for television images of Palestinian children being shot, which are played repeatedly between programs on the station, no one has argued that al-Jazeera fabricated these images. It would probably be better if al-Jazeera also regularly showed clips of Israelis killed and wounded by Palestinian bombers. (Although Hezbollah's satellite channel, al-Manar, which does show Israeli victims, manages to suggest that Israeli deaths ought to be celebrated, which al-Jazeera does not.) But finding a precise balance will never be easy. To Palestinians, *The New York Times* epitomizes pro-Israel bias, even as New York's Orthodox Jewish community calls for a boycott of the *Times* as pro-Palestinian. Al-Jazeera's viewers care more about Arab victims than non-Arab victims, much as local television audiences in the United States are deemed by the media to care more about a single missing child in their town than about whole villages wiped out by disease or genocide in Africa.

In either case, the solution to the problems al-Jazeera creates for American interests is more speech. The ideal is to have al-Jazeera and CNN and a range of other competing media outlets with different perspectives. For better or worse, the Voice of America Arabic-language radio station has been converted to a pop-music format in hopes of attracting listeners to an American perspective. If people want to watch or listen, they will. That is the whole point of a free press. In the long run, though, al-Jazeera sets the precedent that Arab governments will not be able to control the flow of information to all their citizens. On the whole, that is going to be good for the truth. That is the basic theory of free speech and hence of democracy.

Beyond al-Jazeera and a few elected assemblies, though, are there any concrete prospects for more substantive democratization in the oil monarchies? The realistic answer for today is still no. The oil monarchies will not make greater changes unless there is pressure from the West for them to do so. But there may be reasons for such pressure to be applied. That does not mean that the U.S. ambassador would march in to the Saudi crown prince and demand that he abdicate. Outside of storybooks that sort of thing never happens, and it would not work if it were tried. But the United States can respond to democratic gestures by signaling that it favors increased democratization in the oil monarchies. It can make it very clear that more, not less, free speech is desirable, even if that speech criticizes the U.S. It can indicate that it welcomes elections even if in the short run those elections mean the accession of politicians who oppose their governments and the U.S. as well.

The key lesson is the same as the lesson of al-Jazeera. In the short term, greater democratization in the oil monarchies may not appear to serve Western interests. Because the West keeps the rentier states in power, opponents of those states do not much care for the United States. The whole trick of the oil monarchies is to make the West think that the monarchies are the only prospective partners that the West has in the region. But this is a self-fulfilling prophecy so long as the West maintains such close ties to these monarchies.

The oil monarchies are not doomed to collapse. They will likely retain power so long as they keep the oil flowing, the West keeps buying it, and they are able to co-opt or eliminate their internal enemies. But as the Saudis know well and are likely never to forget, everyone was shocked when the shah's U.S.-backed oil monarchy in Iran came to an abrupt end. It is hard for anyone, even the Saudi monarchy, to gauge exactly how stable their rule really is. In the long term, gradual democratization is a far better way to keep one's finger on the pulse of a people and to avoid sudden, violent transfers of power.

For a monarchy, gradual democratization generally means moving in the direction of constitutional monarchy. That development is rather far off for the oil monarchies, none of which have more than token elected assemblies. A constitutional monarchy is a much more real option for the monarchies *without* oil. To these we now must turn to ask what an Islamic constitutional monarchy would mean for Islamic democracy.

KINGS WITHOUT OIL

t must be galling for the kings of Jordan and Morocco when they travel to the West and meet people who know nothing of the Arab world. Westerners assume that any Arab king is richer than Croesus, living in luxury off the limitless oil reserves beneath the Arabian sands, and many no doubt say things to King Abdullah II and King Muhammad VI that imply that they must have no worries about money or the economies of their countries.

Abdullah and Muhammad are hardly paupers, but their countries are not blessed with oil. They themselves are not especially rich, as kings go, and their countries are poor relative to the oil monarchies of the Gulf. They worry about economics all the time; indeed they must sometimes feel they worry about nothing but economics. Jordan has a seaport at Aqaba with access to the Red Sea, but it does not yet have much to export, and its neighbors, Syria, Iraq, Saudi Arabia, Egypt, and Israel, all have ports of their own. As a country whose major trading partner is Iraq, it must constantly consider the possibility that it could lose that partner overnight. Morocco is on both the Mediterranean and the Atlantic, but it is not the gateway to anywhere but the Sahara Desert, and its productivity is not what it should be. The cost of labor is relatively high in both places, making it difficult to break into manufacturing industries.

Jordan and Morocco are popular tourist destinations, especially for Europeans who like the beach. Both are fascinating countries with many beautiful and historically important sites. Petra, the rose red Nabatean city that rises like a mirage from the Jordanian desert, is one of the most dramatic places on earth, and the old city of Fez and the market at Marrakesh make Morocco a magical place to visit. But unlike Egypt, which has the pyramids, or Israel, which has attracted Christian and Jewish pilgrims for millennia, Jordan and Morocco cannot expect that the flow of tourists will ever be a pillar of economic strength. Jordan would like to catch the overflow pilgrims from Israel, but in the long run these tourists would probably rather see Abu Simbel.

If in Saudi Arabia nearly everything comes back to oil, in these countries nearly everything comes back to oil's absence. The economy of Jordan, for example, relies heavily on foreign aid from Gulf states and on remittances, money sent by expatriates working in the Gulf to their families in Jordan. That needs to change for Jordan to be economically viable. Economic development has to occur, and it has to occur from within. Morocco, too, relies on remittances from its citizens who live and work in France.

Both kings, Abdullah and Muhammad, know that education and the cultivation of human capital are keys for economic development. Morocco has a decent system of higher education and is working on improving education across the board. Jordan under King Abdullah recently instituted mandatory English in the schools from first grade, and computer skills from second grade. Both countries have rising rates of literacy.

The more educated people are, the more they seek a say in governing themselves. That is why promoting literacy and education are brave (or risky) strategies for a monarch. One thing people learn when they use their English on the Internet or read books and watch satellite television is that kings are an endangered species in the modern world. A hundred and fifty years ago, it was hard to find any place in the world where there was no king or queen. Latin America was beginning to be an exception, in the wake of Simón Bolívar's wars of liberation and conquest; the United States was another exception, but in 1850 not yet an important one. Today countries with kings are few, and countries where kings actually rule are fewer still. The decline of monarchy has been one of the greatest processes of global political change in all of history.

King Abdullah and King Muhammad are well aware that more education and more access to ideas threaten monarchic rule in their respective countries. For one thing, both men were educated in the West. King Abdullah prepared at Deerfield Academy in Massachusetts, then attended the Royal Military Academy at Sandhurst, the English officers' training school that produced, among other famous graduates, Winston Churchill. He spent a year at Oxford, and later a year at Georgetown University studying international affairs. His English is that of a native speaker, and indeed his mother is English. When Abdullah became king, there was no doubt that he had the capacity to communicate better to Western audiences than had any previous Arab ruler. There was greater concern that he develop connections to ordinary Jordanians. For his part, Muhammad VI got a law degree in Morocco, then spent six years in Europe, first as an aide to Jacques Delors at the European Union, then working on an advanced law degree in Nice.

So these kings know that monarchy is anachronistic in most of the world, and they know that an educated populace will realize the same thing. Why, then, do they continue to promote education? The answer seems to be that both men think that in the long run their countries need to move in the direction of modernity in both economic and political terms. In different ways, these kings without oil hope to lead their countries to develop solutions to integrating tradition and modernization. It is for this reason that these two monarchs may in fact represent the best hope for the development of Islamic democracy in the Arab world.

Democratization in Morocco has followed an interesting path. Muhammad VI's father, King Hassan II, always permitted multiple political parties, but for most of his reign he kept the Moroccan legislature relatively powerless and made certain that the prime minister and his government were royalists. In 1992, Hassan granted a new, more democratic constitution, which he enhanced in 1996. Then in 1998, near the end of his life, Hassan surprised everyone by choosing for the first time a prime minister from what had long been the main opposition party: a socialist named Abderrahmane

Youssoufi, whose coalition had eked out a bare plurality in the 1997 elections. The transfer of power to a new party represented remarkable progress toward democracy.

When Muhammad became king, he immediately fired his father's hated minister of the interior, a man whose job had been the political repression of dissidents. This gave Moroccans further cause for optimism. Since then, Muhammad has only very cautiously begun to deliver the political liberalization that he appeared poised to continue. His room to maneuver has been limited by the entrenched interests of a state that still operates by allocating wealth and power from within the royal sphere. Nonetheless, elections took place in September 2002. The big winners were the moderate Islamic democrats of the Justice and Development Party, who, although permitted to contest fewer than half the districts, finished third, with forty-two seats to Youssoufi's socialists' fifty and the forty-eight seats of the center-left Istiqlal. But a far more popular—and less moderate—Islamist party, the Justice and Benevolence Party, was banned from the elections, which it might well have won, and it is speculated that even the existing official results may have been adjusted to keep Justice and Development out of power. Youssoufi remains prime minister, and free political discussion is far broader than it once was, but both democracy and Islam in Morocco still exist very much within the framework of royal control. While the robust multiparty system holds out hope for increasing legislative power in Morocco, it remains to be seen how Muhammad will rule in the long run, and whether he will expand the scope of democracy to include all the Islamic parties.

Jordan also illustrates dramatically the possibilities and problems of democratization and its interaction with Islamic politics. Jordan's democratic experiment began under the late King Hussein in 1989 and has undergone a number of ups and downs since then. For most of his forty-five-year reign, King Hussein ruled in a world where democracy was not on the front burner of global or regional politics. When he became king in 1952, after the assassination of his grandfather, Abdullah I, the Cold War was new, and neither the Western nor the Communist side was much interested in promoting democracy in the less developed parts of the world. The British Empire, which had presided over the creation of the Hashemite Kingdom of

Jordan, did not press for democracy there. And such were the dangers and internal pressures that King Hussein faced throughout his reign that the idea of democracy would have seemed fantastical for most of it.

In 1948, Jordan joined other Arab states in invading the newly declared State of Israel, and Jordan ended up controlling the West Bank of the Jordan River and East Jerusalem. That meant that the population of Jordan became very mixed. The Palestinians who had lived on the West Bank for many centuries were joined by more Palestinians who had either fled what was now Israel in the false hope that they might someday return, or been pushed out by Israeli regular and irregular forces. When the war ended, these Palestinians could not return home, and many ended up in Jordan, either on the West Bank in refugee camps or in Jordan itself. The demographics of Jordan changed tremendously as a result. There were now not only the Bedouin and other tribesmen who had traditionally lived in Jordan, and the townspeople of the central region around Amman, but also many displaced Palestinians who gravitated toward Jordan's cities.

So from the start, Hussein reigned over a mixed country in which many of his Palestinian subjects, who carried Jordanian passports, did not think of themselves as wholly Jordanian. That fact alone would have made democratization seem implausible. Then, in 1967, Jordan lost the West Bank of the Jordan to Israel. After that debacle, the Palestine Liberation Organization became a real force in Jordan, engaging in attacks across the border on Israel, which brought Israeli reprisals. The PLO hijacked a series of planes to Jordan, which put King Hussein in a delicate position, and in general the PLO's power in Jordan grew to the point at which Yasser Arafat became a major force in the country. What was worse, there were those in Israel, and even among the Palestinians, who suggested that it might be possible to begin to solve the Palestinian refugee problem by creating a Palestinian state—in Jordan. That, of course, would have meant the end of King Hussein and the Hashemite monarchy.

Threatened by the challenge to his authority represented by the rise of Arafat, Hussein directed the military force of the Jordanian state against the PLO in September 1970. After six months of bloody fighting, Jordan managed to eject the PLO; they ended up in Lebanon, where they eventually rebuilt themselves. The upshot was that King Hussein earned the enmity of a large part of the Palestinian people. In a country where there were many Palestinians, that meant democracy was not a viable option for him.

But in 1988, acting with an exquisite sense of realism, King Hussein formally renounced any claim that Jordan might have on the West Bank. The Palestinian uprising against Israel on the West Bank and Gaza made it clear that whatever the future of Palestine, it would not be part of Jordan. Renouncing any claim on the West Bank, and supporting the creation of a Palestinian state, helped King Hussein's relations with the Palestinians considerably. At the same time, internal affairs in Jordan were taking a turn for the worse. April 1989 saw five days of unprecedented rioting, much of it in the southern part of the country, where Palestinians were scarce and support for the king had traditionally been high. The reasons for the riots were mostly economic. The king had introduced austerity measures to save the country from bankruptcy, and that meant higher prices on basic commodities.

Taking his cue from the remarkable events of 1989 in Eastern Europe, King Hussein decided to gamble on instituting democratic measures as a response to the riots. In November 1989 he allowed the first elections for Parliament in twenty-two years. No formal political parties were yet permitted, but loose, party-like structures started to emerge. The cynical reading of the king's rationale was that elections would allow the public to let off steam and to direct their concerns away from the monarchy. A more generous reading would add that King Hussein wanted to be a part of the spirit of 1989 and enjoy any benefits that might bring to Jordan.

The elections revealed that in Jordan, as elsewhere in the Arab world, Islamists had a real political appeal, at least in elections declared before proper parties had time to coalesce. The Islamists in Jordan were mostly affiliated with the Jordanian branch of the Muslim Brotherhood. Candidates associated with the Brotherhood took more than 30 percent of the seats in the new Parliament; other, unaffiliated Islamists took 16 percent or so. The success of these parties had something to do with the electoral system that was adopted, which allowed each voter to cast multiple votes for multiple candidates from the district. If one's region was entitled to five seats, one got five votes. Many voters therefore voted first for a favorite candidate to whom they might have tribal or other local ties, then used the rest of their votes for Islamists.

Notwithstanding their electoral success, King Hussein excluded the Islamists from the government that was formed after the elections; but their presence in Parliament was felt. When political parties were permitted to be formed in 1992, the Brotherhood spun off a party known as the Islamic Action Front, and it immediately became one of the most important political parties in Jordan. But King Hussein was also wary of allowing the Islamists too much political power, partly because of their criticism of financial corruption in the royal family, and partly because he was negotiating a bilateral peace treaty with Israel and knew that the Islamists could make that process more difficult. So the king changed the electoral system before the 1993 elections. Now voters could cast just one vote for one candidate within their region, although the region might be entitled to several seats in Parliament. King Hussein calculated that if a voter had only one vote, he would be more likely to use it on a candidate to whom he had some familial or tribal tie, and less likely to use it on an Islamist candidate.

The king's political calculation proved correct. The total number of Islamic Action Front seats in the 1993 elections was down to 20 percent from the Brotherhood's tally of 30 percent in 1989. Independent Islamists did much worse than they had in 1989. The king did in fact conclude a peace treaty with Israel in 1994. The Islamists didn't like it, but also couldn't stop it. What they could do was express continual frustration over the subsequent peace talks with Israel, which they considered wrong, and the slow pace of the Israeli-Palestinian peace process, which they condemned as both pointless and inadequate.

The most important fact about the Islamic Action Front between 1993 and 1997 is that it remained within the Jordanian democratic framework, such as it was. It spoke out on issues. It took positions about domestic and foreign policy. It opposed the government and, on occasion, the monarchy. In short, it served as the most important opposition party in Jordan. The Islamic Action Front was perhaps the first functioning democratic Islamist party anywhere in the Arab world.

The party's experience in Parliament turned out to be limited. In 1996, with Parliament in recess, the king promulgated a law limiting the free press. Public demonstrations were curtailed. As the 1997 elections approached, the king became increasingly impatient with the party and imprisoned several Islamist activists without trial. Ultimately, the Islamic Action Front decided to boycott the November 1997 election and withdraw from the democratic process temporarily. This did not occur without an internal argument. The Front was skeptical about the boycott, even after the Brotherhood essentially ordered it to occur. And the Front reentered politics in the local elections of 1999. In February 1999, King Hussein died and was succeeded by his son Abdullah. The Islamists are poised to participate in the next elections in one form or another.

The Jordanian experience with limited democracy is a study in the challenges of gradual democratization. Under Jordan's constitutional monarchy, the king's power is structured very much like the president's power under the U.S. Constitution, except, of course, that the king is not elected. Under the Jordanian constitution, the two parts of the legislature—the senate and the assembly—pass the laws, but the king must ratify those laws for them to take effect. (Surprisingly, the constitution provides that the legislature can overrule the king's veto in the same way that Congress can override the president's veto, by a two-thirds vote.) Like the president, the king also has the executive function, empowering him to decide how the laws will be applied; to enact regulations to make sure the laws are applied the way he wants; and to control foreign policy and military affairs.

Notwithstanding this constitution, there had been no elections for the legislature for more than twenty years before 1989. So "democratization" in Jordan meant, first and foremost, giving bite to the constitution as written by allowing the legislature to be elected. That such elections occurred in 1989, 1993, and 1997 is of great significance. None of these elections was perfect, but by most accounts all were basically free. This was certainly progress in the direction of greater democracy, even though there is a general sense that the 1997 elections were less free than those of 1993, and even though the promised 2002 elections have been delayed.

Even so, no one in Jordan right now is speaking openly about shifting any of the king's executive power away from him. Rather, Jordanians who call for democratization—including the Islamists—speak of allowing political parties to operate freely, curtailing arbitrary arrest and torture, ensuring free speech, and allowing the legislature to make laws on its own terms, as the constitution formally provides. The success of democratization in Jordan can be measured by the extent to which government behaves in strict accordance with the constitution and concedes more power to the legislature.

For the foreseeable future, in other words, democratization in Jordan can only happen within the basic structure of constitutional monarchy. Jordan already has a constitutional monarchy in the sense that the king derives his power from a constitution that limits what he can do. The king of Jordan is not an absolute monarch, nor has he been since Jordan was founded in 1924. Still, there are different kinds of constitutional monarchs—some who follow the constitutional rules strictly, usually because the legislature or some other institution has the power to make them, and others who dominate their countries to such a degree that the constitution becomes just a piece of paper. Elections give power to the legislature by investing it with the legitimacy of public will, and so press toward restraint of the monarch. Elections are therefore crucially important for democratizing within the structure of the constitutional monarchy.

How stable is this sort of arrangement? Assume that under King Abdullah, elections proceed and the legislature in Jordan achieves greater influence over affairs of state. Imagine further that the king keeps up liberalization, the economy grows, political parties flourish, and free speech becomes easier to exercise. None of these things is guaranteed to happen, but all seem possible. Can the monarchy survive? Will the Jordanian people agree to allow the king to be, essentially, president for life, or will they start to want the king to recede from politics, to move gradually to make himself more of a figurehead?

Everywhere in the world, the pattern has been similar. According greater power to the people leads them away from rule by kings. There are generally two options: either kings go gracefully, in which case they can become beloved heads of state who exercise relatively little real power, or else they resist, in which case they often end up dead or deposed. Neither is a perfect option for a king who wants to stay in power.

So what is King Abdullah up to in Jordan when he speaks about liberalization and democratization? He undoubtedly wants to lead his country into the modern world. He particularly wants to embrace a modern economy, in which entrepreneurs will create businesses that will generate wealth within Jordan. Abdullah knows that the process of opening up the economy requires opening Jordanian society to the world through education and contact. Both of his signature educational reforms, English and computers in the schools, push Jordan into increased contact with the rest of the world, and especially the West.

Before Western audiences, Abdullah emphasizes his close connection to Jordan's technocratic and business elites. Putting his money where his mouth is, he has appointed ministers and ambassadors from this class. Of course this alliance may be for Abdullah what the alliance with tribal leaders and large landholders was for his father, namely necessary to stay in power. But unlike his father's alliance, this alliance for economic liberalization will likely have the eventual consequence of requiring greater political liberalization. Abdullah says he welcomes political reform once the economy begins to improve, and he may relish the thought of becoming the Juan Carlos of the Arab world, a king who brings his country though a difficult transition into the democratic community of nations. There is a continuum for royal power, in any event. From 1688 to the Second World War, the kings of England passed through that continuum, their constitutional power gradually decreasing. It is very unlikely that King Abdullah would traverse that entire process in a lifetime. He has the capacity to reduce the power of the monarchy over time without making it purely symbolic.

Skeptics would say that Abdullah talks a good game when he is in the West but will rule as a king, not as a proto-democrat. Abdullah cannot act only on his own behalf. There is a royal family and a power structure in Jordan, who will want to keep their power and prerogatives, and who need the monarchy to do so. On this view, democracy in Jordan was born as a sham and will stay one. It sounds very impressive when Abdullah says that because he is not elected, he is free to do the right thing, the brave thing, when it comes to peace with Israel. But the fact that the king is unelected also means he is not responsible to the people, and that he will inevitably want to retain the power of the monarchy above all else.

The skeptics' argument is not without logic. No matter what King Abdullah wants, he has other people to think of, a family, and elites in business, military, and government whom he owes—not to mention the United

States, to whom he is also beholden. But the skeptical view rests on the assumption that no leader ever has a vision for a better and different future if it means a reduction in power. And history does not always bear out that cynical assumption. Mikhail Gorbachev may have unleashed a process that quickly got beyond his control, but he must have known, when he introduced perestroika and glasnost, that he would have less power in a reformed Soviet Union than the power he would have exercised as head of the Communist Party and head of state under an old-style Soviet regime. Yet Gorbachev did introduce a process of reform in the Soviet Union. Admittedly, his example is a cautionary tale for a would-be reformer: leader of the un-free world one day, pitchman for Pizza Hut the next. But King Abdullah is, and would remain, a king. There is a role for kings even when they are not in absolute control.

What is more, there is also ambition, a trait Abdullah does not lack. When you are a king, to what should you aspire? Being a good king, no doubt; being loved by your people, certainly; and being a figure on the world stage. King Hussein achieved some of these goals notwithstanding Jordan's poverty and relative unimportance to the geopolitics of the Arab world. But paradoxically, the only way for a contemporary king to achieve stature is to encourage democratization, a fact that may have had something to do with King Hussein's efforts toward the end of his reign. If King Abdullah were to preside over a process of meaningful democratization in Jordan, he would be remembered as both a great monarch and a great democrat.

Getting there will not be easy, most of all because Abdullah will need help. The United States will play a crucial role in whatever progress he is able to make, and the West more generally must be on the sidelines helping him achieve the goals he sets for himself, in order to encourage democratization in Jordan. The process of democratization is unlikely to succeed if it has to depend solely on spontaneous internal development.

But internal perspectives on government will be critical to making democratization work, and here Islam comes directly into play. Islam matters for the future of democracy in Jordan partly because the king's legitimacy is connected to Islam. Abdullah claims descent from the Prophet. There is even a family tree on the monarchy's official Web site tracing forty-three generations of the king's ancestors back to Muhammad himself, and beyond. Islam is not the only element of the legitimacy of the Hashemites; there are also tribal loyalties that run from Jordanian Arab tribes to the royal family, and there is the legitimacy that comes from having ruled a nation-state for the better part of a century. But Islam is part of the picture, and King Abdullah may be able to use it to advance his agenda internally and in the broader Muslim and Arab world.

Specifically, there is a niche in the Muslim world for a leader who espouses a vision of Islam that is authentic in its connection to Muslim belief and tradition, and also explicit in its commitment to values like justice, peace, and toleration. Moderates all over the Muslim world are frustrated that Islamists have managed to monopolize the language of Islam for purposes of advancing programs that are often radical and extremist. In the Arab world, and also in places as diverse as Indonesia, Turkey, and West Africa, moderate Muslims are looking for a leader who will present Islam as a force for toleration and progress.

King Abdullah might make a strategic decision to become a leading voice of moderate Islam in the world. His heritage gives him the authority to do so. The key would be for Abdullah to articulate his message of expanding freedom and knowledge in Islamic terms. This would begin the process of reclaiming the language of Islam from fundamentalists, which would not be as difficult as it might sound, because so many Muslims around the world have the feeling that radical Islamists cannot be right about what Islam means. The Islamists succeed in large part because they are able to use the language of Islam to capture people's intuitive objections to injustice. A moderate Muslim voice would succeed by capturing people's commonsense moderation in Islamic terms and language.

King Abdullah already does something like this, especially when he speaks in the West. But he could also enhance his position among Muslims by saying what many already believe themselves: that Islam corresponds to their deepest sense of what is right, which is to say justice and moderation, not radicalism or violence. Internally, Abdullah's project of economic and political liberalization would be made much easier and more effective, because he would stand for something, inside and outside Jordan. This would enable him to be identified as more than merely the king of a small and not very rich country that is not taken seriously by other leaders in the Arab world. He would be a visionary with something important to say.

Standing for an authentic, moderate Islam might also help King Abdullah locally, in his relations with the Jordanian Islamists, who make up the second reason that Islam will matter for Jordan's process of democratization. Increasing democratization in Jordan means dealing with Islamist parties like the Islamic Action Front. The Front will not always be so helpful as to boycott elections. They are part of the Jordanian polity and will remain so. Their popularity depends on their message and their reputation for honesty. Their message—that Islam is the answer to social and economic problems—has resonance with the public mostly because people perceive that things need fixing in society, not because the specifics are clear or seem likely to work. By proposing reforms that will improve people's lives, King Abdullah can begin to show that there are good practical alternatives to the Islamists' program. But he can do more, by showing how economic development, knowledge, and technology are part of an authentic Islamic vision of improving society. That will take the wind out of the Islamists' sails, and perhaps even win over some Islamists to his view.

To the extent that Islamists continue to challenge King Abdullah, though, the key to making democratization successful may be to allow them the freedom to express their views publicly. The more they are barred from making their views known, the more popular legitimacy they gain by appearing to be the most vocal opponents of the government. There is a vicious cycle at work here, in which a fringe opposition can become the mainstream just by virtue of being rewarded with repression. In a country like Jordan, where moderate Islam has deep roots, there is little reason to fear that the public will be swept up in a sea of Islamist fervor. There is, however, some reason to fear that Islamists can become the only opposition game in town as a result of being kept out of the public debate. Fighting their speech with more speech is a gamble, but it is a gamble that is worth taking because it will be more effective than shutting them up.

King Abdullah cannot do all this alone, however. The bottom line is that the West must show its support for him when he pursues policies of democratization and liberalization—and not just with money (the United States already gives some aid to Jordan). It means Western governments must facilitate private investment in Jordan. It means they must make clear that the more democratic Jordan becomes, the more it will find itself to be an ally of the West. It means that trade agreements, like the one between the U.S. and Jordan, should be pursued by European partners, too. All of these would begin the work of showing Jordanians and other Arabs that there are tangible, immediate benefits associated with democratization.

The Jordanian experiment with democratization has not followed a simple formula of proceeding from less democracy to more. There have already been steps forward and back, and there will no doubt be others. Abdullah himself has not yet permitted an election during his reign, and until he does, skeptics will be right to question the seriousness of his commitment to democratic liberalization alongside increased economic freedom. But it is possible to see a path that might be followed. So in Jordan as in Morocco, there is reason for guarded optimism. Islamic democracy in Jordan will not be Islamist democracy, but something more moderate and forward-looking. It will have the capacity to become a model for democracy in other Arab states as well.

THE DICTATORS AND THE ISLAMISTS: THE PUZZLE OF EGYPT

Constitutional monarchies like Jordan and Morocco hold out some hope for the prospect of Islamic democracy that comes into being from the top, because both kings are Western-educated reformers who can boast their own Islamic legitimacy. But there are only two such oil-less monarchies in the Arab world. The great majority of Arabs live in countries where kings were deposed more than fifty years ago and replaced by military or quasi-military dictators. Since then, the peoples of Egypt, Syria, Tunisia, and Yemen have lived under a double disadvantage. They have little oil, and they are ruled by dictators who have rarely been benign.

Egypt, in many ways the heart of the modern Arab world, can serve as the model of the dynamics of government in oil-less dictatorships. With 69.5 million citizens, it has by far the largest population of any Arab state, and its television programs, radio shows, and films have long been distributed throughout the Arab world. Under Gamal Abdul Nasser, the colonel who emerged as the undisputed leader of Egypt shortly after the king was deposed in 1952, Egypt was also the center of pan-Arab ideology and politics. Nasser's role as the leading figure in the Arab world in his lifetime, and his commitment to pan-Arabism, had the effect of making Egypt, at one time, the linchpin of the Arab states. Pan-Arabism faded after Nasser's death, and Sadat's pathbreaking decision to make peace with Israel further reduced Egypt's centrality in the Arab world when other Arab states did not follow. Nonetheless, Egypt remains in many ways the archetypal Arab nation. Its problems resemble those of other oil-less dictatorships, even if they are more dire. Egypt remains a trendsetter in the Arab world.

Egypt is the birthplace of both Islamic reformism and modern Islamic fundamentalism. The Muslim Brotherhood, founded in Egypt, remains the largest Islamist organization in the world and has played a role on the Egyptian scene for seventy years. Islamism in Egypt has always opposed the government: the early Islamists opposed the monarchy, which they saw as a tool of the West; when Nasser turned on them, the Islamists opposed Nasser; when Sadat made peace with Israel, the Islamists opposed him, too. Extremist Islamists outside the more moderate Brotherhood founded their own terrorist cells and assassinated Sadat, and Islamists today remain critics of the regime of President Hosni Mubarak.

Despite, or perhaps because of, their critical posture, for much of their history Islamists remained relatively peripheral to Egyptian religious and political life. Most Egyptians had little patience for them. Support for Arab and then Egyptian nationalism was strong among intellectuals and the general public. Many Egyptians, especially the educated, thought of themselves as secular. In the sphere of religion, people attended mosques that were staffed by clerics trained at al-Azhar, the state-run religious university and flagship educational institution of the Sunni Muslim world. These Azharis were trained in the traditional Muslim religious sciences, and they tended to look askance at the Islamists, who typically lacked comparable scholarly training.

It took time for Islamism to get off the ground in Egypt, but eventually it did. In the 1980s, especially in poor villages in Upper Egypt, Islamism started to attract followers in an environment of poverty and hopelessness. The traditional agricultural economy offered little better than subsistence to the peasants; strivers who managed to get an education were unlikely to find jobs. Islamism was brought to the villages by young men who had studied in the big cities, gotten their degrees, and come home to poor prospects and poorer lifestyles. Shaped by their direct experience of the injustice and economic inequality of Egyptian society, they found in Islamism a powerful means for expressing their views. In Lower Egypt, too, especially in poor neighborhoods crowded with Upper Egyptians who had migrated to the cities in search of jobs, similar Islamists were beginning to attract followers.

The growth of Islamism in the poorest parts of Egypt in the 1980s and early 1990s provides the basis for the oft-heard argument that poverty is the "cause" of fundamentalism. Many of the Islamist radicals who committed acts of terror in Egypt in the early 1990s, against tourists and others, came from poor backgrounds, and there is something to the association of poverty and despair with Islamist radicalism. But it is too simple to say that Islamism is "driven" by poverty. Islamist ideologues and leaders have come almost exclusively from the middle classes in Egypt. Many rank-and-file Islamists come from middle-class backgrounds and have university degrees, especially in engineering or the sciences. Ayman al-Zawahiri, infamous as the right-hand man and intellectual inspiration for Osama bin Laden, is (or was) an Egyptian physician from a prominent family. Professionals have long been mainstays of the membership of the Brotherhood. In fact, Islamists have achieved some of their greatest political successes in elections for leadership of professional associations like those for lawyers and doctors.

The simple view that poverty drives Islamism underestimates and misstates the attractions that the Islamist message has for many people in a country like Egypt. Arguing that poverty and desperation drive Islamism implies that no one would embrace Islamism unless he or she were desperate or had nowhere else to turn. Yet Islamism has its own powerful appeal—intellectual, emotional, and spiritual. Many Islamists embrace it because they find its message resonates powerfully with their beliefs, values, and experiences. Poverty is one such experience, but so is alienation from the shallowness of consumerism, and so is the search for meaning that characterizes religious experience everywhere.

Islamism offers a vision of how the universe is structured—in God's oneness—and how the community of Muslims should work together in a united way. These messages have an inherent appeal to people in any place or of any degree of wealth. Monotheism and community solidarity are as appealing in Cairo's bourgeois neighborhoods as in its slums. Such messages have special appeal where social and family structures have been deeply disrupted by population movement. The Islamists' message of restraint in matters of personal morality like sex and the consumption of alcohol sounds very sensible to many in a society shaken by the upheavals of modernity. Islamism also punctures the arrogance of secularist reformers who think they can reorder the world according to a Marxist or purely capitalist economic theory. This criticism has special relevance in Egypt, where the government tried and failed to get the economy going by applying socialist and statist economics, and has now tried and failed to jump-start it using modified free-market principles.

Perhaps most important, Islamism speaks the language of justice in a place where justice is hard to come by. Many ordinary Egyptians have the (accurate) sense that their government does not respond to their needs, that politicians are corrupt, and that their voices count for little compared with the voices of the wealthy. Islamists argue that corruption and inequality are not just wrong but un-Islamic: they violate the word of God. This message transcends petty politics and rises up to the level of moral outrage at the current state of affairs in Egypt.

Islamism, in other words, has supporters in Egypt because it speaks to people's most basic concerns. Poverty is one part of this equation, but only a part. Today, Islamism in Egypt continues to spread, not just among the poor but among some elites. Islamist bookstores have multiplied and offer books written at a variety of levels of complexity and audiotapes of lectures and sermons that are accessible even to people who read a little or not at all. Popular preachers reach not just the poor, but into the villas of comfortable families who find their daughters covering their hair and themselves newly attracted to a message that has been moderated and tailored to them. In an environment where other ideas are not particularly vibrant, Islamist ideas are growing in popularity. One finds Islamism in villages and in universities, among the most educated stratum of the population and among those who have no formal education at all.

What are the practical political consequences of the continuing growth of Islamism in Egypt? Mubarak is deeply opposed to Islamism, and he knows that some radical Islamists think they should finish the job they started when they killed Sadat. He also knows that Islamism has a long history of opposing the government in Egypt. Mubarak heads a dictatorship, where no one else gets to run for president and where elections for parliament are tightly controlled. He can repress all kinds of political dissent, but the Islamists are hard to quiet, because Mubarak cannot close every mosque where Islamists gather to talk. The Egyptian secret police monitor and infiltrate Islamist groups, of course, and many Islamists have spent time in jail and been tortured or killed. But the Islamists cannot be completely suppressed, and any opposition group so resilient has to be a threat to a dictator.

Islamists, even moderate ones not bent on violence, also oppose many of Mubarak's policies. Although Mubarak is not a close friend to Israel, Sadat set Egyptian policy in stone when he recognized Israel in exchange for the return of the Sinai and upwards of $2 billion a year in U.S. aid. Egypt became a dependent ally of the United States and a potential mediator between the Arab states and Israel. Yet anti-Israel sentiment in Egypt seems to be greater now than it was when Sadat first made peace with Israel. The reason is partly that old habits of Israel-bashing die hard, and partly that two Palestinian uprisings, separated by a decade, exposed the Egyptian public to images of Israeli soldiers fighting, and sometimes killing, Palestinian civilians, many of them children. It is not especially surprising that these images have created great anti-Israel sentiment in Egypt. What is perhaps more remarkable is that anti-Israel feeling in Egypt may well be greater than anti-Israel feeling anywhere else in the Arab world, including countries that do not have peace treaties with Israel. The reason may be residual guilt at having abandoned the Palestinians; it may be that Egyptians want to prove to themselves that they are still leaders in the Arab world even though their government has made peace with Israel; and it may also reflect resentment at the undemocratic nature of the peace treaty in the first place. But in any case, Mubarak knows that his alliance with the United States and the policy of cold peace toward Israel, with which he is stuck, do not make him popular with Islamists.

Islamists seem to have a special capacity to criticize Mubarak regarding both Israel and Egypt's alliance with the United States, or at least Mubarak seems especially vulnerable to these critiques when they are made by Islamists. On the question of Israel, Islamists are well placed to argue that religion, not just nationality, plays a direct role in the Middle East conflict. Islamists are prepared to describe the conflict between Israel and the Palestinian people as a conflict between Jews and Muslims. While the Arab nationalists always called Israel "the Zionist entity" and strove to associate Zionism with racism, they did not generally call Israelis "the Jews." In fact, Arab nationalists often protested that they themselves were not anti-Semitic, just anti-Zionist. This distinction, however specious in practice, seemed important to Arab nationalists, and it is still occasionally heard in the Arab world today. The Islamists have no such compunctions. They speak of Israel as a Jewish state and of Israelis as "the Jews." This practice may have started innocently enough. Islamists describe themselves as Muslims, after all, and it is no insult to them to think of others in religious, rather than national terms. But the practice of calling Israelis "the Jews" has become highly charged in Islamist rhetoric. It may well be connected to the disturbing trend of anti-Semitism in the Arabic press, including the occasional revival of the old European blood libel.

Islamists are also effective at criticizing what they see as Mubarak's cozy relationship with the United States They tend not to focus on the immorality of American culture—although one hears that rhetoric occasionally—but on the way that the U.S. supports the Egyptian government while requiring its loyalty in return, regardless of the contrary opinions or interests of the Egyptian people. Thus, for example, the Islamists effectively criticized Egypt's participation in the coalition to remove Saddam Hussein from Kuwait in 1991, participation that went in the face of popular sentiment that opposed siding with America against another Arab state. By extension, any time Mubarak does anything that might possibly be taken as corresponding to American interests, the Islamists attack him as a creature of the United States—and by extension, of Israel. The implication is that Mubarak serves the U.S. to advance his own interests, not his people's.

The Islamists' proven capacity to organize themselves for political purposes has an enormous impact on the process and possibility of democratization in Egypt. Islamists have repeatedly been denied the chance to register themselves as a political party. The Muslim Brotherhood started trying to register as soon as Egypt formally decided to allow political parties under Sadat, but the government has never allowed it. There are a number of elected representatives in Egypt who are known to be affiliated with the Brotherhood, but they do not formally represent the Brotherhood.

Another lively group of Islamic democrats broke with the Brotherhood in 1996 and set out to create their own political party, which they gave the politically savvy name of the Center Party (Hizb al-wasat). Abul-Ela Maadi and Essam Sultan were two of the leaders of this group, educated modern men who proclaimed their commitment to democratic politics and argued that the Brotherhood, mired in its legacy of conflict with the state, was not doing a good job of representing Islamists' political interests and was not deeply enough committed to democracy. The Center Party, Sultan told a reporter, was inspired by faith: "faith in pluralism, faith in democracy, faith in freedom, faith in freedom of opinion, freedom of thought, freedom of creativity, relations with other [political] currents." Threatened more by sophisticated moderate Islamic democrats than by the Brotherhood's informal candidates, the government denied the Center Party the right to register, so Maadi and Sultan created nongovernmental organizations instead.

Blocked from organizing as a formal party, Islamists have engaged the public by providing much-needed social services. Islamist welfare organizations have opened clinics that offer free health care; they assist with food, blankets, and shelter in times of crisis; and they provide financial support for young couples seeking to marry. There are various Islamist social organizations as well. All these organizations, formal and informal, make the Islamists important participants in Egyptian civil society. Providing social services when the state cannot or will not enables the Islamists to occupy the domain of organized non-state activity. Where trade and professional associations already exist, the Islamists have relied on a combination of clever politicking and the absence of a cohesive non-Islamist political movement to win control. As a result, in those realms of Egyptian life where citizens are permitted to organize themselves outside the direct control of the state, Islam invariably plays a major role.

Although the point is not uncontested, many experts on democratic development think that a strong civil society, in which there are many nongovernmental groups and associations through which people can organize, is necessary for democracy to emerge. Egypt has a fairly complex civil society—and much of that civil society is Islamist. Not only do Islamists have their own organizations, but through electoral politics they have succeeded in taking over many associations and trade unions that have no inherent political affiliation. So if in fact civil society is a condition for bringing about democracy, we can expect Islamists to play a big part in any democratization that does occur in Egypt.

What are the prospects for making Egypt more democratic? Egypt has a parliament and has held parliamentary elections since 1984. Political parties are allowed, but only those the government permits to register—and no Islamist party has been permitted. Candidates can express their views on a variety of issues, but only up to a point. During the 1995 elections, candidates were regularly silenced when they criticized the government, and the elections were marked by other forms of gerrymandering and vote rigging. As a result, Mubarak's party, the National Democratic Party, always dominates the Parliament. The 2000 elections, while better than the 1995 elections, again yielded an overwhelming majority for the president's party. The only significant opposition in the Parliament actually comes from Islamists, unofficially affiliated with the Muslim Brotherhood. There were 17 such Islamists elected in 2000, out of a Parliament of 444. The NDP took almost 80 percent of the seats—fewer than the 94 percent it held after the 1995 elections but still enough to testify to the questionable nature of the electoral process.

To make matters worse, democracy advocates in Egypt are not safe from being thrown in prison with little justification. Saadeddin Ibrahim, an Egyptian-American professor who publishes a magazine called *Civil Society* and runs a think tank devoted to democracy issues, was arrested in summer 2000, charged with embezzling European Union funds for his institute. Despite the fact that the European Union denied that any such thing had happened, Saadeddin was convicted in a secret trial, then held in prison for nearly a year before the conviction was reversed on appeal. *The New York Times* put Saadeddin on the cover of its Sunday magazine, highlighting an article that cast grave doubt on the charges against him, but that seems to have had relatively little effect on the disposition of his case, because in 2002 he was convicted in a second trial and sentenced to seven years' hard labor. After the second conviction, President Bush finally decided to exert some meaningful pressure on Mubarak, promising to withhold supplemental aid that Egypt had requested unless something was done for Saadeddin, and in December 2002, the appeals court reversed that conviction, too.

Linking U.S. aid to the treatment of a democracy activist is a step in the right direction where Egypt is concerned. Regardless of whether Saadeddin ultimately is spared further imprisonment, though, his case is telling. Saadeddin had everything on his side—U.S. citizenship, media attention, foreign support—yet was still vulnerable to legalized persecution. That says something about the status of Egyptian democracy activists who are not so well connected. And Saadeddin's case is very far from being the worst instance of Egyptian state repression.

As in any dictatorship, it is hard to know exactly why any one person becomes the subject of special government attention. One speculation about Saadeddin's jailing and arrest, reported in the *Times Magazine* and elsewhere, was that Mubarak was angry that Saadeddin said on al-Jazeera that he could imagine a scenario in which Mubarak's son, Gamal, succeeded Mubarak. Whether this speculation is correct or not, it reveals something about the structure of Egyptian presidential politics. President Mubarak's hold on power is great enough that it is possible to imagine his son succeeding him, just as Bashar al-Asad succeeded his father, Hafez al-Asad, in the presidency of Syria. Needless to say, the Egyptian presidency is not designed to be hereditary. (Nor, to be fair, is the U.S. presidency.) A further reason that speculation follows the well-spoken and intelligent Gamal is that few other major figures have been allowed to emerge in the political environment of contemporary Egypt. If Mubarak were to die, the desire for stability might lead some power brokers to embrace Gamal for lack of another viable option.

The depressing scenario of Egyptian dictatorship continuing unabated is not unrealistic. In fact, it is a little hard to see just how Mubarak could liberalize, or why he would do so unless the pressure from outside or inside his country became much greater than it presently is. On the other hand, there is some basis for hope, even if there is little room for optimism. In fact, Egypt has gotten gradually freer over the past twenty years. There is somewhat more freedom of speech than there was. The 2000 elections were, in fact, an advance over those of 1995, even if the advance was incremental and there was nowhere to go but up. Economic power is beginning gradually to be more diffused, away from the government and toward a newly emerging business class. Perhaps gradually, over time, the business class might begin to seek influence in the sphere of politics, as it has in the sphere of economics.

So real reform may be unlikely, but it is absolutely necessary nonetheless. Egypt managed to change power with a minimum of civil unrest from Nasser to Sadat, then from Sadat to Mubarak. But these were not easy or simple transitions, and they were very rare in the world of dictatorships. Dictatorships are vulnerable to revolution. The Islamists lack the political base necessary for a violent revolution—for now. But if Mubarak were suddenly to die, of natural or other causes, the future of Egypt would be very much in jeopardy.

Egyptians are mostly disillusioned with Mubarak and his government, which has let them down economically and politically. It is obviously in Egyptian interests for greater democracy to develop in Egypt. But it is also in Western interests, because a democratic Egypt could become the centerpiece of an alliance with the West that would be able to exert enormous power in the region. Egypt is still the center of the Arab world, geographically, culturally, and politically. Some American realists will object that the Egyptian public would be less accommodating to U.S. interests than is Mubarak's dictatorship. In the short term, that would no doubt be true. Right now, many Egyptians resent the United States for its support of Mubarak and of Israel. American aid of $2 billion a year since Camp David has bought shockingly little good will. But if American policy were to change, Egyptian public sentiment would very probably change, too. Over time, a stable democracy in Egypt would have a much better chance of acting as a U.S. ally than does an unstable dictatorship; and in time a democracy, too, would understand the benefits of U.S. aid.

An Egyptian democracy would be an Islamic democracy, but it would not necessarily have to be an Islamist democracy. Egypt already makes Islam the official religion of the state. *Shari'a* is named as a source of law under the Egyptian constitution. Islamic law governs in family courts. There is every reason to think that these features would remain if Egypt were to become more democratic. But despite their consistent growth, Islamists in Egypt might not be able to form an electoral majority of the kind that would be able to make *shari'a* the law across the board, in place of existing legal structures. Without proper polling it is difficult to make responsible predictions of the statistical extent of support for Islamists, but many Egyptians remain attached to their tradition of relatively secular government. If Islamist democrats were not able to win majorities, they could be expected to participate in government, seek accommodations where they could get them, and compromise where they could not.

The reason to believe that most Egyptian Islamists would be pragmatic when participating in government is that the Muslim Brotherhood, still far and away the most important Islamist organization in Egypt, has a track record of pragmatism. There are Islamist extremists in Egypt, it is true, but they have receded to the background in recent years. Terrorist attacks have abated. Intimidation of intellectuals, like the stabbing of Nobel laureate Naguib Mahfouz, has become more unusual. The Muslim Brotherhood, by contrast, has emerged as a group willing to participate in elections, even when banned from doing so in its official capacity. The Brotherhood stands for a basically nonviolent strand of Islamism, grounded in a systematic critique of existing power structures—and one can expect support for the Brotherhood to grow. In Egypt, for better or worse, the Islamists are becoming the most viable democratic opposition there is.

That Islamic democracy has become an ideal for some Egyptian reformers says much about the state of politics in Egypt, and about the interaction between democracy and Islam. Islam has deep roots and resonance in Egypt, and so functions as the most effective language to oppose the dictatorship's injustice. Real democracy, on the other hand, has never been tried in Egypt. Yet such is its power as an idea that it has made its way into Egyptian political discourse nonetheless. The government pays lip service to democracy by allowing elections; observing that those elections occur, the Islamists embrace democracy as a means to get their voices heard. To get a chance to participate in self-rule, Islamists like Maadi and Sultan of the would-be Center Party begin to speak the language of democracy. Doing so requires them to work out the relationship between democracy and Islam. The past few years have seen Egyptian Islamists doing exactly that, and it turns out that the merged theory of Islamic democracy has more resonance in Egypt than either Islamism on its own or democracy on its own.

Islamic democracy as a synthesis of mobile ideas may never manage to bring about the reform or downfall of the Egyptian dictatorship. No realist could claim that such a development was imminent. But a realist might grant that just about the only hope for internal democratic development in Egypt is for Islamic democrats to get their voices heard. The synthesis of Islam and democracy is the best option available. The alternative is to imagine that dictatorship will continue indefinitely, until internal revolution or an external push brings it to an end. That is the situation among the oil-rich dictatorships, to which we now turn.

REGIME CHANGE AND ITS CONSEQUENCES: DICTATORS WITH OIL

The forces that move dictators toward democratization are the need to maintain some modicum of legitimacy among citizens at home, and to placate, at least superficially, Western allies abroad. These two forces, internal and external, have little effect on dictators with oil. Inside their countries, men like Saddam Hussein do not need to worry much about keeping the populace satisfied with their rule. They can depend on near-totalitarian state power to keep their citizens in line. What differentiates them from their oil-less counterparts is that they have a steady supply of money enabling them to provide carrots to their supporters even as they beat their opponents with sticks. If the people of Egypt get hungry enough or fed up enough, there is always the chance that they may rise up against the state. Mindful of that possibility, Hosni Mubarak must allow for at least some political freedom; and once he has granted that bit of free speech and elections, he must play the delicate game of repressing just the right amount, and not too much. No such delicacy has been required of Saddam Hussein. Assured of a steady supply of oil revenues, Saddam was long able to gas Kurdish Iraqis, execute his sons-in-law, and ensure that no one—at least no one within Iraq—had the means to overthrow him.

Externally, a regime like Iraq has had even less need to present a facade of legitimacy to the world than it has within. The reason is that the world, the West especially, needs the oil. Declining to buy Saddam's oil was never a viable choice, since Iraq is a large enough oil producer that cutting its supply would drive prices up sharply. Indeed, even as the United Nations imposed sanctions against Iraq during the 1990s, the world found a way to justify continued oil sales through the food-for-oil program. So Saddam acted as if he were a legitimate ruler, and for years the West acquiesced in the fiction of his legitimacy because it served Western interests in keeping the Middle East stable and Saddam's oil flowing. If Saddam had not made the risky and ultimately mistaken calculation that he could conquer Kuwait without the West's objecting, then the United States would, even in 2003, probably have shown little interest in going to war to remove him. Even if Saddam had developed weapons of mass destruction, the United States would have been unlikely to consider war against him had it not thought those weapons were poised to be used against itself, Israel, or its other regional allies.

An oil dictator, in other words, who collects the rent on his oil exports, then uses it to rule, lacks the handful of incentives to democratize that apply to dictators without oil. Within the category of dictatorships, the presence of oil makes democratization less likely. Considered within the separate category of states with oil, oil dictators are also less likely to make even limited progress toward democratization than are oil monarchies. Compared with an oil monarch, an oil dictator is not very susceptible to internal pressure from Islamist activists. Unlike a Muslim monarch, a dictator does not have a claim to legitimacy that is grounded in Islam or in local tradition. Saddam, for example, came to power in the days when secular Arab nationalism was the dominant political ideology, and he typically relied on the rhetoric of nation, not religion, in attempting to bolster his legitimacy. A secularist by inclination and practice, Saddam never even paid lip service to the importance of Muslim scholars. Because he maintained absolute control over what was said in Iraqi mosques, there was never a tradition of criticism on which local Islamists could draw. Indeed, Saddam's Islamist critics would end up in jail or dead much faster than would Islamist critics in oil monarchies, where Islam is often part of the government's claim to legitimacy. As even the legitimacy of Arab nationalism faded, Saddam came to rule by pure force.

All this means that there is little that can push an oil dictator in the direction of democratization. He is not responsible to his people, and he has few real allies. He just has customers, craven ones who want the product and do not especially care whom they have to pay. Saddam, in particular, has also had nervous neighbors. Although somewhat worried about being attacked, despite U.S. protection, Saddam's Arab neighbors have recently worried more about his skill at telling ordinary Arabs and Muslims that since he stands against the United States and Israel, he is a hero. During the Gulf War, Saddam turned his rather ineffectual Scud missiles on Israel mostly for public relations reasons. By becoming the first leader of an Arab country to fire a shot at Israel since 1973, Saddam was able to attract the attention and sympathy of many Arabs who were frustrated by what they saw as their governments' inaction in the face of Palestinian suffering. Saddam also had some success outside Iraq at deploying the rhetoric of Muslim identity in a way that made him seem like a Muslim victim of Western imperial aggression. Despite his long-standing secularism, Saddam added the words *Allah Akbar* to the Iraqi flag when the Gulf War began in order to symbolize that the Muslim cause was in his hands.

Though it could be hard to discern from Western media coverage, as tensions between the U.S. and Iraq grew, Arab rulers were worried that their citizens might side with Iraq in the case of war. That would make things difficult for Arab governments, whether monarchic or dictatorial. These governments have little choice but to side with the United States, at least tacitly, and this renders them susceptible to the argument that they are traitors to the Arab and Muslim cause. To make matters worse from their perspective, Saddam could always point to America's alliance with Israel so as to depict Arab leaders as taking sides against the oppressed Palestinians, a charge to which the rulers are exquisitely sensitive. If, on the other hand, the Arab states failed to support the United States in a war against Iraq, they would lose clout with America, as Jordan did in 1991. The Jordanian foreign minister made it clear that Jordan could not repeat this strategic mistake, but the Saudis have been more circumspect. American frustration with the Arab states can only deepen the division between them that became visible after September 11. Worse, Turkey's cautious willingness to serve as a launching pad for an American attack may cause the Arab states to lose ground against a longtime strategic adversary. Left to their own devices, Arab states would have preferred to see Saddam left alone—and if it had not been for post–September 11 geopolitics, the U.S. would probably have agreed. In the absence of external intervention in Iraq, democracy would have no chance there.

The example that proves the point is Libya, another oil dictatorship. For years, Muammar Qadhafi was a favorite American bogeyman. Libya sponsored terrorism, and the United States responded with sanctions and with occasional bombings. The United States effectively bestowed its imprimatur of chief nemesis on Qadhafi, which afforded an otherwise relatively unimportant dictator stature and cachet in the Arab world. (Making a Muslim into America's public enemy number one is a double-edged sword. Osama bin Laden earned the title after bombing American embassies in Kenya and Tanzania, and there is little doubt that it raised his profile both within and outside the Muslim world considerably, which may have helped him recruit and raise funds.)

In recent years, Qadhafi has apparently decided to ease away from high-profile terrorism and America-bashing. After years of sanctions, he consented to allow two Libyans to be tried in the Hague by Scottish judges on the charge that they planted the bomb that blew up Pan Am 103 over Lockerbie in 1988. (One was convicted, the other acquitted.) Qadhafi insists that he no longer sponsors terrorism, and while that may be an overstatement, the fact remains that George W. Bush left Libya off his "axis of evil" in January 2002. No one today is talking about liberating the Libyan people from Qadhafi's rule. And indeed, the Libyans are not even all that poor. Oil revenues make Libya one of the richest countries in Africa, with a GDP per capita of almost $9,000, more than twice that of Egypt. This money may never make it to the very poorest people, but Qadhafi is in a position to make sure none suffers privation of the kind that might drive people to revolution. The rehabilitation of Qadhafi from enemy to irrelevancy shows that oil dictators who don't step on too many toes can remain in power without the West's caring.

On the other hand, when the United States does decide to pursue the strategy it euphemistically calls "regime change," then both democracy and Islam may become centrally important to the future of the country where

American intervention occurs. The more the United States takes the lead in removing Saddam from power, the more likely that it, or perhaps the United Nations acting as its proxy, will end up establishing a government to replace Saddam's. That seems almost inevitable, since the strongest argument against removing Saddam is that doing so could plunge Iraq into chaos and destabilize the whole region as a result. The U.S. would have as much to lose from such a destabilization as anyone, and more, if the U.S. brought it about by getting rid of Saddam.

Even if the United States were to hand over the government of Iraq to the United Nations, the U.S. would inevitably have a role to play. This is true already in Afghanistan, where the U.S., having brought the Northern Alliance to power, has found that it cannot simply pick up and leave the Afghans to their own devices, but must continue to support Hamid Karzai's shaky interim government, on which it has pinned its hopes. Not only would leaving have the strategic cost of returning Afghanistan to the anarchy that led to the Taliban takeover in the first place, but it would tarnish the international prestige of the United States, which is now seen to have made a real but reluctant investment in the future of Afghanistan. These costs would be even more salient in a post–regime change Iraq, because Iraq, with its oil and prominent location on the Gulf, is much bigger and more important strategically and economically. Civil war in Iraq, even on a modest scale, might spill over to Turkey, Iran, or even Kuwait, and it would drive oil prices sky-high. American prestige would be even more on the line in the wake of a major deployment of ground forces than in Afghanistan, where Northern Alliance surrogates did most of the ground fighting after the American bombardment.

What sort of government will have to come into being in a post-Saddam Iraq? Whether Iraq were broken into pieces, or, as is far more likely, ruled as a unified whole, any government would have to meet some basic standard of democracy to seem even slightly legitimate. Vice President Dick Cheney and Secretary of Defense Donald Rumsfeld have acknowledged as much in conversations with Iraqi opposition leaders, all but promising the creation of democracy in post-Saddam Iraq. There has been no serious political opposition to Saddam within Iraq with the capacity to step in and claim legitimacy after Saddam's fall. Saddam has done too good a job of killing off any potential opponents. The Iraqi National Congress, a body that exists only in exile, has not had the opportunity to be chosen by the Iraqi people, so it is difficult to know how Iraqis will react to it. The only way any government could obtain even the most basic legitimacy would be through elections of some kind. Otherwise, whoever rules Iraq after Saddam will be just another dictator, imposed by the United States or the United Nations.

To justify the removal of Saddam, the United States will have to argue not simply that it is saving itself and Israel from the threat of weapons of mass destruction, but that it seeks to liberate the Iraqi people from an oppressive ruler who has kept them under his thumb for many years. Once the United States makes this argument, it follows that the United States must take account of the decisions and interests of the Iraqi people. That means that the Iraqi people must have a say in ruling themselves: in short, democracy.

To change the regime in Iraq, then, is to set a precedent for open intervention in the internal affairs of a foreign state. Setting that precedent will require the United States to articulate a policy for what happens when regimes are changed. In the light of America's commitment to democratic self-rule for its own citizens, it would be almost impossible for the United States to announce a public policy that would acknowledge that it could impose non-democratic government on other peoples. The imperative to state *some* policy has driven the U.S. toward the position that the new Iraq will be democratic.

A post-Saddam Iraq will inevitably become, in other words, a laboratory for trying out the mobile idea of democracy in front of the whole world. It might be different if there were some other option for the United States to try, such as a plausible government in exile, or an emir like the one in Kuwait whom the U.S. reinstalled after ejecting Saddam in 1991. But no such options exist in Iraq. There can be no restoration, just a glorious revolution. And in the language of democracy, the new order must guarantee the Iraqi people self-government.

That is where Islam will come into play. There are more Shiʻi Iraqis than Sunni Iraqis—a fact sometimes noted by those who fear that a post-Saddam Iraq might fall into a civil war—but both groups are equally likely to look to Islam to derive some political values and ideals. Shiʻis have the

model of Iran next door to consider, and Sunnis have the paradigm of Islamist activism in the Sunni Arab world. While Islamism is not at present a
force in Iraqi life, there is no reason to think that Iraqi Islam is very different
from Islam elsewhere in the Arab world. If Iraqis are freed to make political
decisions on their own behalf, Islamists will no doubt quickly arise to offer
Islamist solutions to Iraqi political problems. Islam is already a fact of life in
Iraq, and freeing the Iraqi airwaves guarantees that developments within
broader Islamic thought would reach Iraq almost instantaneously. Many
Iraqis would probably want Islam to play some role in their new government. Some number of Iraqis—one cannot say just how many—will immediately be interested in voting for new Islamic parties. In a free political
environment, those parties would probably span the range from moderate
and modernist to reactionary and extremist. It would be unwise to predict
how people would vote. The whole point of democracy is that the people
would get a chance to choose for themselves.

Or would they? Will a new democratic order in Iraq permit the participation of Islamic parties? Will it allow Islam to play a part in the ideology
or government of the new state? The United Nations, or the United States,
or whoever is in charge of the transition to democracy in Iraq, would now
face the challenge of asking whether democracy and Islam are compatible.

This may sound like a policymaker's nightmare; indeed, it is the kind
of scenario that has discouraged some realist foreign-policy experts from
counseling replacement of Saddam at all. But confronting the interaction
between democracy and Islam in a post-Saddam Iraq need not be disas-
trously difficult, so long as the powers that be keep in mind the possibility of
synthesis. Post-Saddam Iraq would pose an ideal opportunity for the world to
show its openness to the possibility of Islamic democracy, by embracing any
political parties or organizations that promise to work within the structures
of democratic constitutional government. That would mean that ideas associated with Islam would figure in an Iraqi constitutional convention, and
that Islamic democrats would be able to participate in a subsequent government. The Iraqi people would have to be put in a position where they
could choose. A new government would have little chance of being legitimate if the Iraqi people were denied the opportunity to rely on the ideals
and values of Islam to create it.

One of the problems with politics is that in practice, unlike in theory, one almost never starts from scratch. Many ideal theories of democracy begin by imagining people getting the chance to design their own government in a vacuum. That almost never happens. People live, for the most part, in states where government exists; when a revolution happens, most people get cut out of the decision making. That might not have to happen in post-Saddam Iraq. A coincidence of political and social forces might require the United States or the United Nations to give all the Iraqi people a say in their future government. Ironically, Islamic democracy might be able to emerge peacefully only under these artificial conditions. The U.S. or the West might find itself called upon to act as midwife for a synthesis of mobile ideas that would otherwise have a lot of trouble emerging on its own. Stranger things have happened.

The Big Picture: Islam, Democracy, and the Contact of Mobile Ideas

D
emocracy and Islam are mobile ideas that have come into contact over the course of a century. But only now, in the last
decade, have they entered a period in which self-conscious synthesis is a real possibility. The intellectual dimension of their
synthesis is that people are trying to make sense of the relationship between
democracy and Islam as abstract ideas. That includes a wide range of writers and thinkers in the Muslim world, whose names remain unknown to
most Westerners: Egyptian scholars like Yusuf al-Qaradawi and the late
Muhammad al-Ghazali; the Tunisian intellectual and sometime activist
Rachid Ghannouchi, now living in exile; the Iranian intellectual Abdolkarim Soroush, who travels between Iran and Western universities like
Harvard and Yale; and some young women intellectuals who write about
women and the interpretation of the Qur'an. These thinkers, some formally
trained as Islamic scholars, others self-taught, explore the relationship between democracy and Islam and reach optimistic conclusions. They are trying to work through points of compatibility and commonality between
democracy and Islam. Their ideas are reflected in the chapters in this book
that discuss the compatibility of democracy and Islam.

The intellectual dimension of the contact between democracy and
Islam also includes the thought of many and varied Western writers, academic and journalistic, who think about Islam and democracy from the

Western perspective. These Western writers' ideas, too, have influenced this book, even where that influence registers as respectful disagreement. The intellectual dimension of this historical process, though, is not restricted to writers, whether Muslim or Western or both. It also includes the thoughts and opinions of non-specialists, people in the Muslim world and the West who are trying to figure out how Islam and democracy interact. The historical process of ideas rubbing against one another includes the development of arguments and viewpoints about the ideas themselves.

The political dimension of the contact between democracy and Islam, on the other hand, draws upon abstract ideas, but operates in the real world, where ideas are put into action. In that process, the ideas are changed. Many people in the Muslim world will play roles in the political dimension of this historical process of contact. Islamic democrats who deploy the language and ideals of Islam in their political activities play a major part, of course. The Egyptian Center Party founders, and others like them throughout the Muslim world, are the front line in trying to develop Islamic democracy in practice. People who span the realms of politics and ideas, like President Khatami of Iran, have an especially great capacity to take the ideas they espouse and try to make them work. That ends up involving compromise, which is not always a bad thing. But it can also involve the transformation of the ideas into something entirely different. The Sudanese politician and intellectual Hasan al-Turabi was, during the 1970s and 1980s, one of the most provocative and sophisticated voices advocating the flexibility of Islam and its potential compatibility with some forms of democratic government. But when Turabi's faction took power in a coup in Sudan in 1989, Turabi himself became the ideologue and political operator behind a strongly undemocratic Islamic regime that banned political parties and sought to Islamize the country by a combination of consensus and force. Westerners who had been attracted to Turabi's ideas had to learn afresh the lesson that politics and ideas are connected but are not one and the same.

The political dimension includes more than just Islamic democrats. It also includes those who oppose Islamic democracy, whether from within the governments of the Muslim world or outside them. The argument that Islam and democracy are not and cannot be compatible has political consequences wherever it is made. Muslim monarchs and dictators play their parts here, but so do the foreign offices of Western countries and those who advise them. Former Assistant Secretary of State Edward Djerejian's speech about Algeria, in which he said that the United States was opposed to one person, one vote, one time, formed an important part of an ongoing political process. Huntington's *Clash of Civilizations* had political consequences because of who read it and how it influenced them. And one cannot always predict what the consequences of a work will be. The late Robert Nozick wrote a book of political theory when he was a young man that some treated as a kind of how-to for the Reagan and Thatcher revolutions; but Nozick often said, with characteristic exuberant, good-humored irony, that political conservatives were misreading his book.

In other words, the intellectual and the political dimensions of the contact of mobile ideas are mutually dependent. They are both necessary to a complicated historical process. The historical process has no predetermined outcome, but that is precisely what makes it so exhilarating. Both sides in this debate have the capability to influence the result. Arguing about the contact of ideas can have the effect of moving those ideas in one particular direction or another. We know for certain that some people think and have thought for some time that Islam and democracy are fundamentally incompatible. We also know that a growing number of people think, on the contrary, that Islam and democracy can be moved in the direction of synthesis. In the end, either side could be right. That is the nature of ideas. Perhaps the number and influence of people who consider democracy and Islam incompatible will turn out to be determinative. If so, these thinkers will in some sense have been right. On the other hand, perhaps those who are working toward a synthesis of Islam and democracy will ultimately convince enough people in the domains of the intellect and of politics that Islamic democracy will become a viable phenomenon. In that case, they will have been right.

The situation of Afghanistan in the wake of the American intervention there illustrates some of the challenge of applying ideas to practical circumstances. It would be hard to imagine a country more complicated than Afghanistan: numerous languages and ethnic groups, each enmeshed in a series of alliances and counteralliances with each other and with powers outside the country. Although Afghanistan was always a Muslim state, Islam did not begin to function as the glue holding together many Afghans across tribes and languages until the Soviet invasion. Then Afghans fought back, not just in the name of Afghanistan but in the name of Islam. They got help from the United States, which wanted to weaken the Soviets, and from Muslim countries who saw the Afghans as involved in a jihad against an oppressive, godless, non-Muslim force. When the jihad was over and the Soviets were out, though, the Islamic bond melted and the tribal alliances reasserted themselves. The alliance that defeated the Soviets could not hold the country together or govern it. When the Taliban, who had not liberated the country from the Soviets, entered Afghanistan preaching Islam, they had the capacity to conquer the whole country quickly and impose their extremist strain of Islam throughout.

The Taliban had help from Pakistan; they were largely, though not exclusively, from one ethnic group; and they mixed ethnic Pashtun customs with Islam almost unconsciously. But they were nevertheless drawing on Islam to consolidate their hold over the country. Like the anti-Soviet alliance, they used Islam as a source of cohesion. Then the United States decided, after September 11, to back the Northern Alliance, the rump of the alliance that had liberated Afghanistan a decade before. American bombs brought a quick end to Taliban rule. But bombs, while good for kicking out a government, are not good for building up a new one. Once in power, the Northern Alliance also had to draw on some idea or principle that would command sufficient loyalty to bring the country together.

The challenge facing the interim government installed by the United States is great. The new government cannot use Islam alone to draw the Afghans into one state. The Taliban made that idea look unpalatable to most Afghans, and the United States, which stands behind the government, would be uncomfortable with it, too. On the other hand, Islam will necessarily play a big role in a successful new Afghan state, because it is in some sense the only idea grand enough to create common bonds among Afghans of disparate tribes. The national idea of "Afghanistan" was never powerful enough in the past to create real unity in the country, and it is probably not strong enough today.

This is where the idea of democracy matters. The first major step for the new government, whether it eventually gains control over the warlords who still run various parts of the country or not, was to convene a *loya jirga* of tribal representatives. On its own, the *loya jirga*, a traditional Afghan institution, implies little about democracy as a mobile idea. But this first *loya jirga* will in turn give rise to a constitutional *loya jirga* to draft and perhaps ratify a new constitution for Afghanistan. The *loya jirga* will, in other words, decide what form the new government should take.

What is remarkable is that no one seriously doubts that the constitutional *loya jirga* will propose some sort of democratic government. There may be a symbolic role for the now-returned king, but no one thinks the *loya jirga* could possibly or credibly propose an oligarchy, autocracy, or traditional monarchy. Democracy is the watchword of the day. The idea of democracy has spread so effectively that no one sitting down to plan a new government anywhere today, under the watchful eyes of the world, could propose any different structure of government. Considering the fact that the United States put the new government in place, it will also have a stake in making sure that the government proposed by the *loya jirga* will be democratic.

Writing a democratic constitution at a representative constitutional convention does not guarantee democracy, of course. The world is littered with beautifully drafted constitutions that have been ineffective or ignored in practice. Bringing about democracy in Afghanistan will be an extraordinarily tall order; in fact, just creating a state that monopolizes the use of force may be beyond the capability of the Afghan leadership. Nation building is a tough business in which most fail and only a few succeed. Yet the identity to which the new state will inevitably aspire, right now, is that of Islamic democracy. Surely the fact that Afghanistan will aspire to be an Islamic democracy matters for understanding the interaction of democracy and Islam. At this particular juncture in history, both by contingent luck and as a result of the sheer durability and attractiveness of these two ideas, democracy and Islam now stand face-to-face.

§

PART THREE

The Necessity of Islamic Democracy

WHY DEMOCRACY?
THE PRAGMATIC ARGUMENT

A s Israeli tanks rolled into the West Bank in spring 2002, Muslim anger toward the United States mounted, especially in the Arab world. Composed of equal parts frustration at America's apparent unwillingness to restrain Ariel Sharon, resentment at the impotence of Arab governments in the face of American policy, and condemnation of the unresponsiveness of those governments to popular opinion, this sentiment coalesced into a grassroots boycott of identifiably American products. Anonymous leaflets and chain e-mails went around listing businesses to be avoided; in some places, the same messages also specified Arab-owned substitutes.

The boycott itself received little notice in the Arab or American press, and in economic terms it was not particularly harmful to American interests, mostly because franchises of McDonalds or Starbucks tend to be owned by local businesspeople, not Americans. The significance of the boycott lay in a grassroots conception of political action, relatively new to the Arab world, in which citizens sought to address themselves to what they took to be the underlying causes of policies they disliked. To say, as the boycotters did, that to buy a Coca-Cola was to buy a bullet to kill Palestinian babies, was to make America the cause of Palestinian suffering, and identify American economic interests as the leverage point for affecting U.S. policy.

The boycott also reflected the remarkable effect of technology in form-
ing and galvanizing public opinion. Text-messaging on mobile phones has
spread beyond the very rich to the middle class, allowing political opinion
to diffuse almost instantly. "A mobile in every hand" was the provocative advertising slogan adopted by Egyptian MobiNil in 2001, anticipating, a bit
hopefully, an era in which connectedness is not merely restricted to the
5 million or so disproportionately influential Egyptians who now have mobile
phone service. Where text-messaging does not go, there is unregulated satellite television. These media are fast, to be sure, but the really new element
is the absence of government control of the message, which all too often is
anti-American. The medium cannot be blamed for the message. Yet so long
as there exist reasons for merging anti-American feeling with resistance to
unjust governments, we can expect the technology to be used in ways that
do not correspond to the interests of the United States.

That Arab popular anger, formed in the crucible of the Israeli-Palestinian
conflict, focused itself so directly on the United States frames a familiar
pragmatic challenge to the argument that the U.S. ought to encourage
democratization in the Muslim world. Might Islamic democracy do more
harm than good for the United States? Even if Arabs who participated in the
boycott would probably have said that they hated American policy, not
America, the overwhelming sentiment of the great majority of Arabs toward
the U.S. was unquestionably negative at the moment of the boycott. Arab
governments, by contrast, remained relatively muted in their criticism, generally using back channels to express both their criticism of American support of Israel and their worry that popular Arab anti-Americanism would
soon turn itself into anger at the Arab regimes themselves.

The conflict between Israel and the Palestinian people lies not far below the surface of the concern that democratic Muslim states would elect
anti-American governments. America's close friendship with Israel is now
an accomplished fact, the result of Israel's having formed itself as a democracy, chosen the right side in the Cold War, and built its relationship with
the United States through strategic and military cooperation. The sincere,
vocal, and politically convincing efforts of Jewish Americans and their
sometimes unlikely domestic bedfellows have, over half a century, produced an alliance that has survived repeated changes in political party in

both the U.S. and Israel. It is no longer possible to say with certainty whether Democrats or Republicans are more firmly committed to maintaining what may fairly now be called America's second "special relationship."

Does America's support for Israel doom it to permanent unpopularity in the Muslim world? So long as the cycle of attack and retaliation continues, images of suffering Palestinians will continue to arouse deep anti-Israel feeling among Muslims everywhere. Inevitably the United States, as Israel's patron, will be held responsible. Yet the sincerity of Arab and Muslim sympathy for the Palestinians' plight should not obscure other elements bound up in anti-Israel and anti-American rhetoric. In particular, speaking out on behalf of Palestinians represents one of the only permissible avenues of political protest in much of the Muslim world. To attack Israel is also, more subtly, to criticize Arab governments for doing so little on behalf of the Palestinian cause. Denouncing the United States for backing Israel also implicitly functions as a condemnation of autocratic Arab governments who rely on support from the United States.

This intermingling of anti-Israel and anti-American sentiment with criticism of undemocratic Arab governments percolated to the surface during the round of pro-Palestinian protests in the Arab world in spring 2002. In Egypt, for example, where the protests were reportedly spearheaded by Islamists, chants against Israel and George W. Bush seamlessly transformed themselves into chants against Mubarak. No one was surprised when police intervened to stop the demonstrations, which left some protesters dead and others jailed. In Jordan, the cautious government went so far as to cancel Friday prayers at the largest mosques in Amman during the height of the protests, to avoid the possibility of uncontrolled marchers emerging in the aftermath of inspirational sermons. Even in normally quiet Saudi Arabia, where political protest on a mass scale is essentially unknown, the monarchy apparently arrayed troops on the corniche in the seaside city of Jedda after pro-Palestinian protests took place there, sending the message that further planned demonstrations had better not take place at all. The connection between the rights of Palestinians and the resentment of autocratic rule in Arab states is not obvious in thirty-second television clips, but it was not lost on any of the rulers in the region.

The intensity and trajectory of anti-Israel and anti-American opinion in the Arab world, then, are connected not only to Arab perceptions of Israeli and American actions, but also to the absence of democratic politics in Arab countries. More democracy in the Arab world would, in the short run, probably lead to governments more confrontational toward Israel than those presently in power. Islamists would receive an extra boost from their knack for tapping into anti-American rhetoric to capture the instincts of ordinary people. Yet it is unlikely that a more hostile initial attitude would lead to actual military confrontation, despite recent evidence suggesting that new democracies go to war more frequently than well-established ones. Democratically elected leaders would know just as well as today's Arab leadership that Israel has superior firepower and that any attack would be foolhardy.

Over the long run, one would not expect democratically elected Arab governments to maintain a posture toward Israel any harsher than that adopted by the autocrats. Opening the floodgates of political discourse in the Arab world will reduce the centrality of the Palestinian issue, as Arab citizens get the chance to express their opinions on the full range of government decisions involving domestic and foreign policy. Arab concern for the Palestinians will not disappear but will assume its place in relation to other pressing political and economic needs. Israel will begin to look more like a potential trading partner, and less like the neighborhood bully that it appears to be in the minds of many Arabs. It will no longer be as easy or as attractive for ordinary Arabs to fulminate against the United States when it is perceived as a potential friend to the Arab people, rather than to the dictators alone.

Over time, democracy in the Arab world should actually make lasting peace with Israel more likely. Democratic governments that must respond to public pressure will have to deliver on economic development. Trading relationships and business partnerships with Israel will be efficient ways to make that development happen, as Arab and Israeli businesspeople already know. Commerce is the way for Israel to integrate itself into the Middle East, and commerce will be better served by governments that must stand for reelection. In the end, Israel's hopes for real membership in the Middle Eastern community depend on Arab citizens accepting the normalization of relations. Only in a democratic environment is this outcome possible.

The Israeli-Palestinian conflict must not go on forever. Things look grim as of this writing, but for at least a decade moments of hope and despair have alternated. There remain radicals on both sides who say they will not settle for less than all the land, but clear super-majorities of Israelis and Palestinians say that a two-state solution is the answer. Crown Prince Abdullah of Saudi Arabia proposed normalization of relations with Israel should it accept the creation of a Palestinian state within pre-1967 borders, and the Arab League in principle accepted. Even Ariel Sharon has repeatedly said that a state of Palestine will someday exist. His vision of that state may be minimalist, but as the consternation in his own Likud Party showed, this statement represented an important concession to Palestinian national aspirations. These statements on both sides suggest a quiet recognition by realists of the inevitability of two states and of peace. Peace will come, whether it comes in this decade or in the next, after a new generation of leaders has emerged. Too many have too much to lose by the continuation of the conflict—the United States not least among them.

Democracy in the Arab world may not be, as some on the Israeli right have begun to say, a necessary precondition of peace between Israel and her neighbors. Israel, after all, managed to conclude peace treaties with Egypt under Sadat, and Jordan under King Hussein. But ordinary Arabs will be much less likely to accept normalization of relations with Israel if it is the unilateral decision of governments whose legitimacy they question. If and when Arab democracies reach peace agreements with Israel, Arab citizens will not be able to disclaim responsibility as they would if the peace treaties were made by autocrats. The Arab world will then have to take the psychologically necessary step of acknowledging that Israel is here to stay and that Palestinians will, realistically, have to settle for a state in an area significantly smaller than historic Palestine.

Even before lasting peace comes to pass, the United States can go some distance toward improving its popularity in the Arab world by resuming active involvement in the Israeli-Palestinian peace process. So long as the U.S. is seen to be and actually is concerned to reach a solution that will afford security to Israel and self-determination for the Palestinians, Arabs will accept, in the spirit of realism, that countries like the U.S. should and will stand by their traditional friends. All that the U.S. needs to do is to communicate publicly, by words and deeds, that the Palestinians matter too, and that they have rights that need to be respected alongside Israel's right to security. Calling for democratic reform of the Palestinian Authority, as President Bush has done, makes perfect sense, but only so long as the United States takes action to help bring about this reform. Otherwise the U.S. runs the risk of looking like it is making Palestinian democracy a condition of negotiation in order to avoid engaging at all.

It is often said in explanation of America's support for Israel that the latter is the only democracy in the Middle East. If this is so, and America's natural friends are those who share its political values, then it should follow that the United States would benefit from having more democratic friends in the region. But what concrete benefits will accrue to the U.S. if Muslim countries become increasingly democratic and correspondingly more pro-American? Oil should continue to flow at competitive prices, but that is already true under autocratic government. Security in the region will still have to be kept at a high level over the short term, and so long as there exist non-democratic regimes, it will be necessary to help protect democratic ones against potential threats. American security on the domestic front may improve somewhat as the threat to the U.S. from angry Muslim militants is reduced, but there is no guarantee of this, and as we learned on September 11, it takes only a few extremists to inflict enormous damage.

These benefits, then, are marginal compared with the likelihood that the United States will have gained for itself a set of new allies whose allegiance depends more on shared values than momentary convenience. It would be too simple to claim, as some have, that democracies never attack one another or that their interests cannot diverge sharply. European democracies formed the European Union in no small part in order to avoid being overwhelmed by the international economic and political power of the United States, and the Europeans know perfectly well that their interests and those of the U.S. are not identical. But no one in the United States seriously fears attack from any member of the European Union. The greater the role of democracy in Russia, the less likely it becomes for Russia to make war on democracies elsewhere. This was the theory behind imposing democracy on Germany and Japan after World War II, alongside the economic assistance of the Marshall Plan. And this strategy worked, to a remarkable degree, even though Germany's Weimar experiment with democracy was short-lived and Japan had no tradition of democracy despite the existence of a parliament under the Meiji constitution.

Democracies are also often more predictable than dictatorships when it comes to figuring out how a country will react to a particular event or stimulus. It is always a challenge to predict how a particular election will come out, but no elected party is likely to veer very far away from what it thinks are the wishes of the people it needs to reelect it. Democracies are in the main transparent when it comes to making major decisions; and when they are not transparent there is likely to be internal criticism of that failing. By contrast, autocracies, whether dictatorships or monarchies, make policies behind closed doors and strike alliances with whatever internal and external forces are necessary to maintain their control. Individual leaders may appear to be rational, but that will not always be the case. There are those who maintain that Saddam Hussein's career can be explained by reference to a model of rational choice, and they may be correct after the fact, but even these observers often have not been able to predict what Saddam's next move would be at any point. Qadhafi, too, has been notoriously unpredictable in ways that might be thought irrational. So the benefits associated with the greater predictability of democracies' behavior could be significant for the United States.

On the other hand, if the United States fails to support democracy in the Muslim world, the consequences may prove to be very dire, at least in some of the most important countries in the region. Revolution remains a meaningful possibility in a number of Arab and Muslim states so long as democratization makes no progress. The governments that would come to power through revolution would be far worse than the governments that would be selected democratically—more irrational, more hard-line, more anti-American, and more violent. If the U.S. makes no effort to help develop democratic institutions or practices in the Muslim world, then these are very unlikely to develop entirely on their own. They are still less likely to develop should the United States persist in its policy of actively opposing democratization in the region out of fear of encouraging Islamist parties. Specifically, where democratic development does not occur, the likelihood of eventual violent revolution remains great and can be expected to grow. When that revolution comes, as it did in Iran, those who revolt will take as their archetypal enemy the country that supported the governments that they overthrew: namely, the United States.

It may sound alarmist to compare various Muslim states to the Iran of 1978. The conditions that produce revolution are very particular, and the exact Iranian pre-revolutionary combination of rapid economic growth and widespread disaffection even among elites does not exist in the contemporary Muslim world. But the possibility of revolution is nonetheless real. Egypt, for example, remains so mired in economic hardship and hopelessness that its business elites wonder openly whether their disconnection from the general population is comparable to the disconnection felt by wealthy Iranians just before their revolution. Some 17 million people live in Cairo as of last count. Perhaps 12 million of these have no proper housing; they live in informal squatter communities where they receive only minimal government services, and, lacking legal title to their homes, they are at the mercy of extortionate "landlords" and government officials. Combine this poverty and oppression with a sense of distrust of government, and just enough freedom of the press to enable Egyptians to know how badly their situation compares with that of people elsewhere, and one has, if not the full recipe for revolution, at least many of the necessary ingredients.

Saudi Arabia's oil economy keeps it relatively much better off than Egypt, yet unemployment for Saudi men is near 30 percent. A new "Saudification" policy of reducing the number of South Asian guest workers cannot on its own compensate for this unemployment, particularly as many of those workers fill jobs that Saudis are not prepared to hold. The Saudi monarchy itself does not and indeed cannot know precisely the chances of an uprising of the disaffected, but after September 11, it knows that rejection of the regime is not limited to the poor but extends across all sectors of society. In Pakistan the possibility of a coup is ever present, and although that coup would probably not come from among the grassroots Islamists, it remains possible that Islamically oriented factions within the military and the Inter-Services Intelligence might be the key figures in a move against President Musharraf's government.

The possibility of revolution in one or several Muslim countries calls for a calculation of cost. The options are a gradual transition to democracy, in which Islamists or other anti-American parties might achieve some gains in the short term; or preserving the status quo and hoping for the best, while bearing the significant risk of violent revolution. In the starkest terms, the question is whether to entertain the risk of disaster in the form of a revolution that is not certain but would be extraordinarily costly, or to take on the less costly risk of destabilization that definitely accompanies a process of democratization. This is the kind of risk-management question about which reasonable people could differ; but it is also a question that has an answer. A strong case can be made that it would be better to have gradual democratization, with all its hiccups and uncertainties, rather than take a chance of revolution with its consequences of anti-Americanism and general regional trauma. One lesson of September 11 is that it is less costly to manage known risk than it is to confront unknowable risk. Known risks can be evaluated, planned for, and sometimes avoided.

Of course, democracies can fail just like autocracies; a glance at contemporary Latin America suffices to show that. But there is a further cost that must be added: the cost to Muslims themselves of remaining under autocracy. Without American assistance or encouragement, most Muslims will never have the opportunity to live flourishing lives in which they can pursue their goals and dreams as they would like. The lack of freedom in the Muslim world is not only a circumstance to be condemned or bemoaned or blamed on the Muslims alone. It is also a tragedy of the first order, tragic because it is possible to see how it could be averted. Poverty and disease in sub-Saharan Africa are tragic in a different sense; they might be palliated by increased resources, but their enormity is now such that it is not obvious how the horror could be avoided altogether. Muslims, however, could live freely and relatively well if only they could get out from under their autocratic governments, which remain in place with the complicity of the West.

The path of least resistance for Europe and the United States is to do nothing out of the ordinary, to wash their hands of the Muslim struggle against injustice while telling one another that national character is destiny, and that the Muslims have brought their troubles upon themselves. That distanced stance may salve the consciences of the former colonial powers of Europe and the American superpower today, but it must not be allowed to hide a tragedy for which the West is partly responsible. If nothing changes, or if violent revolution comes, as it did in Iran, it will be because no one was willing to disrupt today's convenience for tomorrow's necessity.

———◦•◦———

Neutralizing Anti-Americanism
by Refuting It

Right now, many of the world's Muslims keenly feel that the West, and particularly the United States, is arrayed against them. Evidence to the contrary, such as the American interventions on behalf of Bosnian Muslims, and later on behalf of Muslim Kosovars, is largely—and unfairly—ignored when this calculus is made. No doubt the reason lies in America's alliances with unpopular and undemocratic governments in the Muslim world and its steadfast support for Israel.

The Muslim perception of U.S. hostility is frustrating for Americans who would like to insist that they bear no ill will toward Muslims, and that the Bosnian intervention, for example, which no country in the world save the United States was prepared to undertake, demonstrates that absence of hostility. Yet the fact remains that the U.S. faces a serious problem of perception in the Muslim world. Suppose, then, that the U.S. does not stand idly by, but shifts policies to encourage democratization in the Muslim world. Such a change in policy, if handled correctly, would likely undermine anti-Americanism among Muslims. It would, in other words, deprive Islamists and others of one of their most reliable weapons: anti-Americanism itself. The more the U.S. pressures Muslim governments to pursue policies of democratization that correspond to what America says are its highest ideals, namely freedom and democracy, the harder it will be for Islamists to

argue that the United States stands in their way and at the side of their oppressors.

How important is it for the United States to begin to convince people
in the Muslim world that it does not stand against their aspirations to self-
government? This question raises a more general problem for America's status as a superpower. If a superpower resembles a traditional empire, then
there is no need for the United States to be liked by anyone outside its borders. The cultures of empires may sometimes be emulated, especially by
colonized elites, but empires themselves are rarely loved. To be effective as
empires they must be feared, and what is feared is generally hated. The subject peoples of the Roman Empire felt little affection for their masters. The
Ottomans, Muslims themselves, were nonetheless hated by many Arabs
and by other non-Turkish subject peoples in the Muslim world. Both foreign policy realists and critics of American power believe it is naive to expect the United States to be well liked so long as it continues to impose its
will on weaker countries. The realists think that the U.S. should accept resentment as the cost of doing business, while the critics think the U.S.
should stop being a superpower altogether; but they agree that superpower
status breeds inevitable resentment.

If, on the other hand, superpower status represents a new kind of
power, one grounded almost as much in good will and influence as in military might, then it matters very much whether the United States is perceived as friend or foe to the peoples of the Muslim world. One billion two
hundred million Muslims cannot be dismissed lightly, and these Muslims
are spread across many countries, unlike the billion-plus Chinese, who,
while they have an important diaspora, are primarily concentrated in main-
land China, or the comparable number of Indians, most of whom live on
the South Asian subcontinent. For those who think that America's position
as a superpower does more good than harm, and should therefore be maintained, a shift in policy that would improve America's place in Muslims'
hearts and minds must be desirable indeed.

There is reason to think that even Islamists, hostile to the United States
since the Iranian revolution made anti-Americanism into a cliché of Islamism, might begin to change their views if American policies changed.
Islamic politics is not inherently anti-American. Although Islamists have

always condemned the governments of the Muslim world as unjust and un-Islamic, they may be perfectly prepared to work alongside the United States if it respects their basic goals and interests. Many of the members of the Afghan Northern Alliance could plausibly be characterized as Islamists—although of course their Islamism is very different from that of the Taliban whom they have replaced. The Northern Alliance was fully prepared to cooperate with the U.S. once the latter turned its attention to Afghanistan on September 12, 2001, and indeed some of its leaders, notably the late Ahmed Shah Massoud, actively sought American assistance even before the Taliban became America's enemy.

Islamist politicians running for office in elections brought about, at least in part, by American pressure, could still try the anti-American slogans and policies that have worked for them in the past. But then they would face the risk that voters would consider these views outdated once American policy had helped bring about the very elections for which the candidates were standing. Islamists might therefore tone down or abandon their anti-American rhetoric in favor of policies that emphasized Islamic values and appealed to a domestically focused constituency.

This has been the strategy of Islamic parties in Turkey, where anti-Americanism is not particularly effective for getting votes, and where most Turks agree that entrance into the European Union must be the lodestar of Turkish economic policy. Turkish Islamists campaign on their incorruptibility and their ability to get things done. Local Islamist politicians claim credit for the improvement of public transit in Istanbul, and the electorate seems to take them at their word. There is nothing in the Qur'an about making the subway trains run on time, but mass transit is good municipal politics, and focusing on it is an effective way of telling people who cannot afford cars that the Islamists put their interests first.

Even if U.S. policy were to change, some extreme Islamists would still hate America. But it is worth noting that even Osama bin Laden did not purport to condemn the United States for what it essentially is, but for the policies it has pursued. Calling the United States and the West "crusaders," as bin Laden did, was intended to impugn the U.S. not for its Christianity, but rather for pursuing policies of intervention in Muslim lands that for bin Laden recalled the Crusades. The rhetoric of "Westoxification" (*gharbzadegi*, in the Persian coinage), so beloved of the Iranian revolutionaries who saw the West as the great Satan, has largely disappeared from Islamist circles. The main reason for this change is that globalization has made Western technology and culture more widely accepted in the Muslim world than they were twenty years ago. It would today seem quixotic even for the most radical Islamists to reject Western influence in Muslim lands altogether. More moderate Islamists, far from rejecting all Western or American culture and ideas, are now prepared to say that democracy itself is not foreign to Islam.

Among Muslims who are not Islamists, the transition away from anti-Americanism will be still easier. Many, probably most, Muslims feel a deep attraction to and admiration for American values of freedom, democracy, and even the free market. After all, the United States has succeeded in generating prosperity for its people and unparalleled world power. In the minds of many Muslims, these are successes to be emulated, not resented.

The criticism that is voiced again and again in the Muslim world is not that the United States is fundamentally flawed, but that it has failed to live up to its own values in its policies toward the Muslim world. Part of this has to do with the perception that the U.S. government has not been sympathetic to the situation of the Palestinian people, but an equal measure derives from American support of undemocratic Muslim governments.

Because Muslims already believe that America in the abstract stands for freedom and democracy, they will be quick to embrace America not simply as an ideal, but as an ally. Muslim anger at the hypocrisy of the United States may be wide, but it is not deep. It is a mistake to think that ordinary Muslims, or even Islamists, are inevitably or unalterably opposed to the U.S. They watch American television, buy American goods—at least when not in the grips of exceptional frustration—and are learning English in schools and on television and the Internet. Indeed, the very fact that so many Muslims say they are prepared to embrace democracy, a system they associate with the United States and its success, provides striking evidence that anti-Americanism may be overcome if the U.S. loosens its embrace of rulers who do not respond to the needs or concerns of their people.

That many Muslims hold the United States to a much higher standard of conduct than their own governments or those of Europe can be frustrating. The U.S. is regularly condemned for simply following its own interests, when it is readily acknowledged that all governments do the same. But arguably, Muslims' readiness to hold the U.S. to a higher standard reflects a latent pro-Americanism, even when it is being deployed to criticize America harshly. It makes sense to criticize the United States for following its own interests only if one believes, as do many Americans, that the U.S. can and must stand for something greater than self-interest. Many Muslims believe that America actually has the capacity to be a new kind of world power, one that stands for principle. This belief compels them to demand that the United States achieve this goal, and it drives them to criticize the U.S. when they perceive it as behaving unfairly. So if the U.S. were to begin to signal to Muslims that it cared about more than its own interests, narrowly defined, and was ready to make self-government for Muslims a part of its general policy, it could expect a transformation in Muslim attitudes.

Encouraging democracy in the Muslim world is not a panacea for all the problems that exist there, nor indeed for all the challenges to American interests in the Middle East and beyond. But it is a beginning, one that could lead to a range of improvements and to a serious attempt to bring greater internal logic to American foreign policy. At present, the Muslim world stands as a remarkable exception to the post–Cold War consistency of that foreign policy. In Africa, America's natural allies are those countries that, like South Africa, have either embraced or substantially expanded their democracies in recent years. In China, the United States has tried, for better or worse, to strike a balance between encouraging reform of the People's Republic via economic liberalization and expressing its support for Chinese rights activists like those who expressed their yearning for democracy at Tiananmen Square. In Latin America, where the United States during the Cold War was not very supportive of democracy, U.S. policy has improved in this regard, albeit with some throwback inconsistencies. The policy of encouraging democratization is a sensible one, and outside the Muslim world it no longer requires extensive justification. With any luck, that will soon be the case in the Muslim world as well.

DOING THE RIGHT THING

The pragmatic and realist arguments in favor of consistency and generating good will toward the United States do not exhaust the range of arguments in favor of encouraging democratization in the Muslim world. There is also the American aspiration to do the morally right thing, shared by many people outside the foreign policy establishment and by a surprisingly large number within. In fighting communism, it was always possible to argue that compromises with respect to the undemocratic behavior of particular allies could be justified by the greater goal of defeating communism; perhaps some of the time this was so. But with the Cold War over, the old ends-justify-the-means argument no longer applies in most of the world.

Cold War habits live on, however, and this has led to a similar attempt to justify America's alliances with Muslim dictators. The argument that we must support dictators or else accept the role of Islamists can be couched in moral terms, and it sometimes is, especially with respect to the rights of women. Yet this argument makes sense only if dictatorships are better than the governments that might replace them. It is unfair to compare the dictatorships that exist to the worst Islamist governments that can be imagined, because those Islamist governments might never come into existence if citizens of Muslim states choose to vote for moderate Islamists or secular government. Even if a radically Islamist government were to come to power through free elections that included women, it is still not obvious that such a government would be morally worse than the unelected dictatorships and monarchies that currently prevail. If women could vote, free elections in Saudi Arabia would at least produce a government that allowed women to drive, which is more than they can do now.

It emerges that very little in the way of moral argument can justify a policy of continuing to back autocratic government when we have the option of exerting pressure toward democracy. The argument that Muslims must get democracy for themselves is spurious in the light of the West's active support for the undemocratic regimes that presently exist. Similarly bankrupt is the isolationism that crops up when the right decides it cannot be bothered with the needs of oppressed foreigners, or the left prefers to keep its hands clean rather than run the risk of neocolonialism. At this late date, no one can reverse either America's superpower status or the pervasive interaction between peoples and states that we call globalization. The United States and the West are already involved in the politics of Muslim states and the lives of Muslims. Western ideas like democracy are affecting the Muslim world, and so is the Western policy that eschews democratization in practice.

That is why the moral dimension of the argument for democratization must not be treated as a luxury that cannot be afforded in an uncertain world: moral ideas are deeply interwoven in the fabric of America's position as a superpower. Today, the familiar observation that morality and self-interest are both at work in American foreign policy has a much richer meaning than is usually supposed. What makes America a superpower, imitated and admired even as it is feared and reviled, is not only its unmatched military strength, but its claim to embody democracy and freedom. To the extent that the United States gives the lie to that claim, it weakens itself as a superpower. This is so in the practical sense that inconsistency makes it more difficult to persuade other countries or peoples to do what the United States wants, and also in the deeper sense that America weakens its own resolve when it fails to live up to the values that define it. In the eyes of the world, America stands for the idea of democracy—an idea that can and must be universalized if it is to make good on its underlying values of liberty and equality. When, far from encouraging the spread of democracy, America impedes it, it becomes a lesser America.

So although the right thing and the pragmatically useful thing cannot always perfectly correspond, in the sphere of American foreign policy, when the spread of democracy is concerned, the two become inextricable. Spreading the idea of democracy serves America's pragmatic interests because it encourages others to see themselves through a prism of values that brings them closer to the way that America wants to see itself. At the same time, encouraging democracy, in the sense of allowing people to choose leaders and government themselves, enables the United States to fulfill the moral values of liberty and equality that lie at the heart of any democracy worthy of the name.

This distinctive combination of realism and idealism merges practicality and morality. It demands that we improve our material condition and status in the service of producing the morally correct outcome. Safety, wealth, and, yes, power are worthwhile only to the extent that they enable us to live in a way that makes us proud. The case of encouraging democratization in the Muslim world, then, is one of those where the right policy and the instrumental policy are mutually dependent. By adopting this policy, the United States can produce results that will enable Americans to look in the mirror and see what, deep down, they want and need to see—a foreign policy informed by the values that Americans would want applied to themselves.

There is a persistent, if sometimes disingenuous, counterargument that is often made against Western intervention to promote democracy in non-Western countries: that democracy is not a one-size-fits-all system of government but is intimately tied to particular Western values, ideals, and historical conditions. The argument is not simply that democracy does not suit non-Western contexts but that it would be hegemonic and wrong, even colonialist or imperialist, for the West to impose democracy where it is not a "naturally growing" form of government. I have perhaps invited this objection by explicitly connecting the encouragement of democracy with America's superpower status. Regarding most of the Muslim world, however, this argument cannot possibly be convincing.

The reason is that the great majority of Muslim countries have constitutions that impose, in theory, a democratic or quasi-democratic system of government. If the Egyptian constitution itself calls for free parliamentary elections, freedom of speech, and the rule of law, then it is not an imposition of foreign values to encourage Egypt to live up to its own basic law. The Jordanian and Moroccan monarchies exist under constitutions that provide for freely elected parliaments and many civil liberties—it is a question of making good on those constitutional promises.

The handful of Muslim countries, most notably Saudi Arabia, that do not have a constitutional structure devoted to democracy may make this argument with more candor and force. But even they must confront the argument that many countries lacking indigenous traditions of democracy have successfully adopted democracy in the modern era. At all events, the Saudis can do no more than assert that their citizens do not want democracy. They show no interest in putting the question up for general discussion. If a referendum, or even a freely conducted opinion poll, revealed that, after reflection, the Saudi public did not want a greater say in ruling itself, then maybe it would be wrong to pressure Saudi Arabia to adopt democratic institutions. But there has been no such poll or referendum, and part of the purpose of the Saudi argument that countries should be left to their own devices is to make sure that there never is. The Saudis also say that gradual change is the hallmark of their society, and that they therefore must be left to proceed at their own pace. Yet history shows that the Wahhabization of Saudi Arabia actually happened rather rapidly, and subsequent changes in the Saudi state structure were only gradual when it was in the interests of the monarchy to make them so.

This is not to assume that every country in the world necessarily wants Western-style democracy. Democracy may not be the only just way to run a government, and many democracies in the real world turn out not to be very just. The point is that as a moral matter, Muslims, like everybody else, should have the opportunity to make basic decisions about government for themselves. The fact that a country is not democratic, however, is not good evidence that its citizens do not wish for it to be more democratic. If Muslims choose democratic government, then they ought to be assisted in achieving it.

If, on the other hand, they choose something else, that, too, should be permitted to exist undisturbed.

To propose that most Muslims would prefer greater democratization to what they have now is not to insist that they wish to be Americanized. The institutions of Islamic democracy will not look precisely the same as American democratic institutions, nor should they, unless that is what Muslims want. Democracy, even in the West, comes in many guises. Democracies disagree about how much liberty and equality citizens should have, and how best to guarantee them. These are legitimate subjects of debate within democratic structures, and one would expect them to be debated in Islamic democracies as well.

As for the argument that democracy is peculiarly Western, and therefore cannot succeed in the Muslim world or cohere with Muslim conceptions of government, the short answer is that Muslims can adopt any view or system that they want and bring it into coherence with Islam by their own efforts. It is certainly true that modern liberal democracy was initially a product of a particular Western historical process. But Indian liberal democracy is a product of Indian political forces interacting with, reshaping, and constructing their own political ideals and institutions. After fifty years, it is not a foreign transplant but a homegrown and vital phenomenon.

It is a distinctive feature of ideas that they can grow and develop in contexts very far from the ones in which they first came into being. Indeed, if the category of mobile ideas has any special historical import, it is because such ideas cannot be restrained or limited to the environments where they began. It is therefore misguided to criticize an idea on the sole ground that it has convinced people of something new and different from what they believed before.

V. S. Naipaul adopts a form of this view when he suggests that Islam has had a particularly deleterious effect in non-Arab countries like Indonesia, Pakistan, and Iran. He calls non-Arabs "converts" to Islam even when that conversion took place more than a thousand years ago, and he blames many of the difficulties in these countries on the domination of pre-conversion cultures by mobile Islam. Naipaul's argument seems inapt when one realizes that many, perhaps most, cultures and civilizations are based on interactions between different ideas; and after all, the Arabs themselves converted to Islam from their preexisting faiths. The argument seems no better when applied to denigrate democracy that has taken root in non-Western countries. True, Indians may in some sense be seen as "converts" to democracy. In this sense, though, so were America's founding fathers, and the black Jacobins of the Haitian revolution. Perhaps everyone who adopts a mobile idea is a convert to it. There is nothing troubling in that notion. The worth of ideas is measured by their content and their effects, not by who had them first.

———————

How to Do It

A year to the day after he left office, Bill Clinton hosted a conference on Islam and America at New York University. After a number of Muslim intellectuals criticized America's failure to encourage democracy in the Muslim world, Clinton rose to respond. "I didn't do as good a job of that as I should have," Clinton said, "but I couldn't figure out how to do it." Alliances with America's non-democratic allies stood in the way. More than an ordinary political excuse, Clinton's unusual admission described a quandary that has long attended efforts to encourage democratization among America's allies. If a country is America's enemy, it is straightforward enough to oppose its government, and that alone may amount to promoting an alternative. But when one is dealing with an ally, particularly an ally vulnerable to violent overthrow, it is a great risk to criticize the ally too intensively. It is also bad manners diplomatically, which may sound trivial, but is not so in a world where governments are repeat players who must establish reputations as cooperative partners.

Clinton's response may also be seen as a challenge to specify a practical way in which the United States can encourage and reward democratization among its Muslim allies without compromising its own interests. In some fundamental sense, no one can force democracy on anyone else; yet unless Muslims who want democracy can obtain help from abroad, it will be all but impossible for them to pressure their governments to afford them the opportunity to participate in decision making. On its own, the Saudi monarchy cannot be expected to offer significant democratic reforms to its people; nor can the government of Egypt, so long as President Mubarak believes that continued limitation on political freedom remains necessary to maintain even a modicum of social order.

There exists a range of ways in which powerful governments like the United States can influence governments like those of the Muslim world. These begin with the creation of positive incentives grounded in economics, trade, aid, and political cooperation; they include counter-incentives such as strengthening alliances with countries that are strategically arrayed against the state one seeks to influence; and ultimately, under certain circumstances, they might even include the use of force—what Clausewitz famously called politics by other means.

If these methods sound interventionist, that is because they are. But interventionism on its own must not be judged to be improper or impolitic until one has thoroughly examined the context in which the intervention will be deployed. There is no neutral position for states that interact with others in the global world. When a superpower trades with one partner, it affects the economy not only of that partner but of all other potential trading partners who have been passed over. The same is doubly true of strategic and military alliances, where the zero-sum game is even more apparent.

The answers to Clinton's challenge, then, do not lie in some radically innovative theory of international politics, nor do I propose to suggest such a theory. What is needed instead is a subtle shift in perspective regarding the deployment of familiar techniques. In particular, this means being prepared to call Muslim allies' bluffs when they insist that they cannot respond to American prodding because of internal pressures. When the United States defers to this excuse, as it frequently does, it encourages bad behavior, creating perverse incentives for undemocratic governments to preserve the most threatening opposition groups while repressing moderate opposition that might look more palatable to the West. Proper incentives, though, can work if they are matched to the particular conditions of the country the United States is trying to affect.

The approach of targeted economic aid in exchange for measurable, sustainable political reform might be extremely effective in Muslim states that are relatively poor, such as Arab states without oil. Egypt, for example, is in desperate need of some way to enable its citizens to generate wealth in order to support themselves. In the early 1990s, there was a brief moment in which Egypt seemed to be focused on structural change, reducing public-sector jobs and streamlining the possibility of the formation of new businesses. There was serious talk of judicial reform, and an air of excitement among Arab businesspeople interested in investing in Cairo. The efforts of the nineties faltered, however, for reasons that are difficult to discern precisely but seemed to relate largely to the entrenched power of the government and military leaders who resisted reform to protect their fiefdoms. Starting a business in Egypt, much less maintaining one over time, remains a daunting challenge for any but the most skilled in manipulating bureaucracy and negotiating the corridors of power.

So Egypt, like other oil-less states, is badly in need of economic development assistance at every level, from educating the poorest people to creating industries in which they can work. American aid today comes mostly in the form of arms, and so does little to stimulate the economy or the creation of jobs. It would not cost much for the United States and Europe to offer further economic assistance in the form of direct aid, expertise, investment, and even debt relief, contingent upon the legalization of a broader range of political parties and the holding of truly free parliamentary elections. This would be meddling, true, but meddling of a sort that one can hardly imagine the Egyptian public resenting. If anything, there is likely to be a rush of other relatively impoverished, undemocratic countries, Muslim and non-Muslim, lining up to see if they too can get help in exchange for opening their political processes. Europe should welcome the opportunity to improve conditions in the Muslim world, if only because of the unappealing European impulse to discourage Muslim immigration to Europe. And it might be easier than one would think to get such assistance approved by Congress. Promoting greater liberty in autocratic countries is a bipartisan idea, one embraced by rock-ribbed Republicans who condemn Arab repression as well as by progressive Democrats who think that America should encourage liberal values abroad.

Pakistan, another poor country, is presently receiving significant U.S. aid simply in exchange for its support of the American intervention in

Afghanistan; but because of concern about President Musharraf's capacity to keep a firm hand on the country, the United States has done relatively little to demand democratization. In the short term, the U.S. may need Musharraf to remain in power in order to continue its fight against terror. But the U.S. should still pressure him to ensure that elected officials have a real say in governing Pakistan, so that over time, a stable, democratic political structure can be built. Increased assistance to Pakistan, which would surely enhance Musharraf's own tenuous legitimacy, could be made contingent on the progress of such meaningful democratization.

The aid can be targeted, furthermore, to purposes that serve the long-term goal of improving the political culture of Pakistan in regard to democracy. Funding the state schools that have fallen into disrepair over the last decade of Pakistan's economic troubles would encourage education that follows the government's relatively secular curriculum rather than the purely religious curriculum of the madrasas. There is no need to tell Pakistan what it must teach in its schools, and indeed such an approach would likely backfire. But imagine the benefit to the United States if it were associated with providing education to young people in Pakistan and elsewhere in the Muslim world. The strategy would be far more effective than standing on the sidelines while complaining that curricula in the schools in Muslim countries speak ill of the U.S. and Israel.

Cash grants are not the only or even the best way to proceed in most contexts. Trade is a further effective tool to the extent that it is followed by serious efforts to establish relations between the private sector in the targeted country and in the United States. Jordan's free trade agreement with the U.S. is an example both of the value of such an incentive and of its limitations when it is not accompanied by serious follow-up. The trade agreement rewards King Abdullah of Jordan for talking a good game about the need for economic liberalization and democratization. Without it, it would be far more difficult for Abdullah to proceed as he has done.

In practice, however, Iraq remains Jordan's largest trading partner, and it has proven difficult for Jordanian industry to find purchasers for its products in the United States. One barrier is the difficulty of setting up methods for payment within the outdated legal structures that obtain in Jordan. A greater barrier is simply the lack of experience and contacts of Jordanian businesses in discovering American markets for their goods. This problem could be rectified at relatively low cost by paying for private-sector middlemen to seek out potential partners for Jordanian firms. In theory, if the market works as it should, such middlemen should present themselves without government help. But the market takes time, and time is especially precious for leaders like King Abdullah who must quickly show results in the form of new jobs in order to build the legitimacy of their reform efforts. Government can help here without significantly distorting market forces. If Jordan lacks the resources to pay for such assistance on its own, then the United States should fill the gap. Jordan knows how important the development of further trading relationships with the United States is, and that is surely one reason that King Abdullah in May 2002 named a businessman with no prior diplomatic experience as his ambassador to Washington, and why the new minister of industry and trade is a sophisticated international lawyer. The United States should do its part to make the incentive of free trade practically useful to Jordanians in Jordan.

The micro-example of Jordanian trade stands for a more basic shift in attitude that is needed if the process of encouraging democratization is to work effectively. The United States must ask how a given piece of economic assistance will fit into the overall goal of creating incentives to democratize. Incentives, after all, only work when directed at the right recipients. And incentives involve initial compromise when directed at monarchs or dictators who presently have the power to promote democracy or repress it. It is always possible to argue that by helping sustain an unelected president, the United States actually delays democracy by staving off internal challenges to governmental legitimacy. The way to avoid this paradox is to insist, at each stage, that greater political openness actually follow on the offer of assistance. Once parliaments become more lively and effective in countries like Egypt, Pakistan, and Jordan, the next stage of incentives will be aimed at encouraging leaders to submit themselves to meaningful election.

Transitions of power at the highest levels are a delicate business, and sensitivity to circumstances is necessary. A president like Mubarak, who has governed for decades and is well into his 70s, cannot realistically be expected to put himself up for general election, but he can be expected to usher in meaningful elections for a successor, on the model of Augusto

Pinochet in Chile. Kings in Jordan and Morocco can be urged to increase the scope of prime ministerial power. President Musharraf must eventually be urged to return the Pakistani presidency to the role that Pakistan's constitution initially envisioned, that of a head of state who chooses the government from among the parties capable of building a coalition. None of these tasks is easy, but where a Muslim country is sufficiently poor to be influenced by foreign aid, none is unimaginable, either.

In a perfect world, countries would democratize instantaneously, with no delicate transitional period in which a leader will be trying to use foreign aid to his advantage without giving up any more of his power than is absolutely necessary. But rapid transition is probably not achievable without creating a great potential for violent upheaval, a result unlikely to serve democracy. A desirable side effect of encouraging parliamentary growth and increased freedom of political speech is that a wider range of political ideas will be expressed than is currently available in most Muslim countries. Some of these ideas will be secular, some moderately Islamic, and some no doubt will call for the establishment of a pure Islamic state. Over time, voters will be able to choose among these divergent views, and over one or two parliamentary cycles, they will be able to form judgments about who was most effective in government. What is certain is that, aided by the technology of television stations like al-Jazeera—run, incidentally, by secularists, not Islamists—ideas of liberal democracy are sure to spread beyond the countries where they are initially given the chance. If these ideas are inherently attractive, they will find adherents all over the Arab and Muslim worlds.

Muslims, it must be remembered, are not pre-programmed to embrace Islamist politics, as indeed most of the history of the twentieth century proves. Only when real political freedom and meaningful electoral choice exist in Muslim countries will it be possible to know for certain whether Muslims would today embrace Islamist parties in numbers. On one hand, free Islamic politics have not yet been tried in the Muslim world. On the other, neither has liberal democracy been tried beyond a few brief moments in places like Lebanon that were plagued by other serious problems. One can expect that Muslims in different countries might be interested in trying out a range of forms of governments, some more Islamic, some less.

That is what free political choice in the marketplace of ideas is meant to be all about.

Countries with oil will be more difficult to influence because their economic needs are less dire. That is not to say that other forms of economic development assistance may not be useful to them. The Saudis understand that they need to diversify their economy beyond oil in order to remain competitive thirty years into the future, and they are carefully watching Dubai's progress toward a diversified economy featuring finance and tourism. So eventually it may be possible to offer certain economic carrots even to the Saudis. For the present, though, the route to influencing governments that do not need money lies in structuring political alliances so as to create incentives for internal change.

Saudi Arabia, for example, must always be looking over its shoulder at the other regional oil producers who seek dominance over the Persian Gulf. Its relationship with the United States is designed to help protect it in the struggle for regional power. Iran and Iraq are the perennial contenders, and over the past two decades both have unintentionally accommodated Saudi interests by alienating the United States. First Iran turned against the U.S. in its revolutionary era; then Iraq, which had enjoyed American support during its war on Iran, managed to mangle its relationship with the United States by invading Kuwait. As a result of these developments, the Saudis drew closer to the U.S., and their influence and prestige in the Gulf rose accordingly.

As we enter a period of change in the Gulf, the Saudis must realize that their alliance with the U.S. could decline in importance. A democratic Iraq—or even a democratic Iran, should things turn out well there—would be a natural ally to the U.S. The implicit, and perhaps even the explicit, message must be that the United States sees its interests aligned with regional democracies. The Saudis would then have little choice but to respond, whether they liked it or not. The pressure need not be crude, and the Saudis are likely to respond better in any case to subtlety than to bombast. Some Saudis already see the writing on the wall in this regard. That explains both the unusual princely public statements in favor of electing the consultative assembly and the Saudi sigh of relief when President Bush distanced the United States from Iran by including Iran in the "axis of evil."

In short, the leverage that the United States holds over Saudi Arabia is its strategic partnership, and that asset can be brought to bear effectively in the push toward greater openness. Encouraging Iranian reform and democracy in post-Saddam Iraq will in any case serve American interests. In essence the goal should be to produce a democracy race between Saudi Arabia and its neighbors, with the stakes of victory being good relations with the United States.

Lest the skeptic object that international pressure is all very well in theory but will not work in practice, there is the example of Turkey, where both the United States and Europe have used the combination of strategic alliance and economic leverage to remarkable effect. Despite its location at the eastern end of the Mediterranean, far from the Atlantic Ocean, Turkey is nonetheless a long-standing member of the North Atlantic Treaty Organization. NATO membership grew from Cold War circumstances and from Turkey's proximity to the former Soviet Union. It was of great use to the United States, but it also benefited Turkey enormously. When it has served American purposes, the U.S. has used its close relationship with Turkey to encourage a gradual process of greater economic and political liberalization there. When the military has intervened in Turkish politics, the influence of the United States has been felt in pressuring the military to give way to renewed civilian government. And the U.S. has regularly, if not continuously, pressured Turkey to improve its human rights record and reduce the repression of the Kurds. This pressure has not been absolutely successful, but it has had a measurable impact.

Europe has in recent years also exerted a powerful influence on Turkish policy by holding out the hope of European Union membership, which would fulfill Ataturk's dream of bringing Turkey fully into Europe. The influence has not been restricted to economic matters and it has not disappeared just because Turkey's possible accession has been long delayed. Thus, for example, European leaders expressed their deep concern about the possible execution of captured Kurdish rebel leader Abdullah Ocalan—and remarkably, he has not been executed despite being Turkey's most wanted man for years. It is unimaginable that Ocalan would still be alive absent European pressure. Europeans called for the abolition of the death penalty altogether in Turkey, a measure that public opinion opposed, yet in summer

2002 the Turkish assembly banned it after ferocious debate. And Europe wants more from Turkey—robust parliamentary democracy, and the economic and legal infrastructure that would permit it to function within the EU. Turkey is doing everything it can to meet these conditions, because most Turks believe that their cost, while significant, cannot compare to the potential benefits associated with EU membership. Even Turkey's one recent deviation from the democratic track, the removal of Necmettin Erbakan from office, was driven in some part by the desire to please Europe and the United States by not appearing to be threateningly Islamic. Anyone who thinks that economic and strategic incentives cannot produce increased democratization, therefore, must reckon with the example of Turkey.

The promise of greater influence in Washington can be also used in concert with economic incentives to convince Muslim governments that democracy would serve their interests. Israel's democratic character provides one basis for its alliance with the U.S. Although Palestinians who live in the occupied territories cannot vote in Israeli elections, and Palestinian Israelis cannot serve in the Israeli army, most Muslims realize that the fact that Israel is a democracy for its citizens—including, albeit imperfectly, its Palestinian citizens who live within pre-1967 Israel—plays a crucial role in strengthening Israel's ties to the United States. The Arab states in particular frequently complain about Israel's disproportionate influence on U.S. policy. They must be made to see that one step toward improving their own ties with Washington is to mitigate the argument that Israel is the only regional democracy by transforming themselves into democracies as well.

This option should look particularly attractive to the Palestinian Authority, which under Yasser Arafat is still struggling for even the most basic legitimacy and acceptance in the United States. Arafat showed some inkling that he understood the necessity of democracy for improved relations with the U.S. when in spring 2002 he announced his intention to reform the Palestinian Authority and hold elections in the next six months. The elections have since been postponed repeatedly, as the Israeli-Palestinian conflict continues to simmer. But even if Arafat is not the man to make reform happen, as President Bush seemed subsequently to say in his own call for Palestinian constitutional reform, the Palestinians will have trouble getting their claims taken seriously in the United States until reform comes. By becoming more democratic, the Palestinian Authority can enhance its position in American public opinion and bolster its position in Washington. Despite the innumerable failings of the early years of the Palestinian Authority, a future Palestinian state still holds out the promise of becoming a democracy. Palestinians have observed Israel's parliamentary democracy, and they want the democratic structures that Israel has even though many consider Israel an enemy. Israel, for its part, knows that a functioning democracy in Palestine would be the best guarantor of its own security. And of course Palestinians are in desperate need of foreign economic assistance, which only the West is in a position to provide.

Incentives of strategic alliance and economic aid may converge here to create a promising opportunity to start from scratch with real democracy—but only if the United States and the West actually help. Palestinians who truly want democracy have three hurdles to overcome: Arafat's now entrenched administration, widely perceived as corrupt inside and outside the Palestinian territories; the conditions of occupation, which make normal processes of democracy difficult or impossible to carry out; and ongoing bombings of Israeli civilians, which harden Israeli and American public opinion while radicalizing Palestinians who are injured or dispossessed when Israel retaliates. Help from abroad means, then, stopping bombings and reprisals, convincing Israel that its own security can be enhanced by facilitating the conditions for Palestinian democracy, and giving reformist Palestinians a platform and realistic hope for eventual statehood. It will not work for the United States, much less Israel, to tell the Palestinians exactly whom they should elect. To be convincing, calls for democracy must focus precisely on the element of self-determination implicit in the democratic idea.

Farther afield, in oil dictatorships like Iraq and Libya, economic incentives and strategic prodding are unlikely to produce democracy. The failure of economic sanctions on Iraq to produce any meaningful change there suggests that even highly coercive economic measures cannot succeed when the dictator is willing to bleed his own people and the world is hungry for the dictator's oil. To make matters worse, the sanctions against Iraq cost the United States dearly in Muslim public opinion. No one disputes that Saddam was diverting oil revenues for his own uses and away from the suffering Iraqi people; but the consensus in the Muslim world is that the U.S. must take some responsibility for putting Saddam in a position in which he could maintain his own regime only at the cost of starving Iraqis.

The predicament of Iraqis living under Saddam poses its own special challenge. When the Gulf War came to an end, the first President Bush made a pragmatic decision not to invade Baghdad but to leave Saddam where he was. That decision was reached on the theory that toppling Saddam would destabilize the region in unforeseeable ways and would strengthen Iran; furthermore, the coalition that the United States had formed was committed to ejecting Saddam from Kuwait, not to replacing him, a precedent that would have sat uneasily in Arab capitals. Those pragmatic considerations still exist today, and the Arab countries that belonged to the coalition are as unhappy about removing Saddam in 2003 as they were in 1990.

So when the United States considers the prospect of changing the regime in Iraq by force of arms, it must ask what justification, whether realist or moral, stands behind that policy. The mere absence of democracy will not suffice to justify an invasion on pragmatic grounds, and perhaps not on moral grounds either when taken by itself. Oppression of Iraq's own citizens begins to look more plausible as grounds for removal, except that Saddam's worst depredations are now sometime in the past. Some five thousand Kurds were gassed at Halabja, and well over twice that number continue to suffer the gruesome aftereffects of the poison, but the Kurds are now relatively safe behind the no-fly zone established and maintained by the United States. Indeed, the Kurds enjoy an autonomy there that they have rarely enjoyed in their history. Ordinary Iraqis are terribly oppressed, to be sure, but the totalitarian state in Iraq is only an exaggerated version of regimes elsewhere in the Arab world. The liberation of the Iraqi people from the weight of Saddam's rule may be one justification for removing Saddam, but it probably cannot be the only one.

The other rationales that the second Bush administration has considered include Saddam's continued production of weapons of mass destruction—the true underlying qualification for Iraq's inclusion in the "axis of evil"—and his connection to international terror, possibly including the attacks of September 11, although this remains unproven. The American people may be willing to trust their president when he says that Iraq is a danger that must be addressed, but they must also wonder if it is pragmatically wise to undertake the risks of an invasion when it seems possible to re strain and control Saddam in much the same way that has worked since the first Gulf War. Some of the same people within the current Bush administration who opposed removing Saddam in 1990 judge that the decision was wisely taken.

Nonetheless, an American decision to change the regime in Iraq, regardless of its underlying motivation, would belong at one end of the continuum of options available to a superpower that seeks to promote democracy in Muslim countries. It stands at the extreme because it is the example of imposition of democracy in the wake of conquest, the model of Germany and Japan, and now, tentatively, of Afghanistan as well. Even if promoting democracy does not on its own provide sufficient rationale for replacing Saddam, once such a strategy of removal has been adopted, it is clear that the United States, probably working through the United Nations, must undertake the project of building democracy in Iraq. This is not precisely nation building, because Iraq is already a nation-state, albeit a heterogeneous one. But it would be democracy building, and that is a task that will require many resources.

Democracy's Muslim Allies

E ncouraging and pressuring Muslim countries to democratize will have little positive effect if the conditions in those countries are not suitable for democracy or if supporters of democracy in the Muslim world turn out to be too weak to make use of well-intentioned American assistance. Much of the academic literature on democratization argues that it is neither enough for elites alone to want democracy, nor for the masses to embrace it. Building democratic institutions that have the capacity to survive requires more. Specifically, it requires citizens, organized into the nongovernmental bodies that make up civil society, to keep elected government honest and prevent it from falling into familiar patterns of corruption and the arbitrary exercise of power. The failure of first-generation democracies in most decolonized countries is often attributed to the weakness of institutions of civil society and to the fact that democracy was typically grafted onto political cultures that had no tradition of democratic government. Arguing that democracy will work in the Muslim world therefore calls for identifying the natural allies and enemies of democracy movements, and the political culture, if any, that might be made to adapt itself to democratic practices.

Ironically or not, the first and most obvious institutional forces with the capacity to take on the job of policing democratic institutions are Islamist organizations. Although their leaders sometimes lack real-world political experience, the Islamists tend to be extremely effective both in understanding conditions right through the social structure and in communicating their message to rich and poor alike. The Islamists also have perhaps the greatest incentive to keep an eye on democratic development because with their relatively advanced political organization, they have the most to gain from democratization. The marriage of the mobile idea of democracy with the mobile idea of Islam has therefore already begun to create one of the most important pieces of the democratization puzzle: a group of civil society institutions with the power of moral suasion and interests aligned with the success of the democratization process.

Herein lies one of the crucial reasons that democracy in the Muslim world will probably have an Islamic character of some sort in its first years. Intentionally or otherwise, Muslim governments have prevented the rise of a vibrant secular civil society of the kind that many theorists of democratization have long believed necessary. Islam and Islamism have filled this gap, drawing upon the reserves of tradition and the commitment of the faithful. But the Islamists have not restricted their organization to traditional forms, as one might have expected from believers who seek to emulate the Prophet and his companions. Instead, the Islamists have brought to the realm of civil society the same flexibility and creativity they have brought to the reconsideration of Islamic tradition, and, in recent years, to the possibility of Islamic democracy. They have formed their own organizations to provide education and social support, and they have proven willing and able to become involved in and even take over those civil society institutions that do exist, such as trade unions and professional associations.

Because of the Islamists, it would be mistaken to say that the Muslim world lacks the civil society that brings about democracy. But to see that this is so, one must first recognize that the Islamists are indeed interested in democracy. Otherwise one will notice nothing but a rising tide of Islamist activity, and miss its political implications. Here academic specialization may have misled some observers. Theorists of democratization have largely neglected the Islamists' institutions and activities because they did not consider religious movements to be properly pre-democratic. Experts on Islamism, for their part, have sometimes declared political Islam dead because it turned away from violent revolution and toward social organization and the realm of quasi-private life. The Islamists have indeed realized, for the most part, that violent revolution will not successfully Islamize society, but their turn to the non-state sphere is not a mark of failure in broader political terms. To the contrary, building civil society through communal organizations puts Islamists in precisely the right place to make democratization happen.

The rise of Islamic civil society also goes some distance to answering the recurrent worry that elected Islamists would abolish democracy and rule as autocrats. Violent Islamist revolutionaries would indeed have had little reason not to rule by force, but Islamists who have achieved popularity through involvement in nongovernmental society would have less reason to do so. This is particularly true to the extent that Islamists have made their political case in democratic terms, a process that both changes Islamists' self-perceptions and allows them to be held responsible to their public embrace of democracy. For an Islamist like the jailed Front Islamique du Salut leader Ali Benhadj to produce an open letter that calls for democracy and free speech by juxtaposing the Prophet and his companions with Voltaire, Jefferson, and Thoreau has powerful effects on the policies his followers might someday adopt in office. It is true that democratic rhetoric does not guarantee democratic practice. But building support by legitimate means can have a transformative effect as Islamists discover that their credibility is enhanced by their adoption of nonviolent means that enable self-government.

Islamist organizations can be expected to have a catalytic effect on others if democratization actually occurs. In a relatively free state, the presence of Islamist civil society will generate competitive organizations of relatively nonreligious Muslims who will see their task as protecting the culture from falling prey to Islamist movements. Saadeddin Ibrahim's Ibn Khaldun Institute for Civil Society in Egypt, now closed by the government, has long viewed itself as responsible for keeping an eye on Islamist movements that might seek to curtail civil liberties, and this organization might serve as a model for others in Egypt and elsewhere in the Muslim world. One would expect such relatively secular private institutions to draw heavily from educated elites, and from the Westernized class that has the most to lose by a curtailment of its freedoms in the wake of Islamist electoral success. Secular civil society institutions are currently thin on the ground in much of the

Muslim world, but more would emerge the moment that Islamists stood in a position to gain democratic power.

Not everyone in Muslim states will be an ally of democratization, of course. Resistance will come initially from two groups: those already empowered by the present autocratic governments, who will see that they have much to lose by an end to their privileges, and secularists who fear, secretly or otherwise, that if they were forced to compete against Islamists in general elections, they would lose. Little can be done about the former group. Governing elites are precisely the people who need to be influenced by outside pressure for the prospect of democratization to be meaningful. It would be very risky to promise them major roles in a new democratic government—a strategy that worked relatively well for Nelson Mandela—because the likelihood seems greater than it was in South Africa that elites remaining in power would seek to subvert the democratic process. On the other hand, the elite secularists will probably go through an initial period of denial, then realize rather quickly that they need to become organized and compete in the electoral marketplace if they want to avoid a scenario in which religious parties defeat them.

It is a gamble to rely on secular moderates to produce democratic parties that are respectful of Islam without being Islamist, but the odds may be better than would appear to the Western imagination. Secularists created and staff al-Jazeera, which embodies an implicit ideology consistent with a mainstream non-Islamist politics, and takes a hard-line position on the Israel-Palestine conflict but not much else. The popularity of al-Jazeera would suggest to a political consultant that there is a market for candidates who would acknowledge the importance of Islam and be prepared to enter dialogue and even coalition with Islamists, but who do not believe that Islam alone offers the solutions to the political, economic, and social problems of the modern Muslim world.

Muslim allies of democracy will have to confront the reality that the political culture of most Muslim countries has not been democratic. But exaggerated claims of the cultural difficulty of introducing democratic institutions in Muslim countries, perhaps unconsciously influenced by the old Western image of the Oriental despot, need to be taken with a grain of salt. One often hears it said, for example, that Arab political culture is authoritarian. Yet the claim of authoritarianism is novel as applied to the Arabs. The classics of political theory in the Muslim world, such as Ibn Khaldun's fourteenth-century masterpiece, *The Prolegomena*, depict the Arabs as preternaturally unwilling to obey unified authority. It was long believed that the tribal structures of desert Arabs encouraged independent-mindedness, skepticism, fluid political allegiances, and an unwillingness to bind oneself to any political alliance for long. T. E. Lawrence rather ruefully endorsed this account after his experiences in World War I; and these characteristics, which were the despair of medieval advocates of monarchy, would seem ideally placed to make good democrats.

The Arab dictatorships of the second half of the twentieth century, then, cannot be blamed on some ancient Arab political culture. More likely, dictators have succeeded in the Arab and Muslim worlds for the same reasons that they have succeeded elsewhere: Muslim dictators have grown from the army, and the army has the means and opportunity to hold the population at bay. As for Arab monarchies, the very word *king* constituted an innovation in Arab political forms when it was introduced at the beginning of the twentieth century. Novelty, not well-established correspondence to political culture, characterizes the Arab monarchies. Only Iran, of all the Muslim countries, had an ancient monarchic tradition; yet whatever he may be, the Supreme Leader is not a king.

So while the political culture in Muslim autocracies and dictatorships will have to change for democracy to succeed there, this change should be no more drastic or difficult than any of the other changes in the politics of the Muslim world over the last century. Politics turns out to be highly mutable and political culture highly malleable, even where leaders try to deny it. What is more, the effectiveness of the mobile idea of democracy in spreading to Muslim countries already provides some indication that Muslim peoples are prepared to experiment with the institutional arrangements that correspond to it. Especially when married to an idea of Islam that has enormous prestige and influence in the Muslim world, democracy may be poised to introduce significant changes to Muslim political culture.

Democracy will need local allies to succeed in the Muslim world. But one of the key claims of this book has been that many Muslims are already prepared to embrace democracy, and that it is their governments that stand in the way. Democracy will find civil society allies among moderates and secularists, and also, more remarkably, among Islamists who have spent much of the past decade building up social and charitable institutions that meet all the criteria political scientists use to identify civil society. To the extent that Islam and democracy succeed in producing a synthesis, American efforts to encourage the growth of democracy in the Muslim world will not be sown in barren ground.

Imagining an Islamic Democracy

What would an Islamic democracy look like in practice? Would it regulate the private lives of Muslims who, while professing love and respect for their religion, choose not to adhere to the strict dictates of Islamic law? This question pits the many proud, committed Muslims who occasionally drink a glass of wine or prefer a T-shirt and jeans to *hijab* against the "volunteer" religious police who, in Saudi Arabia and Iran, urge the faithful to attend the mosque at prayer times and enforce Islamic codes of dress. It is conceivable that in some countries, in the first flush of elections, legislators and leaders might be elected who would insist on precisely such a policing of personal religious practices. Yet it is extremely unlikely that such measures would be put in place or long maintained in the major part of the Muslim world. The evidence shows that most Muslims do not want or need such religious enforcement, and few varieties of Islam judge that it is required. A great majority of Muslims do not believe that Islamic practices should be enforced by the state. Even were the volunteers to continue their exhortations, a democratic state could and likely would deprive them of enforcement power.

In the public, political life of an Islamic democracy, many Muslims would want Islam to function as a moral guide to keep domestic and foreign policies just and ethical. No doubt an Islamic democracy would think twice before aligning itself with a non-Muslim power against another Muslim country—but throughout history, from medieval Spain to the modern Middle East, Muslim states have been prepared to make convenient alliances with non-Muslim partners when necessary, and Islamic democracies would doubtless do the same. In an Islamic democracy, principles of political equality would likely be couched in Islamic terms, as would the condemnation of corruption. Yet when it comes to structuring institutions or deciding what road or power plant should be built and where, one can expect decisions to follow pragmatic, not religious lines. Islamic values may be invoked to call for protection of the environment and a social safety net for less fortunate citizens, but Islam does not dictate particularized solutions to these general problems. Muslims are obligated to give to charity, but this need not be an exclusive or exhaustive remedy to problems of poverty.

So an Islamic democracy would no doubt look distinctively Islamic, with mosques and religious language and religio-cultural tradition all prominent. But this does not mean that an Islamic democracy would need to be mired in backward-looking or simplistic social and political practices. Even a restrictively Islamic democracy has the capacity to enhance the degree of thoughtfulness and sophistication that have gone into the theory of political Islam by working out various problems in the light of experience and reality. In any Islamic democracy, one could expect many, and perhaps eventually most, citizens to choose political and social values that emphasize individual freedom and rational collective decision making.

Muslims, in other words, are not fundamentally different from anybody else. That fact would not need stating if it were not so often the case that writers on the Muslim world seem to suggest otherwise. Muslims are not inherently less inclined toward individual freedom in matters of politics or indeed religion than are the practitioners of any other religious tradition. *Islam* does mean something like "submission," but it is submission to God, not to man. Such submission follows logically from recognition of God's sovereignty, and indeed is inseparable from it in Islamic thought. English-speaking writers on Islam often mistakenly conflate submission to God with a submissive political attitude. But in fact a Muslim offers his ultimate allegiance to God alone, and never submits to man. Islam counsels obedience to legitimate government, defined by reference to respect for God's justice.

The contact of Islam and democracy should help explain how Muslims can and will embrace the basic structures of the political system known as democracy alongside their great and rich religious tradition. Islam has long proven tremendously flexible in its engagement with different political theories and systems. When the century-old religion of Islam first came to Iran, it took less than a single generation for newly converted Muslim Persian intellectuals to draw on ancient Persian political theory while giving advice to the caliph who ruled the Muslim community. Some Muslim countries have kings, although monarchy is absent from the earliest Muslim tradition. Some have presidents, although the concept was new when the French and the Americans adapted it to their purposes in the late eighteenth century.

The interaction between Islam and political ideas that originated outside the Muslim sphere has affected both. Imagining that the ideas associated with Islam are unchangeable or unchanging may be inspiring for authenticity-seeking Islamists, and convenient for opponents of Islamism who would like to sustain the status quo in the Muslim world. But the world cannot afford this myth, because it constructs a false dichotomy for Muslims, in which they must either deem democratic freedom inconsistent with Islam, or else reject their religious heritage. Neither option is tenable for the long term. Muslims are beginning to step outside the false dichotomy, and it remains for the powerful governments of the West to follow suit. But following will not be enough, because unless the West and the United States actively encourage democratization in the Muslim world, Muslims may never have the opportunity to shape Islamic democracy for themselves.

Muslims themselves no doubt bear much responsibility for the lack of political freedom in their countries. It has repeatedly been observed by both outsiders and some Muslims that the habit of blaming the rest of the world for their problems has not served Muslims well. But at the same time, it is worth remembering that people do not always get the government they deserve. Not every autocracy can be blamed on its subjects, a truth that the United States implicitly acknowledges every time it supports a democratic opposition or opposes an autocratic government in the name of the people whom that government is repressing.

Muslims deserve the chance to have the assistance of the world in achieving meaningful self-government. The Iraqi people deserve democracy, and maybe, with the intervention of the United States, they will eventually get it. Iranians deserve democracy too, and it is not beyond the power of the United States to help facilitate that process by encouraging legitimate democrats in Iran and opposing the hard-liners who seek to foreclose the democratic option. The peoples of other non-democratic Muslim countries deserve no less, and it makes little sense to leave them to their fates simply because their leaders, unlike Saddam Hussein, are politic enough to support the U.S. rather than oppose it.

Picture, then, a state recognizably Islamic, populated by Muslims, and committed to the political principles of democracy. Such a state might get its start in a number of different places by a variety of different means. It might grow out of the constitutional monarchies of Jordan and Morocco. It might emerge in Turkey, where democracy is rooted and now needs only to overcome its hostility to Muslim religious expression. It might come about in a future state of Palestine, where the very newness of the enterprise, the scrutiny and assistance of the world, and the political experience of self-realization might combine to produce democracy inflected by Islam. Islamic democracy might somehow, against the odds, develop in an autocracy like Egypt or even Algeria, where the shell of democracy exists and needs to be filled by its spirit. Pakistan could be an Islamic democracy, if its experiment with federalism pays dividends and its latest military leader proves better than those who came before. The oil monarchies of the Gulf might even surprise the world by making good on the election of newly empowered legislatures and becoming mini-democracies to inspire Saudi Arabia. Islamic democracy might arise in any of these contexts—or none. Whether it does will matter to all the world's Muslims, and it should matter to all the world's democrats.

After Jihad

S ince September 11, the small army of books with the word *jihad* in the title has been supplemented by still more explaining the origins and ideology of violence stemming from the Muslim world. These books share an underlying tone of warning: Islam is coming, and it is carrying the banner of holy war.

This alarmist argument is behind the curve. There are still some prepared to do violence in the name of Islam, who will doubtless make continued attempts to terrorize the West. But many, perhaps most, Muslims are, instead, entering a confirmed period of post-jihad, "post" in the sense that the option of holy war now seems spent, peripheral, unrealistic, and indeed distasteful in the light of the violence of September 11. They are turning toward another kind of jihad that is embedded in Islamic thought and tradition, a type of jihad explicated in the well-known hadith that forms the epigraph of this book. In one version of this received tradition, the Prophet Muhammad preceded a band of his followers in the return from a battle against the infidel. Observing the battle-weary Muslims approaching camp, the Prophet delivered a sobering message: you have returned from the lesser jihad to embark upon the greater jihad.

In the orthodox interpretation of the anecdote, incorporated in some versions of the tradition, the greater jihad is the inward struggle to perfect one's moral qualities. Sufi mystics have long embraced this interpretation, which they extend to mean that life's central task lies in overcoming the ego. So affecting was this metaphor of inward struggle as the true and highest calling for humans that one medieval writer included the story—suitably bowdlerized for Jewish readers by the replacement of Muhammad with a generic pious man—in an important Jewish work of moral theory and guidance. This interpretation of the hadith remains vital among modern Muslims.

More broadly, inward jihad means any worthy struggle infused by the principles of religion. One might say it was this more general type of struggle that the Prophet described as the greater jihad, as opposed to the lesser jihad of actual war. Jihad can also mean, then, by association, Islam's struggle to create a just system of political government. After all, the Muslims whom the Prophet addressed were returning to the bosom of their community, presumably to take up its affairs. Jihad is a collective duty of all Muslims—but it is a special collective duty under classical Islamic law, one resting squarely on each individual until the community has fulfilled it. The greater struggle the Muslims were to take up may have begun individually, but surely individual morality also has great consequences for communal organization. This must be especially true when there is no living Prophet who can convey the word of God directly when new circumstances arise. The medieval Muslims who read Aristotle, themselves no strangers to synthesis between Islamic and Greek ideas, saw an intimate connection between individual ethics and the political community. So perhaps it is not taking too great a liberty to suggest that this connection may be implicit in the Prophet's call to the greater jihad.

The violent sort of jihad is still with us, and will be so long as there are people who can benefit by invoking a religious justification for the strategy of violence. Perhaps Muslims who understand themselves to be acting in self-defense or in a struggle for liberation will always fit this description. But the greater jihad, the jihad of personal struggle to do good, and for a viable collective solution to bringing the values of Islam into the structure of the state, is on the rise. This peaceful jihad is the way of a future pregnant with the possibility of Islamic democracy.

America should not wage its own violent jihad either, not in the sense of jihad as holy war pursued by Americans to impose their beliefs on people whose values are deemed fundamentally incompatible with their own. Violent jihad in the cause of democracy is oxymoronic, as the United States had occasion to learn during the Cold War. On the other hand, jihad as a struggle waged to make sense of one's own values might not be the worst way of thinking about future American efforts to encourage Islamic democracy. By working to enable Muslims to make real democratic choices for themselves, the U.S. can convey the message that its interest in the Muslim world is not to create an empire, but to promote liberty. Through this sort of struggle, Americans might express their own deepest values abroad and thereby clarify what America stands for to itself.

Jihad waged as a struggle to act justly and well does not require any opposition between one's own group or community and another. This jihad may reach its fullest expression in cooperation among peoples and ideas. After the option of violent jihad disappears, perhaps Muslims will not see the United States as a force to be overcome, and perhaps Americans will begin to see Muslims not as inevitable adversaries nor as enemies to be feared, but as people whom the U.S. may be able to help to achieve their own higher aspirations. If there is to be a jihad of the peaceful sort, it will have to be one waged by Muslim democrats and America in tandem.

After jihad comes a turn within, to self and to community. It is a turn away from opposition and toward combination. The mobile ideas of Islam and democracy have the flexibility, universality, and simplicity to make their encounter into a struggle for synthesis rather than supremacy. This vision is not utopian. Its realistic beginnings exist. But the outcome of this historical process is not predetermined, for either good or ill. To make the encounter of Islam and democracy peaceful and creative instead of violent and destructive will require patience, courage, and self-knowledge. That would not have surprised the Prophet. The greater struggle, he promised, comes after jihad.

NOTES

I follow standard academic transliteration conventions except for proper names, which appear according to their usual journalistic spellings.

vii   *Epigraph*: The translations are my own. The two versions of the tradition may be found in several collections of hadith and hadith criticism. One accessible source is *Al-Asrar al-marfu'a fi-l-akhbar al-mawdu'a*, also known as *Al-Mawdu'at al-kubra*, of 'Ali al-Qari (d. 1605 or 1606), ed. Muhammad al-Sabbagh (Beirut: Dar al-amana, 1971), 206–07. The longer version is introduced as follows: "Al-Suyuti said: Al-Khatib reports in his History from among the hadith of Jaber . . ."

   The shorter version is said to appear in the *Revival of the Sciences of Religion* of the great Abu Hamid Muhammad al-Ghazzali (d. 1111); al-'Iraqi attributed it to Ahmad ibn Husayn al-Bayhaqi on the authority of Jaber and said that the chain of transmission had a weak link. Ibn Hajjar al-'Asqalani attributed the tradition to one Ibrahim ibn 'Abla. It is recorded that Hamza ibn Rabi'a said that he had never seen a tradition more eloquent. See *Al-Asrar al-marfu'a* 206, n. 5.

   For a parallel presentation of both traditions, see the *Kashf al-khafa'* of Isma'il al-Jarrahi (d. 1748 or 1749), vol. 1 (Beirut: Dar ihya al-turath al-'arabi, 1932–33, reprint 1968), 424–25.

3   On Algeria, see Lisa Garon, "The Press and Democratic Transition in Arab Society: The Algerian Case," in Rex Brynen, Baghat Korany, and Paul Noble, eds., *Political Liberalization & Democratization in the Arab World*, vol. 1 (Boulder, Colo.: Lynne Reiner, 1995), 149–65; Baghat Korany and Saad Amrani, "Explosive Civil Society and Democratization from Below: Algeria," in Rex Brynen, Baghat Korany, and Paul Noble, eds., *Political Liberalization & Democratization in the Arab World*, vol. 2 (Boulder, Colo.: Lynne Reiner, 1995), 11–38; Martin Stone, *The Agony of Algeria* (New York:

Columbia University Press, 1998); Emad Eldin Shahin, *Political Ascent: Contemporary Islamic Movements in North Africa* (Boulder, Colo.: Westview, 1997); Michael Willis, *The Islamist Challenge in Algeria: A Political History* (Ithaca, N.Y.: Ithaca Press, 1996). On democratization in North Africa more generally, see John P. Entelis, ed., *Islam, Democracy, and the State in North Africa* (Bloomington, Ind.: Indiana University Press, 1997).

4 *Islamists*: There is an enormous literature, growing by the minute, on Islamism, also known as Islamic fundamentalism and political Islam. For a taste, see R. Scott Appleby, ed., *Spokesmen for the Despised: Fundamentalist Leaders of the Middle East* (Chicago: University of Chicago Press, 1997); Abdel Salam Sidahmed and Anoushiravan Ehtteshami, eds., *Islamic Fundamentalism* (Boulder, Colo.: Westview, 1996); Bassam Tibi, *The Challenge of Fundamentalism: Political Islam and the New World Disorder* (Berkeley, Calif.: University of California Press, 1998). The best general introduction to the topic is still the essays in Martin E. Marty and R. Scott Appleby, eds., *The Fundamentalism Project*, vols. 1–5 (Chicago: University of Chicago Press, 1991–95).

8 On former Soviet Republics, see Olivier Roy, *The New Central Asia: The Creation of Nations* (New York: New York University Press, 2000); Ahmed Rashid, *Jihad: The Rise of Militant Islam in Central Asia* (New Haven, Conn.: Yale University Press, 2002).

On the failure of Islamists to take over governments, see Olivier Roy, *The Failure of Political Islam* (Cambridge, Mass.: Harvard University Press, 1994); Gilles Kepel, *Jihad: The Trail of Political Islam* (Cambridge, Mass.: Harvard University Press, 2001); Emmanuel Sivan, "Why Radical Muslims Aren't Taking Over Governments," *Middle East Review of International Affairs Journal*, vol. 2, no. 2 (May 1998).

On the takeover of Sudan by Islamists, see Kepel, *Jihad*.

On the Taliban, see Ahmed Rashid, *Taliban: Militant Islam, Oil and Fundamentalism in Central Asia* (New Haven, Conn.: Yale University Press, 2000).

9 *between 5,000 and 30,000 civilians*: Estimates vary widely. See, for example, Moshe Maoz, Joseph Ginat, and Onn Winckler, eds., *Modern Syria: From Ottoman Rule to Pivotal Role in the Middle East* (Portland, England: Sussex Academic Press, 1999), 8 (citing 10,000 to 30,000 civilians); Patrick Seale with the assistance of Maureen McConville, *Asad of Syria: The Struggle for the Middle East* (Berkeley, Calif.: University of California Press, 1989), 339 (reporting 5,000 to 20,000 civilians); Daniel Benjamin and Steven Simon, *The Age of Sacred Terror* (New York: Random House, 2002), 86 (giving "best estimates" as 18,000 killed).

11 *Internet discussions*: For an off-line guide to the subject, see Gary R. Bunt, *Virtually Islamic: Computer-Mediated Communications and Islamic Cyber-Environments* (Cardiff: University of Wales Press, 2000). Hundreds more Web sites have of course been added since 2000.

19   *democratic possibilities*: See, for example, Samuel Huntington, *The Clash of Civilizations and the Remaking of World Order* (New York: Touchstone, 1996), 114; Yahya Sadowski, "The New Orientalism and the Democracy Debate," in *Political Islam: Essays from Middle East Report*, eds. Joel Beinin and Joe Stork (Los Angeles: University of California Press, 1997), 35.

21   *some academic writers prefer to speak of "Islams"*: See Akbar S. Ahmed, *Postmodernism and Islam: Predicament and Promise* (New York: Routledge, 1992) and *Islam Today: A Short Introduction to the Muslim World* (New York: I. B. Tauris, 1999).

22   *definition of democracy*: A modern definition that has exerted great influence is that of Robert Dahl, *Polyarchy: Participation and Opposition* (New Haven, Conn.: Yale University Press, 1971). According to Dahl, democracies grant their citizens certain procedural rights, including the right to vote and the right to be elected. Political candidates compete for support and votes in free and fair elections. Democratic institutions exist to ensure that government policies are dependent on votes and other expressions of constituent preference. Dahl also describes democracies as guaranteeing certain freedoms: freedom of association, freedom of expression, and freedom of information, including access to alternative sources of information besides those under government control.

24   *mandatory modesty will facilitate women's greater participation in public life*: See Leila Ahmed, *Women and Gender in Islam: Historical Roots of a Modern Debate* (New Haven, Conn.: Yale University Press, 1992), 223–31.

24   On the decline of Iran, see 'Ali M. Ansari, *Iran, Islam, and Democracy: The Politics of Managing Change* (London: Royal Institute of International Affairs; Washington, D.C.; distributed worldwide by the Brookings Institution, 2000); David Menashri, *Post-Revolutionary Politics in Iran: Religion, Society, and Power* (Portland, Oreg.: Frank Cass, 2001); Behzad Yaghmaian, *Social Change in Iran: An Eyewitness Account of Dissent, Defiance, and New Movements for Rights* (Albany, N.Y.: State University of New York Press, 2002).

24   *Distinctively Islamic economics*: The most influential book in this context is probably Muhammad Baqir al-Sadr, *Iqtisaduna*, 1st Arabic ed. (Beirut: Dar al-fikr, 1969); in English, *Our Economics* (Tehran: WOFIS, 1982–84). For a thoughtful assessment, see Chibli Mallat's brilliant work *The Renewal of Islamic Law, Muhammad Baqer as-Sadr, Najaf, and the Shi'i International* (Cambridge: Cambridge University Press, 1993). Comparably influential is Sayyid Qutb, *Al-Adala al-'ijtima'iyya fi-l-islam* (Cairo: Al-Bai, 1958); in English, *Social Justice in Islam*, trans. John B. Hardie, rev. Hamid Elgar (Oneonta, N.Y.: IPI, 2000).

26   *Samuel Huntington*: "The Clash of Civilizations" appeared as an article in *Foreign Affairs* 72, no. 3 (Summer 1993), 22–49. It became a book, *The Clash of Civilizations and the Remaking of World Order* (New York: Touchstone, 1996).

     Bernard Lewis: *The Arabs in History*, 6th ed. (Oxford: Oxford University Press, 1993); P. M. Holt, Ann K. S. Lambton, and Bernard Lewis, eds., *Cambridge History of Islam* (Cambridge: Cambridge University Press, 1978); *What Went Wrong? Western Impact and Middle Eastern Response* (Oxford: Oxford University Press, 2002).

     See also Lewis's interesting essay "Islam and Liberal Democracy: A Historical Overview," *Journal of Democracy* 7, no. 2 (1996), 52–63, in which he argues that the concept "freedom" has not been well developed in the Muslim world, and that separation of church and state is the right direction for Muslim states. The categorization of Muslim regimes is also instructive.

27   *Why the Muslims Have Lagged Behind*: Amir Shakib Arslan, *Limadha ta'akhkhara al-muslimun wa-li-madha taqaddama ghayruhum* (Cairo: 1930); in English, *Our Decline and Its Causes*, trans. M. A. Shakoor (Lahore, Pakistan: Ashraf, 1952).

28   *Orientalism*: Edward Said, *Orientalism* (New York: Pantheon Books, 1978).

28   *1.2 billion Muslims*: This has become a standard estimate, but of course such estimates are very imprecise.

     Islam is growing quickly: While exact statistics are difficult to obtain, one reliable source reports that between 1990 and 2000, the Muslim population, including converts, grew at a rate of 2.13 percent per year, compared with a global population growth rate of 1.41 percent. "World Summary," *World Christian Encyclopedia* (New York: Oxford University Press, 2001).

29   *Algeria . . . under the age of 20*: Derived from "Distribution of Population by Age and Dispersion," National Organization of Statistics of Algeria, http://www.ons.dz/ English/ Demogr/population.htm.

33   *one famous definition*: Joseph Schumpeter defined democracy as a system "for arriving at political decisions in which individuals acquire the power to decide by means of a competitive struggle for the people's vote." Joseph Schumpeter, *Capitalism, Socialism, and Democracy*, 2d ed. (New York: Harper, 1947), 269. For elaboration, a very useful review of the issues surrounding democratization, and a guide to some of the vast democratization literature, see Larry Diamond, *Developing Democracy* (Baltimore: Johns Hopkins University Press, 1999).

34   Thomas Friedman, *The Lexus and the Olive Tree* (New York: Anchor Books, 2000).

35   *creolization*: My presentation of creolization is heavily influenced by Jeannie Suk, *Postcolonial Paradoxes* (Oxford: Oxford University Press, 2001). One foundational text of the *créolité* movement is Jean Bernabé, Patrick Chamoiseau, and Raphaël

Confiant, *Eloge de la Créolité: Edition bilingue français/anglais*, trans. M. B. Taleb-
Khyar (Paris: Gallimard, 1993); see also Edouard Glissant, *Discours antillais*; in En-
glish, *Caribbean Discourse: Selected Essays*, translated and with an introduction by
J. Michael Dash (Charlottesville, Va.: University Press of Virginia, 1989).

36   *creolization has . . . produced thrilling music*: Joan Gross et al., "Rai, Rap, and Ramadan Nights," in *Political Islam*, Beinin and Stork, eds.

37   Compare the argument about synthesis with the description of the dialectics of globalization in Clement M. Henry and Robert Springborg, *Globalization and the Politics
of Development in the Middle East* (Cambridge: Cambridge University Press, 2001),
15–21. On issues relevant to religion as a mobile idea, see Susanne Hoeber Rudolph
and James Piscatori, eds., *Transnational Religion & Fading States* (Boulder, Colo.:
Westview, 1997). I owe the example of liberal democracy as a synthesis to Richard
Primus.

38   On Ottoman reform and early Arab nationalism in the late Ottoman Empire, see
Hasan Kayali, *Arabs and Young Turks: Ottomanism, Arabism, and Islamism in the Ottoman Empire, 1908–1918* (Berkeley, Calif.: University of California Press, 1997).

39   On Islamic modernism, the classic work is still Albert Hourani, *Arabic Thought in the
Liberal Age, 1798–1939* (Cambridge: Cambridge University Press, 1983). Also very useful is Malcolm H. Kerr, *Islamic Reform: The Political and Legal Theories of Muhammad 'Abduh and Rashīd Rida* (Berkeley, Calif.: University of California Press, 1966).

40   *a controversial Arabic book*: 'Ali 'Abd al-Raziq, *Al-Islam wa-usul al-hukm* (Cairo:
Matba'at Misr, 1925).

41   *a failed intellectual movement*: On the other hand, there has been an outpouring of recent work in the modernist vein, much of it explicitly feminist. A few notable exam-
ples include Farid Esack, *Qur'an, Liberation, & Pluralism* (Oxford: Oneworld, 1997);
Charles Kurzman, ed., *Liberal Islam: A Sourcebook* (New York: Oxford University
Press, 1998); Mahmoud Mohamed Taha, *The Second Message of Islam*, trans. Abdul-
lahi Ahmed An-Na'im (Syracuse, N.Y.: Syracuse University Press, 1987); Amina
Wadud, *Qur'an and Woman* (New York: Oxford University Press, 1999).
       On rumors of the death or failure of political Islam, see Kepel, *Jihad*, and Roy,
Failure of Political Islam.

41–43   On Banna, the Brotherhood, and Qutb, see Ibrahim M. Abu-Rabi', *Intellectual Ori-
gins of Islamic Resurgence in the Modern Arab World* (Albany, N.Y.: State University of
New York Press, 1996); Ahmad S. Moussalli, *Radical Islamic Fundamentalism: The
Ideological and Political Discourse of Sayyid Qutb* (Beirut: American University of
Beirut, 1992).

44   *Milestones: Ma'alim fi-l-tariq* (Milestones) (Cedar Rapids, Ia.: Unity, 1981–85).

45   On the Shi'i ideologues, see Mallat, *Renewal of Islamic Law*.

46   On the beliefs of Sadat's assassins, see Johannes J. G. Jansen, *The Neglected Duty: The Creed of Sadat's Assassins and Islamic Resurgence in the Middle East* (New York: Macmillan, 1986).

48   *No Arab state . . . adopted political Islam*: see Kepel, *Jihad*; Roy, *Failure of Political Islam*; and Sivan, "Radical Muslims."

48–49   On Islamist political parties in Jordan, see Quintan Wiktorowicz, *The Management of Islamic Activism: Salafis, the Muslim Brotherhood, and State Power in Jordan* (Albany, N.Y.: State University of New York Press, 2001).

51   *various proposals for Islamic democracy*: One engaged treatment of some of these—and an undertaking in its own right—is Ahmad S. Moussalli, *The Islamic Quest for Democracy, Pluralism, and Human Rights* (Jacksonville, Fla.: University Press of Florida, 2001). See also Fathi Osman, *Islam in a Modern State: Democracy and the Concept of Shura* (Washington, D.C.: Center for Muslim-Christian Understanding Occasional Papers, 2001). The final chapter of Nathan J. Brown, *Constitutions in a Nonconstitutional World: Arab Basic Laws and the Prospects for Accountable Government* (Albany, N.Y.: State University of New York Press, 2002), entitled "Islamic Constitutionalism," offers a good overview, with reference to specific countries.

51   For a sampling of Ghannouchi's views, see Azzam Tamimi, *Rachid Ghannouchi: A Democrat Within Islamism* (Oxford: Oxford University Press, 2001).
        For a sampling of Khatami's views in English, see Mohammad Khatami, *Islam, Dialogue and Civil Society* (Canberra: Centre for Arab and Islamic Studies, Australian National University, 2000); *Islam, Liberty, and Development* (Binghamton, N.Y.: Institute of Global Cultural Studies, Binghamton University, 1998); *Hope and Challenge: The Iranian President Speaks* (Binghamton, N.Y.: Institute of Global Cultural Studies, Binghamton University, 1997). See also Ansari, *Iran, Islam, and Democracy*.

52   *question that remains unresolved*: See the controversial and provocative book by Patricia Crone and Martin Hinds, *God's Caliph: Religious Authority in the First Centuries of Islam* (Cambridge: Cambridge University Press, 1986).

52   For more on how Islamic governments have historically chosen leaders, see L. Carl Brown, *Religion and State: The Muslim Approach to Politics* (New York: Columbia University Press, 2000); W. Montgomery Watt, *Islamic Political Thought* (Chicago: Edinburgh University Press, 1968).

52   On loosing and binding, see Brown, *Constitutions in a Nonconstitutional World*, 172.

53 *Medieval political theorists*: Ghazzali prominent among them. See Noah Feldman,
"Religion and Political Authority as Brothers: The Islamic Constitution and the Ethi-
cal Literature," in *Islamic Constitutionalism*, eds. H. E. Chehabi and Sohail Hashmi
(Cambridge, Mass.: Harvard University Press, forthcoming).

53 *a conference on the subject of* shura *and democracy*: The conference took place in
Cairo, May 23–25, 1997. The volumes are *Al-Shura fi-l-fikr wa-l-mumarasa* (Shura in
Theory and Practice), *Ishkaliyyat al-'alaqa bayna al-shura wa-l-dimuqratiyya* (Problematic of the Relation Between Shura and Democracy), and *Tajarib mu'asira fi mu-
marasat al-shura wa-l-dimuqratiyya* (Contemporary Experiments in the Practice of
Shura and Democracy), published jointly under the auspices of al-Azhar and the
World Center for the Study and Investigation of the Green Book, in Tripoli. In other
words, Qadhafi was behind the publication and probably the funding of the conference; strange bedfellows indeed, Qadhafi and al-Azhar.

See also Tawfiq Muhammad al-Shawi, *Al-Shura: a'la maratib al-dimuqratiyya*
(Shura: The Highest Level of Democracy) (Cairo: Al-zahra' li-l-'ilam al-'arabi, 1994);
Abd al-hamid Isma'il al-Ansari, *Al-'Alam al-Islami al-mu'asir bayna al-shura wa-l-
dimuqratiyya: ru'ya naqdiyya* (The Contemporary Islamic World Between Shura and
Democracy: A Critical Perspective) (Cairo: Dar al-fikr al-'arabi, 2001).

54 *obligatory for the ruler to follow the people's will*: See, for example, the very influential
fatwa of Yusuf al-Qaradawi on the compatibility of Islam and democracy, in *Min fiqh
al-dawla fi-l-islam* (Of the Law of the State in Islam) (Cairo: Dar al-shuruq, 1997), 146,
where he insists on the obligatory nature of *shura* with the binders and loosers. If the
ruler could ignore the consultation, he asks, then in what sense would those who provided it have the power to bind and loose? Qaradawi concludes that "Islamic consultation (*shura*) comes close to the spirit of democracy; or if you prefer: the definition of
democracy comes close to the spirit of Islamic consultation." See also 136 on *shura*.
For an overview on Qaradawi, see Armando Salvatore, *Islam and the Political Discourse of Modernity* (London: Ithaca Press, 1997), 197–216.

56 *Saudi Arabia uses . . . classical Islamic law*: On Saudi law in action, see Frank E. Vo-
gel, *Islamic Law and Legal System: Studies of Saudi Arabia* (Leiden, Netherlands:
Brill, 2000).

57 *recognition of God's sovereignty*: For a review of various Islamist theories of sovereignty,
see Ermin Sinanovic, "The Majority Principle in Islamic Legal and Political Thought,"
in Center for the Study of Islam and Democracy Second Annual Conference Proceedings, April 7, 2001, 72–90, http://www.islam-democracy.org.

See also Qaradawi's fatwa, 140–41, where he analyzes the differences between
sovereignty and governance.

The Rule of God, the Rule of the People: Raja Bahlul, *Hukm allah, hukm al-
sha'b: hawla al-'alaqa bayna al-dimuqratiyya wa-l-'almaniyya* (The Rule of God, the
Rule of the People: On the Relation Between Democracy and Secularism) (Amman,

Jordan: Dar al-shuruq li-l-nashr wa-l-tawzi', 2000). This sophisticated work seeks to disentangle democracy from liberal democracy in its inquiry.

58   *"there is no coercion in religion"*: Qur'an 2:256.

59   *The Iranian writer Abdolkarim Soroush*: See *Reason, Freedom, and Democracy in Islam: Essential Writings of Abdolkarim Soroush*, trans. and eds. Mahmoud Sadri and Ahmad Sadri (Oxford: Oxford University Press, 2000).

60   *Sufi mystics*: See Annemarie Schimmel, *The Mystical Dimensions of Islam* (Chapel Hill, N.C.: University of North Carolina Press, 1985); Idries Shah, *The Sufis* (New York: Anchor Books, 1971).

60   *separation of church and state*: There is a sizable Arabic literature on the relationship between secularism, democracy, and Islam. See, as representative examples, Ibrahim Bashir al-Ghawil (or al-Ghuwayyil), *Al-Dimuqratiyya wa-l-'almaniyya wa-huquq al-insan: al-marji'iyya al-gharbiyya wa-l-marji'iyya al-islamiyya* (Democracy, Secularism, and Human Rights: Western Authority and Islamic Authority) (Beirut: Dar al-afaq al-jadida, 1999); Abd al-Razzaq 'Id and Muhammad 'Abd al-Jabbar, *Al-Dimuqratiyya bayna al-'almaniyya wa-l-islam* (Democracy Between Secularism and Islam) (Beirut and Damascus: Dar al-fikr, 1999) (this is two books in one); Raja Bahlul, *Dawlat al-din, dawlat al-dunya: hawla al-'alaqa bayna al-dimuqratiyya wa-l-'almaniyya* (Theocratic State, Secular State: On the Relation Between Democracy and Secularism) (Ramallah, West Bank: Palestinian Institute for the Study of Democracy, 2000) (like his *The Rule of God, the Rule of the People*, an extraordinarily sophisticated treatment of the issues); Munir Shafiq, *Al-Dimuqratiyya wa-l-'almaniyya fi tajriba al-gharbiyya: ru'ya islamiyya* (Democracy and Secularism in the Western Experience: An Islamic Perspective) (London: Maghreb Center for Researche [sic] and Translation, 2001). One title that leaves no doubt about its point of view is Ghazi 'Anaya, *Jahiliyyat al-dimuqratiyya* (The [Non-Islamic] Ignorant Barbarism of Democracy) (Amman, Jordan: Dar zahran li-l-nashr wa-l-tawzi', 1999); and indeed the work abounds in rejection not only of democracy but of all manner of peace or cooperation with Israel.

61   *The government can support*: I explore these issues more fully in Noah Feldman, "From Liberty to Equality: The Transformation of the Establishment Clause," *California Law Review* 90 (May 2002), 673.

62   *Islamic commitment to equality*: A thoughtful treatment of issues concerning equality in Islam can be found in Louise Marlow, *Hierarchy and Egalitarianism in Islamic Thought* (Cambridge: Cambridge University Press, 1997). See also Ann Elizabeth Meyer, *Islam and Human Rights: Tradition and Politics*, 3d ed. (Boulder, Colo.: Westview, 1999).

   "O mankind!": Qur'an 49:13.

63 *women . . . serving as heads of state*: Narrated on the authority of Abu Bakr: "During the battle of Al-Jamal Allah benefited me with a word. When the Prophet heard the news that the people of Persia had made the daughter of Khosrau their queen [ruler], he said, 'Never will such a nation succeed as makes a woman their ruler.'" See *The Translation of the Meanings of Sahih Al-Bukhari, Arabic-English*, vol. 9, trans. Muhammad Muhsin Khan (Medina, Saudi Arabia: Dar al-fikr, 1981), 170–71.

For a general discussion of discrimination against women's political participation in Islam, see Meyer, *Islam and Human Rights*, 91 ("Conservative Muslims generally claim that the *shari'a* excludes women and non-Muslims from most, if not all governmental positions").

On Bahraini elections, see Neil MacFarquhar, "In Bahrain, Women Run, Women Vote, Women Lose," *New York Times*, May 21, 2002; "Bahrain Holds Elections, and Women Are Included," *Washington Post*, May 10, 2002.

64 For Qaradawi's statement of September 12, 2001, see Reuven Paz, "Shaykh Dr. Yousef al-Qaradawi: Dr. Jekyll and Mr. Hyde," *Policywatch*, no. 576 (Washington, D.C.: Washington Institute for Near East Policy, October 18, 2001), available at http://www.washingtoninstitute.org/watch/Policywatch/policywatch2001/576.htm.

64 *"If one of them shall forget . . .":* Qur'an 2:282.

65 On Islamic divorce and inheritance law, see Ziba Mir-Hosseini, *Marriage on Trial: Islamic Family Law in Iran and Morocco* (New York: I. B. Tauris, 2000); Ziba Mir-Hosseini, *Islam and Gender* (Princeton, N.J.: Princeton University Press, 1999).

65 *Muslim women activists*: See Susan Sachs, "Egypt Makes It Easier for Women to Divorce Husbands," *New York Times*, January 28, 2000.

66 On Islamist claims that Islam can unleash women's full potential, see Ahmed, *Women and Gender in Islam*.

67 *compulsory uncovering of the head*: On *l'affaire du foulard*, see Kepel, *Jihad*. There is a very large French literature on the controversy and the court cases surrounding Muslim girls' desire to wear head scarves and the response of French schools and the government.

"We are a religious people": Zorach v Clauson, 343 US 306 at 313 (1952).

67 *a compact that still survives*: The so-called constitution of Medina appears as an appendix to Watt, *Islamic Political Thought*.

For a helpful review, see Jorgen S. Nielsen, "Contemporary Discussions on Religious Minorities in Islam," 2002 *B.Y.U.L. Rev.* 353, 360–69; for the historical view, see Bernard Lewis, *The Jews of Islam* (Princeton, N.J.: Princeton University Press, 1984). For a range of Islamist views, see Abul Ala Maududi, *Rights of Non-Muslims in*

Islamic State, trans. Khurshid Ahmad (Lahore: Islamic Publications, 1961); Fahmi Huwaydi, *Muwatinun la dhimmiyyun: mawqi' ghayr al-muslimin fi mujtama' al-muslimin* (Beirut: Dar al-shuruq, 1985) (Citizens, Not Protected Persons: The Status of Non-Muslims in the Community of Muslims); Rachid Ghannouchi, *Huquq al-muwatana: wad'iyyat ghayr al-muslim fi-l-mujtama' al-islami* (The Rights of Citizens: The Situation of the Non-Muslim in the Islamic Community) (Tunis, 1989, reissued Herndon, Va.: International Institute of Islamic Thought, 1993).

68   For more (far from unbiased) discussion on "protected persons," see Bat Ye'Or, *The Dhimmi: A Historical Survey of Jews and Christians under Islam*, trans. David Maisel (Rutherford, N.J.: Fairleigh Dickinson University Press, 1984); Bat Ye'Or, *Islam and Dhimmitude: Where Civilizations Collide*, trans. Miriam Kochan and David Littman (Madison, N.J.: Fairleigh Dickinson University Press, 2002).

70   *"O you who believe!"*: Qur'an 24:27.

70   *"Sahl bin Sa'd . . ."*: See *The Translation of the Meanings of Sahih Al-Bukhari*, vol. 8, Book 74, no. 258: Narrated Sahl bin Sa'd: A man peeped through a round hole into the dwelling place of the Prophet, while the Prophet had a Midray [an iron comb] with which he was scratching his head. The Prophet said, "Had I known you were looking [through the hole], I would have pierced your eye with it [i.e., the comb]." Verily! The order of taking permission to enter has been enjoined because of that sight [that one should not look unlawfully at the state of others].

71–72 *hudud*: see Rudolph Peters, *Islamic Criminal Law: Theory and Practice from the Sixteenth to the Twentieth Century* (New York: Cambridge University Press, forthcoming).
       For more on how tribal customs and Islamic customs have become enmeshed in Afghanistan and elsewhere, see Rashid, *Taliban*.

72   *symbol of the new order*: See Ruud Peters, "The Reintroduction of Islamic Criminal Law in Northern Nigeria," conducted on Behalf of the European Commission (Lagos, 2001), available at http://europa.eu.int/comm/europeaid/projects/eidhr/pdf/islamic-criminal-law-nigeria_en.pdf.
       For examples of legal ways out, see Peters, *Islamic Criminal Law*.

78   On Indonesia, see Robert Hefner, *Civil Islam* (Princeton, N.J.: Princeton University Press, 2000). I also follow Hefner's transliterations, including Nahdlatul Ulama instead of Nahdatul Ulama.

81   Clifford Geertz, *Islam Observed* (New Haven, Conn.: Yale University Press, 1968).

83    $99^{44}/_{100}$: For the election results, see http://www.electionworld.org/election/tunisia.htm.

84 *democratization . . . through gradual processes*: For more details on why these gradual processes are best and how they might occur, see Catharin E. Dalpino, *Deferring Democracy: Promoting Openness in Authoritarian Regimes* (Washington, D.C.: Brookings Institution Press, 2000).

85 *loya jirga*: Carlotta Gall, "Afghans Gather to Choose Grand Council," *New York Times*, June 3, 2002.

87 On modern Iran and the origins of the revolution, there is a great deal of writing, much of it excellent. To cite some works would inevitably slight others. For what remains the classic introduction to the subject, see Roy Mottahedeh's classic, *The Mantle of the Prophet: Religion and Politics in Iran* (Oxford: Oneworld Publications, 1985).

90 For the Iranian election results, see http://www.electionworld.org/iran.htm. For the 1997 results, see Ansari, *Iran, Islam, and Democracy*, 108.

On Khatami's views, see Daniel Brumberg, *Reinventing Khomeini: The Struggle for Reform in Iran* (Chicago: University of Chicago Press, 2001), 195–201, and Ansari, *Iran, Islam, and Democracy*.

90 On newspaper closings, see Nazila Fathi, "Iran's President Trying to Limit Power of Clergy," *New York Times*, August 29, 2002.

92 *Mohammed Mossadegh . . . had been displaced*: Kermit Roosevelt, *Countercoup: The Struggle for the Control of Iran* (New York: McGraw-Hill, 1979).

96 *Khatami has recently spoken out*: See Fathi, "Iran's President."

101 On Turkey generally, a useful introduction is Stephen Kinzer, *Crescent and Star: Turkey Between Two Worlds* (New York: Farrar, Straus and Giroux, 2002). See also the essays in *Turkey in World Politics: An Emerging Multiregional Power*, eds. Barry Rubin and Kemal Kirişci (Boulder, Colorado: Lynne Rienner Publishers, 2001); and see Heinz Kramer, *A Changing Turkey: Challenges to Europe and the United States* (Washington, D.C.: Brookings Institute Press, 2000).

Turkey's 66 million citizens: United Nations Development Program, 1999, available at http://www.undp.org/hrd2001/indicator/indic_44_1_1.html (citing 65.7 million citizens).

laws broadening civil liberties: "Turkish Parliament, Looking to Europe, Passes Reforms," *New York Times*, August 4, 2002, 12.

104 For more on the Ottoman *millet* system that allowed minority religious communities some degree of self-government, see Bernard Lewis, *Christians and Jews in the Ottoman Empire: The Functioning of a Plural Society* (New York: Holmes and Meier, 1982).

106   *the Welfare Party drew 21.4 percent of the total vote*: Arthur S. Banks and Thomas C. Muller, eds., *Political Handbook of the World 1999* (New York: CSA Publications, 1999), 988; Fawaz A. Gerges, *America and Political Islam: Clash of Cultures or Clash of Interests?* (Cambridge: Cambridge University Press, 1999).

113   All statistics from *Dorling Kindersley World Atlas* (New York: Dorling Kindersley, 2000).
    Indonesia: 206.5m people total, 87% Muslim = 179.66 million Muslims
    Pakistan: 147.8m, 97% (77% Sunni; 20% Shi'i) = 143.37 million Muslims
    India: 976m, 11% = 107.36 million Muslims
    Bangladesh: 124m, 87% = 107.88 million Muslims
    Malaysia: 21.5m, 53% = 11.40 million Muslims
    Philippines: 72.2m, 5% = 3.61 million Muslims
    Burma/Myanmar: 47.6m, 4% = 1.9 million Muslims
    Cambodia: 10.8m, 2% = .22 million Muslims

114   On Bangladeshi elections and the Jamaat-e-Islami, see "Zia's Victory," *AsiaWeek* (October 12, 2001), available at http://www.asiaweek.com/asiaweek/magazine/Dateline/0,8782,178033,00.html.

115   On corruption, see "Study Rates Bangladesh Most Corrupt Country," *New York Times*, August 29, 2002, A15.

116   See Hefner, *Civil Islam*.

117   On Megawati, see "Trading on Her Father's Image," *Economist*, April 13, 2002.

119   On Pakistan generally, there has been a spate of recent books: Mary Anne Weaver, *Pakistan: In the Shadow of Jihad and Afghanistan* (New York: Farrar, Straus and Giroux, 2002), and Owen Bennett Jones, *Pakistan: Eye of the Storm* (New Haven: Yale University Press, 2002), are both readable introductions to the subject. Dennis Kux, *The United States and Pakistan, 1947–2000* (Washington, D.C.: Woodrow Wilson Center Press, 2001) is a useful treatment of the international dimension; and a collection of essays, *Pakistan: Nationalism Without a Nation*, ed. Christophe Jaffrelot (New York: Zed Books, 2002) provides an exploration of a range of themes on the diversity and complexity of the country.

125   *The constitutional changes that Musharraf unilaterally announced*: David Rohdey, "Musharraf Redraws Constitution," *New York Times*, August 22, 2002, 1.
    The first set of changes are outlined in proposed amendments at http://www.pak.gov.pk/public/const_amend.pdf.
    For a discussion, see Ronald L. Watts, "Constitutional Proposals for Pakistan," *Comparative Federalism Newsletter* 17:1 (2002), available at http://www.indiana.edu/~speaweb/IPSA/article14.html.

126   For Pakistan's economic growth and literacy rate statistics, see Asian Development Bank, http://www.adb/org, accessed August 22, 2002. For its population growth, see UNESCO E-9 Initiative statistics, available at unesco.org.

        For October 2002 election results, see http://www.electionworld.org/pakistan/htm.

127   *madrasas*: See Douglas Jehl, "A Nation Challenged: Islamic Militants," *New York Times*, March 9, 2002.

129   On Pakistan's federalism, see http://www.pak.gov.pk/public/const_amend2.pdf.

132   *280 million Arabs*: United Nations Development Programme Arab Human Development Report: Creating Opportunities for Future Generations, 2002, 35. According to the report, page 37, 38 percent of the Arab population is under the age of 14.

134   On Yemen, see Jillian Schwedler, "Islam, Democracy, and the Yemeni State," in Center for the Study of Islam and Democracy Second Annual Conference Proceedings, 20–42, available at http://www.islam-democracy.org.

135   For a table of oil exports by country, see Henry and Springborg, *Globalization and the Politics of Development in the Middle East*, 40.

138   Nadav Safran, *Saudi Arabia: The Ceaseless Quest for Security* (Ithaca, N.Y.: Cornell University Press, 1988).

142   *Prince Talal*: Eric Rouleau, "Trouble in the Kingdom," *Foreign Affairs* 81, no. 4 (July/August 2002): 75–89.

145   Fouad Ajami, "What the Muslim World Is Watching," *New York Times Magazine*, November 18, 2001, 48.

146   *radio station . . . converted to a pop-music format*: Felicity Barringer, "U.S. Messages to Arab Youth, Wrapped in Song," *New York Times*, June 17, 2002, 8; "Towers of Babelaganda," *Economist*, August 24, 2002, 36–38.

150–51 On Morocco, see Abdo Baaklani, Guilain Denoeux, and Robert Springborg, *Legislative Politics in the Arab World: The Resurgence of Democratic Institutions* (Boulder, Colo.: Lynne Reiner, 1999), 111–32; Baghat Korany, "Monarchical Islam with a Democratic Veneer: Morocco," in Brynen, Korany, and Noble, eds., *Political Liberalization & Democratization in the Arab World*, vol. 2, 157–84; Laurie A. Brand, *Women, the State, and Political Liberalization: Middle Eastern and North African Experiences* (New York: Columbia University Press, 1998); and John P. Entelis, "Political Islam in the Maghreb," in *Islam, Democracy, and the State in North Africa*, 50–56.

        For election results, see http://www.electionworld.org/morocco/htm.

See also John P. Entelis, "Morocco: Democracy Denied," *Le Monde Diplomatique*, October 2002, at http://mondediplo.com/2002/10/13/morocco.

151 A fascinating perspective on democracy and Islam in Jordan may be found in Wiktorowicz, *The Management of Islamic Activism*. See also Zakki Attahleh, *Al-Islam al-siyasi fi-l-urdun wa-l-dimuqratiyya* (Political Islam in Jordan and Democracy) (Amman, Jordan: Al-Urdun al-Jadid Research Center, 1996). For a recent essay, see Timothy J. Piro, "Islam and Democracy in Jordan: The Limits of Political Inclusion," Center for the Study of Islam and Democracy Second Annual Conference Proceedings, 8–19, available at http://www.islam-democracy.org.

152 *Palestinians who had . . . fled*: See Benny Morris, *The Birth of the Palestinian Refugee Problem, 1947–1949* (Cambridge: Cambridge University Press, 1987).

158 *pitchman for Pizza Hut*: "Gorbachev's Pitch for Pizza Released," December 23, 1997, at http://www.cnn.com/WORLD/9712/23/gorby.pizza/.

158 *the monarchy's official Web site*: http://www.kingabdullah.jo/hashemites/hashemites .html.

162 *largest population of any Arab state*: Egypt's population is 69,536,644 (July 2001 est.), *CIA World Factbook 2001*, http://www.cia.gov/cia/publications/factbook/index.html.

164 *growth of Islamism*: There is a large literature on Islamism in Egypt. Two recent, thoughtful, highly readable books that deal with the subject are Geneive Abdo, *No God but God* (Oxford: Oxford University Press, 2000), and Anthony Shadid, *Legacy of the Prophet: Despots, Democrats, and the New Politics of Islam* (Boulder, Colo.: Westview Press, 2002).

167 *blood libel*: For a discussion of anti-Semitism in the Arab press, see Anti-Defamation League, "Anti-Semitism in the Arab World," http://www.adl.org/main%5Fas%5Farab.asp.

168 *The Center Party . . . was inspired by faith*: The interview is quoted in Shadid, *Legacy of the Prophet*, 262. Shadid's discussion of the Center Party is excellent and instructive. See also Omayma Abdel-Latif, "Avoiding Confrontation" (interview with Abul-Ela Maadi), *Al-Ahram Weekly On-line*, October 12–18, 2000, no. 503, available at http://www.ahram.org.eg/weekly/2000/503/el2.htm, and Ivesa Lubben and Issam Fawzi, "A New Islamic Party Pluralism in Egypt? (Hizb at-Wasat, Hizb al-Sharia and Hizb al-Islah as Case Studies)," *Orient* no. 2 (2000).

169 *There were 17 such Islamists*: On the election of the so-called Group of 17 Islamists, see "Egypt's Parliamentary Elections: An Assessment of the Results," *Estimate*, vol. 12, 23, November 20, 2000, http://www.theestimate.com/public/111700.html.

    Saadeddin . . . Sunday magazine: Mary Anne Weaver, "Egypt on Trial," *New York Times Magazine*, June 17, 2002, 46.

169   *President Bush finally decided*: Peter Slevin, "Bush, in Shift on Egypt, Links New Aid
        to Rights," *Washington Post*, August 15, 2002, A1, A20.
                reversed that conviction, too: Neil MacFarquhar, "Egyptian Court Frees Rights
        Advocate and Orders Retrial," *New York Times*, December 4, 2002.

175   On Saddam's past relationship with the U.S., see Sandra Mackey, *The Reckoning: Iraq
        and the Legacy of Saddam Hussein* (New York: W.W. Norton, 2002).

177   *GDP per capita of almost $9,000*: $8,900 GDP (2000 est.), from the *CIA World Fact-
        book 2001*, at http://www.cia.gov/cia/publications/factbook/index.html.

179   "Bush Administration Intent on Democracy for Iraq," *New York Times*, August 11, 2002, A2.

182   *writers and thinkers in the Muslim world*: For a discussion of some of these figures, as
        well as others mentioned in this book, see John L. Esposito and John O. Voll, *Makers
        of Contemporary Islam* (Oxford: Oxford University Press, 2001).

182   *Western writers, academic and journalistic*: Such writers include, prominently, Bernard
        Lewis, Samuel Huntington, Gilles Kepel, Olivier Roy, John Voll, John Esposito, Carl
        Brown, James Piscatori, and Dale Eickelman; commentators like Thomas Friedman;
        talented journalists like Geneive Abdo and Anthony Shadid, two Arab Americans of
        Lebanese Christian descent who have lived in Egypt and written fascinating books about
        democracy and Islam—see Shadid, *Legacy of the Prophet*, and Abdo, *No God but God*.
                Other relevant writers whose works I have not otherwise cited above include Ab-
        dullahi Ahmed An-Na'im, whose numerous works include *Toward an Islamic Refor-
        mation: Civil Liberties, Human Rights, and International Law* (Syracuse, N.Y.:
        Syracuse University Press, 1990); Fatima Mernissi, *Islam and Democracy: Fear of the
        Modern World*, trans. Mary Jo Lakeland (Cambridge, Mass.: Perseus Books, 1992);
        Shireen T. Hunter, *The Future of Islam and the West: Clash of Civilizations or Peace-
        ful Coexistence?* (Westport, Conn.: Praeger, 1998); and Abdulaziz Sachedina, *The Is-
        lamic Roots of Democratic Pluralism* (Oxford: Oxford University Press, 2001).

184   Robert Nozick, *Anarchy, State, and Utopia* (New York: Harper and Row, 1974). For
        just one of his comments on the reception of the work, see the introduction to Robert
        Nozick, *Socratic Puzzles* (Cambridge, Mass.: Harvard University Press, 1997).

184–85 On Afghanistan, see Barnett Rubin, *The Fragmentation of Afghanistan* (New Haven,
        Conn.: Yale University Press, 1995) and *The Search for Peace in Afghanistan* (New
        Haven, Conn.: Yale University Press, 1995).
                On the Taliban, see Ahmed Rashid, *Taliban*.

190   "*A mobile in every hand*": See http://www.internationalreports.net/middleeast/egypt/2001/
        mobinil.html, estimating 5 million users by the end of 2002; also, personal communi-
        cation with Osman Sultan, CEO of MobiNil, Cairo, May 2002.

191 *pro-Palestinian protests*: See "Demonstrations in Saudi Arabia," from al-Jazeera Web site, trans. Eric Mueller, http://www.zmag.org/content/Mideast/aljazeera_saudidemos-april5-2002.cfm: "Al-Quds al-'Arabi has learned that the Mosque of Lady Fatimah the Radiant in the city of Jedda on Saudi Arabia's west coast was the scene of a demonstration after evening prayers Wednesday. That demonstration was broken up by Saudi security by force. A number of the participants in the action were arrested. Saudi sources in Jedda said that the call to demonstrate was spread by means of written messages on portable cell phones, particularly among women. The call was answered by more than a thousand men and women who crowded the courtyard of the mosque and the surrounding area. After the end of the evening prayers the women came out carrying Palestinian flags and wearing black and white checkered Palestinian scarves. They chanted slogans in support of the intifada and condemning Arab inaction. The Saudi security forces, which had been deployed in force around the mosque, charged the marchers. They seized the Palestinian flags that were being carried by the women who were at the front of the marchers."

192 *new democracies go to war*: See Jack Snyder, *From Voting to Violence: Democratization and Nationalist Conflict* (New York: Norton, 2000).

195 *a model of rational choice*: For a recent attack on the idea that Saddam's behavior can be modeled rationally, see Kenneth M. Pollack, *The Threatening Storm: The Case for Invading Iraq* (New York: Random House, 2002).

196 *unemployment for Saudi men*: Rouleau, "Trouble in the Kingdom," 83.

197 On the human costs of lack of freedom in the Arab world, see *UNDP Arab Human Development Report*, passim.

203 *a new kind of world power*: The most prominent advocate of this view is surely Joseph Nye Jr. See *The Paradox of American Power: Why the World's Only Superpower Can't Go It Alone* (New York: Oxford University Press, 2002), and *Bound to Lead: The Changing Nature of American Power* (New York: Basic Books, 1990).

210 For the Clinton quote, see the videotape of the conference "America and Islam in a Global World," January 24, 2001, available through New York University School of Law Special Events Office.

211 *targeted economic aid*: The United States Agency for International Development (US-AID) plans to spend $624,500,000 in Pakistan in fiscal year 2002 and has requested $250,000,000 for fiscal year 2003. For the actual numbers spent in 2001, and the amounts earmarked for democracy and governance in each of these years, see USAID Bureau for Asia and the Near East, "Pakistan Briefing," http://www.usaid.gov/regions/ane/newpages/one_pagers/pak01a.htm.

214 *businessman with no prior diplomatic experience*: Ambassador Karim Kawar. For his appointment, see James Morrison, "Embassy Row," *Washington Times*, July 3, 2002, http://www.washtimes.com/world/20020703-77693085.htm.

    sophisticated international lawyer: Dr. Salaheddin Bashir. For his appointment, see "Profiles of New Ministers," *Jordan Times*, October 28, 2001, http://www.jordanembassyus.org/10282001003.htm.

222 *civil society*: For a comprehensive discussion of civil society in the Middle East, see the two volumes of *Civil Society in the Middle East*, ed. Augustus Richard Norton (Leiden: Brill, 1995, 1996). Particularly valuable on Islamists' civil society is the chapter by John P. Entelis, "Civil Society and the Authoritarian Temptation in Algerian Politics: Islamic Democracy vs. the Centralized State," in vol. 2. Entelis relies heavily on Rabia Bekkar, "Taking Up Space in Tlemcen: The Islamist Occupation of Urban Algeria," *Middle East Report* 179 (November/December 1992). On civil society in rentier oil monarchies, see Jill Crystal, "Civil Society in the Arabian Gulf," in *Civil Society in the Middle East*, vol. 2.

224 *Ali Benhadj*: Sometimes spelled Belhadj. Benhadj's remarkable open letter of July 31, 1999, may be found in translation on the FIS website. See http://www.ccfis.org/doc/ABLetter310799.pdf.

    Ibn Khaldun: "Arabs are the least willing of nations to subordinate themselves to each other, as they are rude, proud, ambitious, and eager to be the leader." Ibn Khaldun, *The Muqaddimah: An Introduction to History*, trans. Franz Rosenthal (New York: Bollingen Foundation, 1958), vol. 2, 305.

233 *medieval . . . Jewish work*: See Bahya Ibn Paquda, *Kitab al-hidaya ila fara'id al-qulub* (Duties of the Heart), ed. A. S. Yahuda (Leiden: E. J. Brill, 1912), 232 and notes at 95–96. For an English edition, see *The Book of Direction to the Duties of the Heart*, ed. and trans. Menahem Mansoor with Sara Arenson and Shoshana Dannhauser. (London: Routledge & Kegan Paul, 1973), 277. I owe the reference to Professor Bernard Septimus.

ACKNOWLEDGMENTS

I have been very fortunate to have friends and colleagues willing to read the manuscript of this book and to offer their thoughts on every aspect of it. None agrees with everything I have to say; some agree with almost nothing; and all have improved the book immeasurably, so that the remaining faults cannot help but be my own. Richard Primus, Nader Mousavizadeh, Maureen McLane, Jay Furman, Shahab Ahmed, Scott Wilkens, Bill Nelson, Abdulaziz Al Fahad, and Chibli Mallat merit special thanks in this regard. Jill Goldenziel provided wonderful research assistance while simultaneously editing and challenging my ideas.

My editor, Paul Elie, was a steady—and steadying—source of insight; the entire book bears his imprint. Don Gastwirth kick-started my writing and brought me together with Paul, for which I am deeply grateful. Heather Schroder has encouraged and educated me at every turn; she also made terrific suggestions on the manuscript. Heidi Zehngut Lubov worked as tirelessly, cheerfully, and effectively on this project as on the many others that she manages. Diana Morse's friendship and counsel have been constants in my life for three years and I hope they shall remain so.

I presented sections of the book in the form of papers at the Yale Middle East Legal Studies Seminar and the New York University School of Law Faculty Colloquium and gained much from the participants in both places. Both the Society of Fellows at Harvard and NYU Law have given me remarkable freedom to write. Conversations with my colleagues in Cambridge, both at Lowell House and at the Society, helped the book enormously; I am lucky to have found such stimulating intellectual companionship. Daniel Schwartz, the kind of loyal friend one would think is found only in books, introduced me to the Young Presidents Organization, which in turn sponsored several trips to the Middle East, where I learned much and made many new friends. YPOers all over the world have challenged me to defend or expand on the ideas I present here, and for that and their unflagging hospitality I thank them individually and collectively.

In my teachers I have been no less fortunate. Owen Fiss challenged me to make the central argument of the book, and traces of my conversations with him are on every page. Harold Hongju Koh has taught me more than anyone about the relation between the moral and the practical. The late Robert Nozick kept a watchful eye on me from my freshman year until this past one; watching him play with ideas gave me my model for what the life of the mind should be. Nur Yalman's wisdom, encouragement, and confidence in me have been invaluable. Bernard Septimus, who once warned me about temporal vanities, taught me rigor in thinking about ideas in contact. The late Isadore Twersky was in some sense the inspiration for the whole project. Fritz Zimmermann did what he could with an American in Oxford. Gregg Stern was my guide into the Middle Ages, whence he never grudged my return. Wilson Bishai joyfully opened the world of Arabic language to me when I was a boy of fifteen. Muhsin Mahdi revealed to me the suppleness and subtlety of Islamic political thought. My experiences working for Judge Harry T. Edwards and Justice David H. Souter, two very different men with a profound shared commitment to reasoned judgment, have left influences so deep that I will never be able to identify them fully. Those who taught me during my twelve years at the Maimonides School gave me an extraordinary education in the possibilities and limitations of synthesis; I hope the book reflects the spirit of their undertaking. My parents, Roy and Penny Feldman, raised me in a world of multiple and complicated ideas, for which I can never thank them enough.

Finally, all undeserved, I have had the unmatched intellectual engagement of my wife, Jeannie Suk, in every imaginable aspect of the book. Her ideas and arguments pervade it. My gratitude for that, though deep, cannot begin to approach the happiness that I have found in being with her.

INDEX

Abduh, Muhammad, 39
Abdullah, Crown Prince of Saudi Arabia,
    144, 193
Abdullah I, King of Jordan, 151
Abdullah II, King of Jordan, 148–50, 155–60,
    213–14
Abu Bakr, 88, 243n
Afghani, Jamal al-Din al-, 39
Afghanistan, 15, 85–86, 131, 178, 184–86, 201,
    213, 221; loya jirga in, 85, 186; Saudi Arabia
    and, 47–48; Soviet occupation of, 7,
    46–47, 85, 127, 185; under Taliban, 8,
    13–14, 49, 72, 85, 127, 145, 185
Ajami, Fouad, 145
Algeria, 3–6, 10, 13, 21, 29, 78, 184, 231; anti-
    colonialist movement in, 134; Berbers in,
    131; nationalism in, 132; oil in, 137
'Ali, 88
al-Qaeda, see Qaeda, al-
Anglican Church, 54, 60, 67
anti-Americanism, 5, 13, 91–92, 191–92, 197,
    199–302
anti-Semitism, 167
Arab Afghans, 46–47
Arabia, 133; see also Saudi Arabia
Arab League, 193

Arabs in History, The (Lewis), 26
Arafat, Yasser, 144, 218, 219
Aristotle, 233
Armenian genocide, 103
Asad, Bashar al-, 9, 170
Asad, Hafez al-, 9, 12, 170
'Askari, Hasan al-, 88
Ataturk, Mustafa Kemal, 103–5, 112, 217
Athens, ancient, 32
Austro-Hungarian Empire, 102

Bahrain, 12, 28, 63, 82, 84, 142, 144
Bali nightclub bombing, 117
Balkans, 39
Bangladesh, 63, 83, 101, 113–15, 121, 122, 135, 139
Banna, Hasan al-, 41–48, 121
bay'a (contractual agreement), 52
Benhadj, Ali, 224
Berbers, 131
Bhutto, Benazir, 63, 124–26
Bhutto, Zulfikar, 123, 124
Bible, 42
bin Laden, Osama, 7, 8, 14, 46, 49, 138, 141,
    143, 145, 164, 177, 201
Bolívar, Simón, 149
Bosnia, 199

Brazil, 77–78
Britain, 34, 35, 83, 92, 134, 150; Egypt and, 42, 133; Hashemite kingdoms and, 132, 133, 151–52; India and, 119, 120, 126, 134; monarchy in, 140, 157; religion, 54, 55, 60, 67; Yemen and, 135
Buddhists, 115
Bulgaria, 102
Burma, 113
Bush, George, 220
Bush, George W., 10, 117, 169; "axis of evil" described by, 99, 177, 216, 220–21; Palestinian policy of, 10, 191, 194, 218

Calvinism, 59
Cambodia, 113
Cambridge History of Islam, The (Lewis), 26
Central Intelligence Agency (CIA), 92
Chechnya, 8
Cheney, Richard, 178
Chile, 215
China, 135, 200, 203
Christians, 37, 38, 54, 59, 68, 149, 201; Arab, 39; Indonesian, 116, 117; in Islamic states, 72, 77; Lebanese, 13; reconquista of Spain by, 31; Turkish, 104
Churchill, Winston, 150
Ciller, Tansu, 63, 106, 107
Civil Islam (Hefner), 116
Clash of Civilizations, The (Huntington), 26, 184
Clausewitz, Carl von, 211
Clinton, Bill, 128, 210, 211
CNN, 146
Cold War, 4, 19, 26, 203, 204, 234; Iraq during, 135; Israel during, 190; Jordan during, 151; Turkey during, 217
Congress Party, Indian, 119–20
Crusades, 201

Dahl, Robert, 237n
Declaration of Independence, 56
Delors, Jacques, 150
Democratic Party, U.S., 10, 191, 212

Djerejian, Edward, 5, 184
Druze, 134
Dubai, 134, 135, 144, 216

Egypt, 7, 9, 64, 134, 148, 162–73, 182, 211, 214, 224, 231; in British sphere of influence, 133; constitution of, 207; economy of, 177, 196, 212; Islamic law in, 55; Israel and, 44, 46, 135, 162, 163, 166, 191, 193; mobile phones in, 190; Muslim Brotherhood in, 42–44, 49; nationalism in, 132; oil in, 137; in Ottoman Empire, 103; tourism in, 149; women's rights in, 63
Erbakan, Necmettin, 106–9, 218
Erdogan, Recep Tayyep, 108, 110
European Union (EU), 108, 150, 169, 194, 201, 217–18

Farouk, King of Egypt, 42, 43
Forum for Democracy, Indonesian, 116
France, 5, 35, 132, 133, 139
Friedman, Thomas, 34, 35
Front de Libération National (FLN), 3–5
Front Islamique du Salut (FIS), 4, 5, 224

Gandhi, Mohandas K., 119
Garibaldi, Giuseppe, 132
Gaza, 12, 145, 153
Geertz, Clifford, 81
Gerges, Fawaz, 107
Germany, 60, 68, 85, 194–95, 221
Ghannouchi, Rachid, 51, 68, 182
gharbzadegi ("Westoxification"), 201–2
Ghazali, Muhammad al-, 182
Gorbachev, Mikhail, 158
Graham, Billy, 110
Greece, 102, 103; ancient, 31, 233
Gulf War, 49, 135, 138, 143, 167, 176, 220, 221

Haiti, 209
halakha (Jewish law), 65
Hamas, 64
Hashemites, 132, 133, 151
Hassan II, King of Morocco, 150

Hefner, Robert, 116
Hezbollah, 8, 24, 47, 99, 146
Hidden Twelfth Imam, 88
hijab (women's head scarves), 35, 66, 67, 228
Hindus, 34, 120, 121, 125, 126, 128; Afghan, 85; in Bangladesh, 114, 115; in Mughal Empire, 73
Hizb al-wasat (Egyptian Center Party), 168, 172, 183
Holland, 115
hudud (certain crimes under Islamic law), 71–72
Hungary, 102
Huntington, Samuel, 26, 27, 184
Husayn, Faysal ibn, 133
Husayn, Sharif, 132–33
Hussein, King of Jordan, 48–49, 84, 134, 151–55, 157, 158, 193
Hussein, Saddam, 45, 85, 135, 137, 174–77, 195, 220–21, 231; invasion of Kuwait by, 9, 143, 167; Iraq after, 15, 178–81, 217; and September 11 terrorist attacks, 177, 221

Ibn Khaldun Institute for Civil Society (Egypt), 224
Ibrahim, Anwar, 114
Ibrahim, Saadeddin, 169–70, 224
India, 8, 59–60, 113, 115, 125, 200, 208–9; Mughal, 73, 120; Pakistan and, 83, 119–22, 126, 128
Indonesia, 7, 20, 49, 81–83, 114–18, 131, 159; Naipaul on, 208; women in, 63, 66–67
Iqbal, Mohammed, 120
Iran, 12, 21, 24, 51, 87–100, 141, 178, 180, 182, 183, 217, 220, 228; anti-Americanism of, 5, 23, 91–92; Indonesia and, 115; Islamic Revolution in, 7, 45, 87–89, 91–93, 97, 143, 196, 198, 200, 202, 216; Kurds in, 101; Naipaul on, 208; oil in, 147; in Ottoman Empire, 102; Palestinians and, 8, 99; religious coercion in, 70; Saudi Arabia and, 47; secular nationalism in, 20, 44–45; Turkey and, 107, 109; war with Iraq, 89, 94, 216; women's rights in, 35, 63, 94

Iraq, 3, 45, 85, 131, 132, 134, 148, 174–81, 231; Bush administration and, 10, 99, 220–21; during Cold War, 135; Hashemite kingdom of, 133; Jordanian trade with, 49, 213; Kurds in, 101, 174, 220; Kuwait invaded by 9, 86, 143, 167, 175, 216; oil in, 137, 174–76, 219–20; in Ottoman Empire, 102, post-Saddam, 15, 178–81, 217; Shi'i majority in, 82; war with Iran, 89, 94, 216
Islamic Action Front, 154–55, 160
Israel, 14, 62, 67, 105, 143, 148, 152, 167, 213; invasion of Lebanon by, 8, 134; Iraq as threat to, 175, 176; law of return in, 68; Palestinians and, 8, 13, 99, 144–46, 153, 154, 166, 189–94, 218, 219, 225; peace treaties with, 44, 46, 84, 157, 162, 163, 166; religion-based family law in, 73; tourism in, 149; U.S. support for, 23, 171, 189–91, 199, 218
Italy, unification of, 132

Jamaat-e-Islami, 114, 122
Jamaat Ulema-e-Islami, 122
Japan, 194–95, 221
Jazeera, al- (television station), 144–46, 170, 215, 225
Jefferson, Thomas, 224
Jews, 68, 72, 149, 166–67, 233; Afghani, 85; American, 146, 190; Arabic-speaking, 39; Turkish, 104; *see also* Judaism
Jinnah, Mohammed Ali, 120, 121
Jordan, 9, 12, 48–49, 84–85, 176, 213–14; Israeli peace treaty with, 84, 193; monarchy of, 7, 132, 133, 137, 148–62, 207, 215, 231; PLO ejected from, 134, 152–53; women's rights in, 63
Judaism, 33, 34, 62, 65, 67, 73, 77, 94
Justice and Benevolence Party, Moroccan, 151
Justice and Development Party; Moroccan, 151; Turkish, 108, 110

Karzai, Hamid, 178
Kashmir, 8, 128

Kenya, bombing of U.S. embassy in, 177
Khaldun, Ibn, 226
Khamene'i, Ayatollah 'Ali, 90
Khan, General Ayub, 123, 124
Khan, General Yahya, 123
Khatami, Mohammad, 51, 89–91, 95–98, 100, 183
Khomeini, Ayatollah Ruhollah, 45, 87–88, 93
Kollek, Teddy, 105
Korea, 104
Kosovo, 199
Kurds, 101, 102, 108, 109, 174, 217, 220
Kuwait, 63, 78, 178, 179, 220; Iraqi invasion of, 9, 86, 143, 167, 175, 216

Lawrence, T. E., 226
League of Nations, 85
Lebanon, 8, 24, 47, 99, 131, 215; in Ottoman Empire, 103; PLO in, 134, 152; Shi'i minority in, 82
Lewis, Bernard, 26–27, 238n
Libya, 85, 107, 134, 137, 177, 219
Likud Party, Israeli, 193

Maadi, Abul-Ela, 168, 172
Mahfouz, Naguib, 172
Majalla, 56
Malaysia, 81, 113–15, 131
Malcolm X, 77
Manar, al- (television station), 146
Mandela, Nelson, 225
Marshall Plan, 195
Marxism, 19, 135, 140, 165
Massoud, Ahmed Shah, 201
Maududi, Abul Ala, 45, 121–22
Milestones (Qutb), 44
Mohamad, Mahathir, 114
Morocco, 7, 12, 13, 28, 81, 131, 132; monarchy of, 133, 137, 148–51, 161, 162, 207, 215, 231; women's rights in, 63
Mossadegh, Mohammed, 92, 93, 96
Mu'awiya, 88
Mubarak, Gamal, 170

Mubarak, Hosni, 135, 163, 165–67, 169–71, 174, 191, 211, 214
Mughal Empire, 73, 120
Muhammad, Prophet, 38, 41, 43, 131, 224, 232, 234, 244n; blasphemy laws and, 70; and coexistence with non-Muslims, 67; death of, 88; descendants of, 76, 158–59; Islamic law and, 56; unification of tribes by, 51–52; Wahhabi beliefs about, 47; on women's role, 63, 243n
Muhammad V, King of Morocco, 133
Muhammad VI, King of Morocco, 133, 148–51
Musharraf, General Pervez, 49, 125–27, 129–30, 196, 213, 215
Muslim Brotherhood, 47, 121; in Egypt, 42–44, 163; in Jordan, 49, 153, 154, 164, 167–69, 172
Muslim League, 120, 126
Mutahhida Majlis-e-Amal (MMA), 122, 126
Myanmar, 113

Naghrela, Samuel ibn, 67
Nahdlatul Ulama, 82, 116
Naipaul, V. S., 208
Nasser, Gamal Abdul, 43, 44, 162–63, 171
National Democratic Party, Egyptian, 169
National Socialism, 37
Nationalist Party, Bangladesh, 114
Nawaz Sharif, Mian, 125, 127
Nazism, 110
Nehru, Jawaharlal, 119
New York Times, The, 122, 145, 146, 170
Nicaragua, 47
Nigeria, 49, 72, 135
Nixon, Richard M., 110
North Atlantic Treaty Organization (NATO), 217
North Korea, 99
Nozick, Robert, 184

Orientalism, 28, 29
Ottoman Empire, 27, 38–39, 56, 75, 102–4, 132, 200

Pahlavi, Mohammad Reza Shah, 45, 87–89, 91–93, 96, 143

Pakistan, 7, 13, 28, 45, 49, 83, 113, 115, 119–30, 214, 215, 231; creation of, 83, 119–21; Inter-Service Intelligence (ISI) in, 127, 196; Islamic law in, 55, 122; Kashmir and, 8, 128; Naipaul on, 208, Sunni majority in, 82; Taliban and, 185; U.S. aid to, 212–13, 250n; women in, 63

Pakistan People's Party (PPP), 125, 126

Palestine, Arab conquest of, 131

Palestine Liberation Organization (PLO), 134, 152–53

Palestinians, 13, 14, 64, 145, 146, 189–94, 225, 231; demonstrations in Saudi Arabia in support of, 191, 250n; Egypt and, 166; Iran and, 8, 99; Iraq and, 176; in Jordan, 152–53; in Ottoman Empire, 103; peace process of Israel and, 144, 154, 193; U.S. policy toward, 10, 189–91, 194, 202, 218–19

Pan Am flight 103, 177

Paul, St., 77

Pentagon, terrorist attack on, see September 11 terrorist attacks

Persia, 76, 131

Philippines, 113, 131, 139

Pinochet, Augusto, 214–15

PKK (Kurdistan Workers' Party), 102

Poland, pro-democracy movement in, 19

Prolegomena, The (Ibn Khaldun), 226

Protestantism, 37, 73

Qadhafi, Muammar, 85, 107, 177, 195, 241n

Qaeda, al-, 7, 8, 14, 117, 127, 143

Qaradawi, Yusuf al-, 64, 182, 241n

Qatar, 64, 144

Qur'an, 41–44, 53, 56, 58, 62, 64–65, 70, 76, 131, 182, 201

Qutb, Sayyid, 43–46, 121

Raziq, 'Ali 'Abd al-, 40

Reagan, Ronald, 184

Republican Party, U.S., 191, 212

Rida, Rashid, 39

Roman Catholicism, 36–37, 60, 73, 94

Roman Empire, 37, 200

Rule of God, the Rule of the People, The (Bahlul), 57

Rumsfeld, Donald, 178

Russia, 8, 194

Sa'ud, 'Abdulaziz Ibn, 133

Sadat, Anwar, 7, 44, 46, 135, 162–63, 165–67, 171, 193

Sadr, Ayatollah Muhammad Baqir al-, 45

Said, Edward, 28

Saudi Arabia, 21, 28, 63, 81, 84, 148, 176, 217, 231; Islamic law in, 56, 57, 228; Israel and, 193; monarchy in, 5, 7, 211; oil in, 137–38; 142–44, 147, 149, 196, 216; pro-Palestinian protests in, 191, 250n; religious coercion in, 70; Wahhabism in, 47–48, 207; women in, 35, 66, 205

Saudi Arabia: The Ceaseless Quest for Security (Safran), 138

Sejong, King of Korea, 104

Senegal, 28, 81

September 11 terrorist attacks, 6–8, 12, 26, 46, 64, 145, 176, 194, 197, 232; Iranian response to, 91; and popular perception of Islamists, 10; retaliation against Taliban for, 85, 127, 185; Saddam Hussein and, 177, 221; Saudi Arabia and, 143–44

shari'a (Islamic law), 49, 55, 111, 117, 171

Shariati, 'Ali, 45

Sharon, Ariel, 189, 193

Shi'i Muslims, 8, 33, 45, 47, 82, 88–89, 134, 179–80

shura (consultation), 53, 241n

Solidarnosc, 19

Soroush, Abdolkarim, 59, 182

South Africa, 203, 225

Soviet Union, 8, 9, 19, 44, 135, 158, 217; Afghanistan occupied by, 7, 46–47, 85, 127, 185; fall of, 105, 139

Spain, medieval, 31, 67, 131

Stalin, Joseph, 105

sub-Saharan Africa, 131, 135, 197

Sudan, 8, 183
Sufi mystics, 60, 232–33
Suharto, 49, 82, 116
Sukarno, Ahmad, 116
Sukarnoputri, Megawati, 63, 117
Sultan, Essam, 168, 172
Sunni Muslims, 33, 38, 41, 45–47, 82, 88, 134,
    141, 163, 179–80
Syria, 88, 107, 131, 134, 148, 170; Hashemite
    kingdom of, 133; oil in, 137, 162; in
    Ottoman Empire, 103; Soviet Union and,
    9, 139

Talal, Prince, 142
Taliban, 8, 13–14, 49, 72, 85, 127, 145, 178, 201
Tanzania, bombing of U.S. embassy in, 177
Thatcher, Margaret, 184
Thoreau, Henry David, 224
Tiananmen Square uprising, 203
Transjordan, 133; see also Jordan
True Path Party, Turkish, 106
Tunisia, 51, 63, 82, 134, 137, 162, 182
Turabi, Hasan al-, 183
Turkey, 7, 13, 101–12, 159, 231; anti-
    Americanism in, 201; European Union
    and, 217–18; guest workers in Germany
    from, 68; Iraq and, 176, 178; Kurds in,
    101–2, 108, 217; secularism in, 40, 82,
    102–12; women in, 63, 66

Ukraine, 78
'Umar, 88
umma (Muslim community), 51, 67
United Arab Emirates, 84
United Nations, 85, 175, 178–81, 221
United States, 9–16, 110–11, 149, 195, 197–98,
    204–6, 210–14, 222, 227, 230; Afghanistan
    and, 46–48, 85–86, 127, 178, 184, 185, 201,
    213; Agency for International Development
    (USAID), 250n; al-Jazeera and, 145–46; Al-
    geria and, 5; Bosnian intervention of, 199;
    during Cold War, 19, 203, 204, 217, 234;
    Constitution of, 58, 69, 110, 155; Egypt and,
    135, 166, 167, 169–71; founding fathers of,

209; hostility toward, see anti-American-
    ism; Indonesia and, 116; Iran and, 91–94,
    99, 100, 147; Iraq and, 135, 143, 175–81,
    219–22, 231; Israel and, 23, 189–94, 199, 218;
    Jordan and, 157–58, 160, 213–14; legal sys-
    tem in, 56, 57; Pakistan and, 123, 127, 128,
    212–13, 250n; Palestinian Authority and, 194,
    218–19; post–World War II, 194–95; Saudi
    Arabia and, 137–38, 143–44, 216, 217; sepa-
    ration of church and state in, 74; Supreme
    Court of, 67; terrorist attacks on, see Sep-
    tember 11 terrorist attacks; Turkey and,
    107, 108, 217, 218; war on terror of, 10, 117
'Uthman, 88

Virtue Party, Turkish, 108
Voice of America, 146
Voltaire, 224

Wahhabism, 47–48, 133, 207
Wahid, Abdurrahman, 82, 116–17
Wajed, Sheikh Hasina, 63
Welfare Party, Turkish, 106–8
West Bank, 12, 145, 152, 153, 189
"Westoxification," 201–2
What Went Wrong? (Lewis), 26
Why the Muslims Have Lagged Behind and
    Why Others Have Advanced (Arslan), 27
World Trade Center, terrorist attack on, see
    September 11 terrorist attacks
World War I, 102, 103, 132, 226
World War II, 119, 157, 194

Yemen, 134–35, 137, 162
Yilmaz, Mesut, 107
Young Turks, 103
Youssoufi, Abderrahmane, 150–51
Yugoslavia, 102

Zawahiri, Ayman al-, 164
Zia, Khaleda, 63, 114
Zia al-Haq, General Mohammed, 123–24,
    127, 129
Zionism, 105, 167

ML